The New York Times

STEEPED IN CROSSWORDS

The New York Times

STEEPED IN CROSSWORDS
180 Easy to Hard Puzzles

Edited by Will Shortz

ST. MARTIN'S GRIFFIN ❧ NEW YORK

DIFFICULTY KEY

Easy:

Medium:

Hard:

ACROSS

1 Tennessee team, for short
5 Acknowledge as true
10 Pole or Czech
14 Admit openly
15 Often-maligned relative
16 ___ mind
17 Blue-skinned race in "Avatar"
18 With 50-Across, it's represented by 15 squares in an appropriate arrangement in this puzzle
19 Some Monopoly purchases. Abbr.
20 French pupil
22 Grandpa on "The Simpsons"
23 Boot
24 Live it up
26 N.F.L. player with a black helmet
28 Hebrew month when Hanukkah starts
30 Richard Branson's airline company
33 Hundred Acre Wood resident
34 Place to hear fire and brimstone
38 Personal question?
39 Washing machine contents
41 David of "The Pink Panther"
42 Rear half of a griffin
43 Writer Katherine ___ Porter
44 Barely adequate
45 Iams competitor
46 1943 penny material
48 Suffix with meth- or prop-
49 What you might buy a flight with
50 See 18-Across

53 Place with complimentary bathrobes
56 Pronoun for Miss Piggy
57 Rodeway ___
58 Past the expiration date
61 Ship sinker
63 Pep up
65 "Not my call"
66 Words of encouragement
67 Calls it quits
68 Weatherproofing stuff

DOWN

1 Revolver with the letters N-E-W-S
2 Speed skater's path
3 Make-out session spot
4 Spin, as an office chair
5 It might be bummed
6 Basketball player who starred in "Kazaam"

7 Commoner
8 Police stun gun
9 "I ___ you one"
10 Barber, at times
11 Medical directive
12 With, on le menu
13 Item under a jacket, maybe
21 At any time
23 Nefarious
25 Roulette bet
27 ___-garde
28 Caffeine-laden nuts
29 "Not gonna happen"
31 Comment made while crossing one's fingers
32 Pitchers' hitless games, in baseball slang
35 Experienced through another
36 The first Mrs. Trump

37 Shakespeare's Antonio and Bassanio, e.g.
40 Judge
42 Reclined
47 British sailors
49 One of the friends on "Friends"
51 No-show in a Beckett play
52 Certain belly button
53 Tuxedo shirt button
54 St. Peter was the first
55 B.A. part
58 Cabo's peninsula
59 Lots
60 Thing often of interest?
62 Hawaiian dish
64 Blanc or Brooks

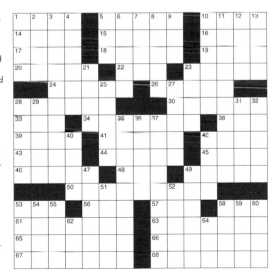

by Joel Fagliano

ACROSS

1 Pat down, as pipe tobacco
5 Trade
9 Carpenter's file
13 Grammy winner McLachlan
14 Heading on a list of errands
15 Salt lake state
16 1959 hit by the Drifters
19 Stock market index, with "the"
20 Collaborative Web project
21 Helpers
22 What children should be, and not heard, they say
24 Pudding or pie
27 1970 hit by Eric Clapton
32 Barbie and others
34 180 degrees from WNW
35 Close by
36 Letter after pi
37 Belly muscles, for short
40 Magazine with an annual "500" list
42 ___-la-la
43 Forever and ever
45 "___ in apple"
47 Nutso
49 1978 hit by Journey
53 Something to scribble on
54 "Hurry!," on an order
57 11- or 12-year-old
60 Therefore
62 One may be under a blouse
63 What the artists of 16-, 27- and 49-Across are doing (in reference to the last words of their hits)?
67 "___ and the King of Siam"

68 On the Adriatic, say
69 Brings in, as a salary
70 Piece of fly-casting equipment
71 Roseanne, before and after Arnold
72 Exercise that may involve sitting cross-legged

DOWN

1 California/Nevada border lake
2 "Can anybody hear us?"
3 Feb. follower
4 "Close call!"
5 Bram who created Dracula
6 "Alas!"
7 Billboards, e.g.
8 Certain lap dog, informally
9 Gloat

10 Slightly
11 Kemo ___ (the Lone Ranger)
12 ___ ed. (gym class)
13 Norms: Abbr.
17 Nobel-winning author André
18 Fisherman's tale
23 Org. for the Bears and Bengals
25 "But of course, amigo!"
26 Garden of ___
28 Fed. air marshal's org.
29 Locale for an 1863 address
30 "B.C." creator Johnny
31 A waiter carries plates on it
32 Sketched
33 Cry before "I know!"
38 Worms, to a fisherman

39 Not at all nutso
41 Network with an "eye" for entertainment
44 Dakar's land
46 Pearly Gates sentinel
48 Alias letters
50 Anderson of "WKRP in Cincinnati"
51 "That's so funny I forgot to laugh"
52 Rim
55 ___ football
56 Fail's opposite
57 Bygone Kremlin resident
58 Cabernet, for one
59 Feminine suffix
61 Follow, as orders
64 Arrest
65 Fed. property manager
66 Philosopher ___-tzu

by Amy Johnson

ACROSS

1 With 1-Across, toy train
5 Set of values
10 Half of cuatro
13 ___ mark (#)
14 Texas city
15 Messenger ___
16 Introductory drawing class
17 Old game consoles
18 Early Tarzan Ron
19 Not found
21 With 21-Across, "I'll believe it when I see it!"
23 With 23-Across, CBer's opening
26 With 26-Across, #1 hit for the Mamas & the Papas
27 ___ Doone (cookie brand)
28 Prefix with center
31 Jobs at Apple
32 Six-pointers, in brief
33 Med. exam involving an injection into the forearm
36 "Washingtons"
37 With 37-Across and 37-Across, a holiday song
39 Lead in to girl
42 Tots
43 ___ Records
46 Play lazily, as a guitar
48 Rap's Dr. ___
49 Thai or Taiwanese
51 With 51-Across, town crier's cry
53 With 53-Across, "Nothing's changed"
55 With 55-Across and 55-Across, real-estate catchphrase
58 Real nerve
59 ___ Records
60 Montana's capital
62 "The lady ___ protest too much"
65 "Perfect" number
66 Part of a train headed to a refinery
67 Drama award since 1956
68 The "E" in E.S.L.: Abbr.
69 Drenches
70 With 70-Across, #1 hit for Billy Idol

DOWN

1 With 1-Down and 1-Down, lively Latin dance
2 With 2-Down, "Ver-r-ry funny!"
3 Stable employees
4 Buckeye
5 Sup
6 "Shut yer ___!"
7 Title for Goethe
8 "Green thumb" or "purple prose"
9 Universe
10 German city rebuilt after W.W. II
11 Temporarily away
12 Agrees
14 With 14-Down, like some talk shows
20 Play in the N.H.L.
22 Being pulled
23 Diner inits.
24 Curtain holder
25 Made tighter, as a knot
29 With 29-Down, nursery rhyme starter
30 Debatables
34 "As an aside," in chat lingo
35 Big inits. in C&W
37 First lady before Michelle
38 ___ bin Laden
39 Jock
40 1976 horror film whose remake was released, appropriately, on 6/6/06
41 Copying exactly, as a sketch
43 1970 John Wayne western
44 Baseball's Ripken
45 &
47 Collection of legends
50 Hardly ever
52 Farm letters?
54 With 54-Down, food gelling agent
56 Spanish pot
57 Bottle part
61 "Illmatic" rapper
63 With 63-Down, title boy in a 2011 Spielberg film
64 With 64-Down and 64-Down, Fat Albert's catchphrase

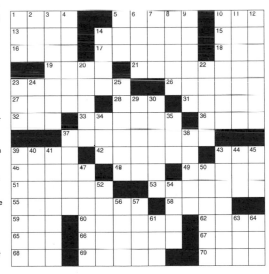

by Tim Croce

4

ACROSS

1 Scotch ___
5 Stare dumbfoundedly
9 Simba's best friend in "The Lion King"
13 Nyet : Russian :: ___ : German
14 More than some
15 Engine
16 Jamaican sprinter nicknamed "The Fastest Man on Earth"
18 Story for storage
19 Polynesian kingdom
20 Nothing daring in terms of offerings
22 Ostentatious displays
24 Sounded like a horn
25 Washtub
27 Indian dress
28 Mediterranean and Caribbean
30 Winter pear
32 Having painterish pretensions
36 Golf course target
37 PC outlet
39 Had supper
40 Firebug's crime
42 Lovett of country music
43 Title beekeeper in a 1997 film
44 "Dies ___" (hymn)
46 Brand of dinnerware with a Scandinavian design
48 Bandleader Glenn
51 Roger who played 007
53 Service charges
57 Apple tablets
59 "Dig?"
60 Heralded, as a new era
62 Rum drinks for British sailors
63 Subway support

64 Companion of the Pinta and Santa Maria
65 Cravings
66 Pig's grunt
67 "General Hospital," e.g.

DOWN

1 Letter-shaped fastener
2 Fable writer
3 Nightspots for cocktails and easy listening
4 Mysteries
5 Yak
6 Baseball's Matty or Jesus
7 D.C. types
8 "___, Brute?"
9 Sore loser's cry
10 Fragrance of roses
11 France's longest river

12 Shaped like a rainbow
15 Teen hanging out among shoppers
17 Dozes
21 "The ___ Daba Honeymoon"
23 Brothers and sisters, for short
26 Aristocratic
27 Bawl out
28 Place that might offer mud baths
29 Pointy part of Mr. Spock
31 007, for one
33 Rush Limbaugh medium
34 Sault ___ Marie, Mich.
35 "___-haw!"
37 Turmoils
38 500 sheets
41 Structures in the Gulf of Mexico

43 Annual tournaments . . . or a description of the starts of 16-, 20-, 37-, 53- and 60-Across?
45 Terrier's sound
47 Roulette bet that's not rouge
48 Hot and humid
49 River of Grenoble, France
50 Divulge
52 Minneapolis suburb
54 It replaced the franc and mark
55 Actor Morales
56 Body part that's often bumped
58 Partner of Crackle and Pop
61 "Benevolent" club member

by Zhouqin Burnikel and D. Scott Nichols

5

ACROSS

1 Cowboy chow
5 Distresses
9 Word from the Arabic for "struggle"
14 Simpson who said "Beneath my goody two shoes lie some very dark socks"
15 See 16-Across
16 With 15-Across, preparing to pop the question, say
17 Cash dispensers, for short
18 "___ first you don't succeed . . ."
19 What a star on a U.S. flag represents
20 Subject of the book "Revolution in the Valley"
22 Beset by a curse
23 Pinocchio, periodically
24 Snarling dog
25 Poisonous
28 Person who works with dipsticks
33 Not much, in cookery
34 Powerful org. with HQ in Fairfax, Va.
35 Shine, commercially
37 People in this may have big ears
42 Shot ___
43 "Criminy!"
44 Actress Watts
45 Sioux shoe
49 Metaphor, e.g.
50 "Whazzat?"
51 Employs
53 Meal with Elijah's cup
56 Journalist of the Progressive Era
61 Kick out
62 Vogue alternative
63 Starting score in tennis
64 Techie sorts
65 From the top

DOWN (continued)

66 Managed, with "out"
67 Unable to hold still
68 Speaker's place
69 Like Lindbergh's historic trans-Atlantic flight

DOWN

1 Glitz
2 Meter maid of song
3 Gomer Pyle's org.
4 Legendary lizard with a fatal gaze
5 Japanese dog breed
6 Notify
7 Pastures
8 Brother of Cain and Abel
9 Book after Deuteronomy
10 Person getting on the job training
11 Snopes.com subject
12 Up-front stake
13 Monopoly card
21 Specialty
24 Cartoonist Addams
25 Pack down
26 Detestation
27 ___ knife
29 Japanese mushroom
30 Grand ___ (wine of the highest rank)
31 Eskimo home
32 Stick together
36 Theater award since 1956
38 Word repeatedly sung after "She loves you . . ."
39 "___ amis"
40 Opposite of exit
41 Deals at a dealership
46 Partner of balances
47 Girl's show of respect
48 Cell centers
52 Twists, as facts
53 Gaming giant
54 Smooth
55 Lighten up?
56 Quaff for Beowulf
57 Bone next to the radius
58 Gorilla pioneering in sign language
59 Knievel of motorcycle stunts
60 Make over

by Patrick Blindauer and Andrea Carla Michaels

ACROSS

1 Slyly spiteful
6 The "D" of PRNDL
11 Easy-to-chew food
14 Mutual of ___ (insurance giant)
15 Aid in detecting speeders
16 ___ Direction (boy band)
17 John Cusack thriller based on a Grisham novel
19 "Golly!"
20 Inviting
21 "Gimme ___!" (start of an Iowa cheer)
22 Southward
23 "___ Misérables"
24 Santa's little helper
26 Snouts
28 Newly famous celebrity
32 ___ date (make some plans)
35 Tuna container
36 Lying on one's back
37 Conductors of impulses from nerve cells
39 Grazing area
41 Judicial statements
42 Fought like the Hatfields and McCoys
44 Abbr. after a lawyer's name
46 Lose traction
47 Stipulation that frees one of liability
50 Minor difficulty
51 Bit of butter
52 "He said, ___ said"
55 Praise
57 Nautical record
59 Nautical unit of measure
61 Swiss peak
62 Part of a ski jump just before going airborne
64 Bronx ___

65 Pop concert venue
66 Strong, seasoned stock, in cookery
67 Japanese money
68 Military cap
69 Run-down, as a bar

DOWN

1 Atoll composition
2 Tell jokes, say
3 Oxygen suppliers for scuba divers
4 Spicy Southeast Asian cuisine
5 Show that's bo-o-oring
6 Unmoist
7 Indian nobleman
8 "Can't say"
9 Sundry
10 Suffix with crock or mock
11 Toy that hops
12 All over again
13 Ball-___ hammer
18 Shoelace end
22 Hate, hate, hate
25 "Words ___ me!"
27 Macho sort
28 Quick but temporary fix
29 Prepare for prayer
30 Voting against
31 What library patrons do
32 How the cautious play it
33 Mates who've split
34 Mention in passing
38 Aug. follower
40 Inits. on a rush order
43 State openly, as for a customs official
45 Drink, as of ale
48 Tight necklace
49 Fills with personnel
52 Disgrace

53 ___ in on (got closer to)
54 "E" on a gas gauge
55 Indolent
56 ___ vera
58 Trait transmitter
60 Factual
62 File extension?
63 Grain in Cheerios

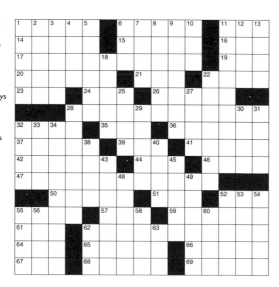

by Gary Cee

ACROSS

1 Now, in Acapulco
6 Like a college course labeled "101"
11 551, once
14 One using Yelp or TripAdvisor, perhaps
15 Prefix with biology
16 Suffix with planet or fuel
17 Overcome an unpleasant misunderstanding
19 Fall mo.
20 Bit of crew equipment
21 ___ tai
22 Actor Milo
24 Left-brain activity
29 "Anderson Cooper 360°" channel
30 Asimov and Newton
31 March honoree, for short
34 "And ___ bed"
36 "The Wonder Years" teen, for short
38 2004 film featuring Dustin Hoffman
42 Half a bikini
43 Accompanying
44 Final approval
45 Anderson Cooper, e.g.
48 Midpoint: Abbr.
49 Reason to see a rheumatologist
54 Instrument played by George Harrison
55 Gulf state: Abbr.
56 Loony
58 ___ Paulo, Brazil
59 "The Lord of the Rings" setting . . . or a feature of 17-, 24-, 38- and 49-Across?
64 Young Darth Vader, to friends
65 Filmmaker Morris
66 He-Man's sister
67 Initials of fashion

68 Oracles
69 Point toward

DOWN

1 Instruction to play with the bow
2 Special-request flight meal option
3 Cheri formerly of "S.N.L."
4 "The Crying Game" actor Stephen
5 Sheet music abbr.
6 Joy formerly of "The View"
7 Failed in a big way
8 "___ Na Na"
9 Common pasta suffix
10 Mexican beer
11 Thingamajig
12 Royalty payers, say
13 Collar attachment
18 Certain Fed
23 Reggae precursor

25 Org. with Lions, Tigers and Bears
26 ___'acte
27 Thumb a ride
28 Escapes injury
31 Fam. member
32 Allies of the Trojans in the "Iliad"
33 What pad Thai is often cooked in
34 Bake, as eggs
35 Not closeted
37 Letters on brandy
39 Old draft category for civilian workers
40 Italian wine area
41 Cartoon boy who can be described by an anagram of his name
46 It runs the "L"
47 Mercury counterpart
48 Native Canadian
49 Test, as ore

50 Mary or Elizabeth
51 Cough drop brand
52 Like some legal proceedings
53 Kama ___
57 Word said while pointing
60 Dander
61 Dr. ___
62 Spanish 57-Down
63 Tuna type

by Kevan Choset

ACROSS

1 Concealed
4 It's wide in a May-December romance
10 Quaint words of worry
14 "I love," to Ovid
15 Elaborate architectural style
16 Mineral in thin sheets
17 With 62-Across, question in a children's song
20 Seoul's land
21 Yoko who loved John
22 Hellish suffering
23 Yukon S.U.V. maker
25 Justice Sotomayor
27 Entertain in a festive manner
30 *It's a happening place
34 *Sophocles tragedy
37 Ram's mate
38 Rants
39 Action before crying "You're it!"
40 Full political assemblies
42 Summer: Fr.
43 *British luxury S.U.V.
45 *Star-making title role for Mel Gibson
48 Oozed
49 ___ the Cow (Borden symbol)
52 TV forensic series
53 Old Olds model
56 TiVo, for one
58 Words often after the lowest-priced in a series of items
62 See 17-Across
65 Sorority's counterpart, for short
66 Infuse with oxygen
67 Extra periods of play, in brief
68 1970s–'80s sitcom diner

69 Secret get-togethers
70 Oink : pig :: ___ : cow

DOWN

1 Dove's opposite
2 "If you ask me," in chat rooms
3 Thinker's counterpart
4 Localized charts
5 Liquidy gunk
6 Verbal feedback?
7 Fancy dresses
8 Sneezer's sound
9 "The Raven" writer
10 Pricey watches
11 Song syllables before "It's off to work we go"
12 Thom ___ shoes
13 "Duck soup"
18 Jackson a.k.a. Mr. October
19 Reason for a game delay

24 Gulager of "The Last Picture Show"
26 Veto
27 Rodeo rope
28 Sidled (along)
29 "¿Cómo ___ usted?"
31 "Pet" annoyance
32 Possessed
33 Tiny bit of crying
34 City near Provo
35 Managed
36 Messy Halloween missiles
40 Forewarns
41 Cantering
43 Doc's written orders
44 Common Market inits.
46 Scouts earn them
47 Tons
50 Aesop's grasshopper, for one
51 The "E" in EGBDF
53 Having two bands, as most radios

54 Apollo plucked it
55 Airline to Israel
57 Food label figs.
59 "Indiana Jones and the Temple of ___"
60 "Do ___ others as . . ."
61 Cuban money
63 Tit for ___
64 Giant among baseball's Giants

by Ed Sessa

ACROSS

1 "Ad __ per aspera" (Kansas' motto)
6 Fine pillow stuffing
11 Car with a checkered past?
14 Turkish money
15 Parkinson's treatment
16 Egg: Prefix
17 Audibly shocked
18 Military muscle
20 Sign of change at the Vatican
22 Prell rival
23 Ogle
24 Ship slip
25 RR stop
26 Chief Norse god
28 Saffron and ginger
32 Functional lawn adornment
36 Per person
37 Word that can follow both halves of 18-, 20-, 32-, 40-, 54- and 57-Across
39 Plus
40 Take every last cent of
42 Inflatable safety device
44 Curt denial
45 10 Downing St. residents
46 Scoring 100 on
49 One who keeps plugging along
53 Fade
54 "Go" signal
57 Using all of a gym, as in basketball
59 Eagle's home
60 Network that aired "Monk"
61 007, for one
62 News that may be illustrated by a graph
63 Fictional detective __ Archer

64 Like the north side of some rocks
65 __ Park, Colo.

DOWN

1 "There oughta be __!"
2 "Alas" and "ah"
3 Curly hair or hazel eyes
4 Haile Selassie disciple
5 Bad-mouth
6 Actress Jenna of "Dharma & Greg"
7 Moron
8 Almost any character on "The Big Bang Theory"
9 Fencing blade
10 Radio format
11 Shrink in fear
12 Deflect
13 Word with canal or control

19 Place to get free screwdrivers, say
21 Free throw, e.g.
24 Said, as "adieu"
26 "__ for octopus"
27 "Yeah, like you have a chance!"
28 Regulatory inits. since 1934
29 __ around with
30 Winter driving hazard
31 Wide strait
32 Word of qualification
33 Priest's garment
34 Org. with a prohibited-items list
35 Sharer's opposite
38 Parisian assent
41 Yule libation
43 Quarantine
45 & 46 Quite bad
47 Effect's partner

48 Something acquired by marriage?
49 Shore fliers
50 Shore fixtures
51 "Snowy" wader
52 __ Valley, German wine region
54 __ girl
55 Regrets
56 Senators Cruz and Kennedy
58 Machine part

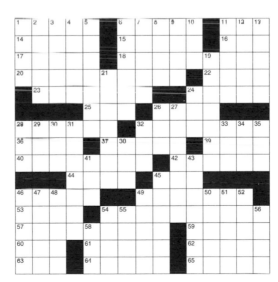

by Robert Cirillo

ACROSS

1 Tree with acorns
4 Garment under a blouse
7 Expresses derision
13 "___ Mir Bist Du Schön" (1938 hit)
14 Dress that covers the ankles
16 Lassie, for one
17 ___ and tonic
18 Droop in the heat
19 Set off from the margin
20 Lead-in to Bear or Berra
22 Post-monologue spot for Jay Leno
24 Male and female
25 Shade of meaning
27 Diatribes
29 German coal region
30 Former penitentiary in San Francisco Bay
34 "___ luck!"
36 Japanese camera
37 Anger
38 One with a leading role?
39 Santa ___ winds
40 Tex-Mex fare with shells
42 East Lansing sch.
43 Get access, as to a protected site
45 "___ the Sheriff" (Eric Clapton #1 hit)
46 Grated cheese
48 Ancient Peruvian
49 In the midst of
50 "Oh my stars!"
53 Miata maker
56 Prefix with present
58 BlackBerrys and Palms, for short
59 Mark that might be left with greasy fingers
61 Supply-and-demand subj.
63 Monthly entry on a bank statement: Abbr.
64 Say O.K., begrudgingly
65 Western mil. alliance
66 Wedding words
67 Dried plums
68 Imbecile
69 Prankster

DOWN

1 Maternity ward doc
2 Group to which "Y" is sometimes added
3 "Monty Python and the Holy Grail" protagonist
4 Mini Cooper maker
5 Oakland N.F.L.'er
6 Wheel turner
7 Astron., e.g.
8 Eponym of the city now known as Istanbul
9 Like St. Augustine vis-à-vis all U.S. cities
10 Show off at Muscle Beach
11 Alternative to a jail sentence
12 Tennis units
15 Camp classic by the Weather Girls . . . or a homophonic hint to 3-, 8-, 26- and 31-Down
21 Occupied, as a bathroom
23 Alpo alternative
26 So-called "Father of Europe"
28 Sgt., e.g.
31 Shakespeare play that begins "Now is the winter of our discontent"
32 Suffix with buck
33 Joie de vivre
34 "One ___ or two?"
35 Greece's Mount ___
36 1998 Winter Olympics host
41 Musical alternative to B.M.I.
44 Bear: Sp.
47 Infuriate
48 Imbeciles
51 Bit of candy that "melts in your mouth, not in your hand"
52 Legally prevent
53 Car showroom sticker inits.
54 The "A" in U.S.A.: Abbr.
55 South African native
57 Sweet 16 org.
60 Many "Star Trek" extras, for short
62 1, 2, 3, etc.: Abbr.

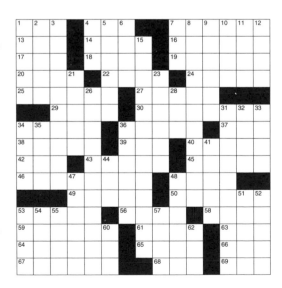

by John Lieb

ACROSS

1 Fed. procurement overseer
4 Boito's "Mefistofele," e.g.
9 "Delta of Venus" author Nin
14 Giver of a hoot
15 Remove, as a spill
16 Bendel of fashion
17 *Migratory flock
19 Couldn't stand
20 Small French case
21 Appear
22 Plenteous
23 Cuckoo in the head
25 Dada pioneer
28 Heart
29 Greek letter traditionally associated with Earth Day
30 *Singer Amy with six Grammys
33 Drought ender
35 Group of papers
36 *Pegasus, notably
39 Asian capital that was from 2004–07 home of the world's tallest building
41 ___ Minor
42 *"Regardless of the outcome . . ."
44 News items often written years in advance
49 Directional suffix
50 D.C. V.I.P.
51 Dim sum dish
52 Yale Whale players
54 Blarney Stone home
57 Stat for A-Rod
58 Take care of a fly?
60 Witticism . . . or, literally, a description of the answer to each of the four starred clues?

62 Año's start
63 Facing the pitcher
64 Who said "The revolution is not an apple that falls when it is ripe. You have to make it fall."
65 "Hollywood Nights" singer Bob
66 Bronx Bombers
67 Le Mans race unit: Abbr.

DOWN

1 Head toward the setting sun
2 Trade, as places
3 Attraction
4 "Yipe!," online
5 Wordsworth words
6 Sporting weapon
7 Artifice
8 Hypothetical primate

9 "Yes . . . that's the spot . . . yes!"
10 Approaching
11 Like a "Better active today than radioactive tomorrow" sentiment
12 "You can't make me!"
13 Not the main action
18 Course-altering plan?
24 Brothers of old Hollywood
26 Auto take-backs
27 Mummy, maybe
30 Golfer Michelle
31 River through Pakistan
32 Training acad.
34 Like a ballerina
36 Manitoba's capital
37 Big W.S.J. news
38 Charlemagne's domain: Abbr.

39 Plucks, as brows
40 Fleet operator
43 Like a relationship with a narcissist
45 Historical subject for Gore Vidal
46 "It's me again"
47 Chinese martial art
48 Onetime colleague of Ebert
51 "___ Previews" (onetime show of 48-Down)
53 Not doubting
55 Journalist Skeeter of the Harry Potter books
56 Amazon.com ID
59 ___ favor
61 Amt. to the right of a decimal point

by Paula Gamache

ACROSS

1 "The Lord of the Rings" creatures
5 Sprinkle with holy water
10 Number in a quartet
14 Muck
15 Preceded, with "to"
16 Loll
17 New ___ (Enya type)
18 Licoricelike flavor
19 Colored part of the eye
20 Friendly comment after providing information
23 Sports stadium
24 Lesser-played part of a 45
25 Cellist Casals
28 Puccini opera or its heroine
32 Put ___ happy face
34 Goes "pop!," as a jack-in-the-box
38 Shakespeare in the Park founder/producer Joseph
40 Italian birthplace of Paganini
41 Captain ___ (pirate)
42 Rome's nickname, with "the"
45 Lock unlocker
46 The king, in France
47 Volleyball star Gabrielle
49 Cuckoo ___
53 French words describing how roast beef is often served
56 Author of the verse that starts with the beginnings of 20-, 34- and 42-Across
59 Coca-___
61 Bramble
62 ___ about (approximately)
63 Prefix with lock

64 Whiskered creature
65 Loaned
66 Dynamite sound
67 Insects with big stingers
68 Where sailors go

DOWN

1 Nebraska's largest city
2 Severity
3 Party streamer material
4 One of the Williams sisters
5 Lacking pizazz
6 Sultry singer Horne
7 Does some magazine work
8 Fish-on-rice serving
9 Put the pedal to the metal
10 Simple means of animation

11 They're in locks on a boat
12 Israeli-made gun
13 In medias ___
21 Keep ___ on (watch)
22 Tennis do-overs
26 Org. for women drivers
27 Pitcher Hershiser
29 Quirky bandleader with the City Slickers
30 Give up
31 Handy-___
32 German automaker
33 Kids' detective ___ the Great
35 "Monsters, ___"
36 Alternative to rouge in roulette
37 Box-office take
39 Declare loudly
43 River near the Pyramids
44 2013, e.g.

48 Domelike top
50 U-shaped bend in a river
51 Magna ___
52 Makes woolen bootees, e.g.
54 Slightly leading in score
55 Mattress brand
56 Voice below soprano
57 Shallow's opposite
58 Makes mistakes
59 Hack's vehicle
60 Yoko who married John

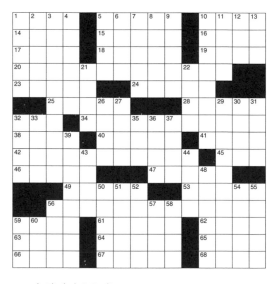

by Elizabeth C. Gorski

ACROSS

1 767s, e.g.
5 Tame, as movies go
11 Move like a bunny
14 Wyatt out West
15 Farthest point of a 50-Down
16 Goof or go off
17 1960s dissident
19 ___ de la Plata
20 Suffix with Tao or Mao
21 Fend (off)
22 "You've gotta be kidding!"
23 1987 movie with the hit "Hungry Eyes"
27 Bodies of rules
30 In other words, in old Rome
31 Checkup
32 More together
34 He's no gentleman
37 Smash-hit entertainment?
41 K.C.-to-Nashville direction
42 Tests for many Ph.D. candidates
43 Farm unit
44 Boxer Roberto with "hands of stone"
46 Like some schoolbook folders
48 Fast-food chain with an orange and pink logo
52 "Dies ___"
53 Series of golf courses that host the British Open
54 Carrier to Oslo
57 Co. whose logo includes Leo the Lion
58 Jump-rope style
62 ___ jeans
63 Like some job training
64 Grp. whose members account for more than 50% of the world's defense spending

65 Abbr. on a golf scorecard
66 Solid, liquid and gas
67 Lacking depth . . . or like 17-, 23-, 37-, 48- and 58-Across?

DOWN

1 Darth Vader, once
2 Corny things?
3 Public transport option
4 Letters on a beach bottle
5 Some control tower equipment
6 To the left, at sea
7 Winter warmer
8 Flan ingredient
9 Actor Billy ___ Williams
10 Neighbor of Lux.
11 Creature that adopts a seashell

12 Figure of myth known for his belt
13 Tine
18 Minnesota player
22 IV units
23 "___ arigato, Mr. Roboto"
24 T. rex and others
25 Mideast port
26 Mathlete, stereotypically
27 Surrender
28 Lumberjacks' tools
29 Acted the fink
32 Lectern, e.g.
33 Suffer
35 Skilled
36 Like orange hair
38 Actress Singer
39 Hassan Rouhani's land
40 Goes back
45 Lanai strings
46 Students taught alone

47 Slightly
48 How romantic dinners are lit
49 Encouraged
50 Satellite's path
51 Nick of "Cape Fear"
54 Persian suffix that ends seven country names
55 When the balcony scene occurs in "Romeo and Juliet"
56 Like racehorses' feet
58 Opposite of no-nos
59 Prov. bordering Manitoba
60 Winner of more than half of all the World Puzzle Championships
61 Prefix with lateral

by Mike Doran

ACROSS

1. Conks on the head
5. Old Russian ruler
9. Drummer Ringo
14. Israel's Abba
15. Charles Lamb's pen name
16. Place to keep a hibachi
17. Prefix with dynamics
18. Lambs' fathers
19. Diplomatic representative
20. Part of a bushel belonging to Dick?
23. Chaney who played the hunchback of Notre Dame
24. Greek letters before rhos
25. Facial expression
29. Serving between appetizer and dessert
31. S-shaped molding
33. Prefix with Atlantic
34. Car belonging to Rex?
37. Professional charges
39. Catch, as a criminal
40. New York's Giuliani
41. Lite beer belonging to Bea?
46. The last King Richard
47. "Cheerio!"
48. Facial socket
51. Put another layer on, as of paint
53. Exploit
54. Column's counterpart
55. Rock belonging to Ariel?
59. Waikiki welcome
62. "___ upon a time . . ."
63. Taylor boy of Mayberry
64. Actress Sophia
65. Gomer of Mayberry
66. "Darn it all!"
67. Doghouse infestation
68. Former spouses
69. Lairs

DOWN

1. Long-eared dog
2. King of the fairies, in Shakespeare
3. Like the end of this clue (in terms of punctuation)
4. Kiss, to Brits
5. Wirehaired dog
6. Leaves rolling in the aisles
7. Prepares to shoot a gun
8. Filing tool
9. Homo sapiens, for humans
10. Goes suddenly from success to failure, in slang
11. Off-road goer, for short
12. ___ de Janeiro
13. Artist Lichtenstein

21. Abbr. above 0 on a phone
22. Tied, scorewise
26. Self-esteem, as the French would have it
27. Encircle
28. Small whirlpool
30. Too hasty
31. ___ bin Laden
32. Mongolian desert
35. The "I" of M.I.T.: Abbr.
36. Center square of a bingo card
37. Not foul
38. Lake ___, source of the Niagara River
42. Salt Lake City residents, e.g.
43. Pro ___ (proportionally)
44. Tenants
45. Cleaning solutions

49. ___ Sea, body of water south of Italy
50. Messages limited to 140 characters
52. Milo of "The Verdict"
53. "I give up!"
56. 1948 Hitchcock thriller
57. Cameo gem
58. Mrs. Lincoln's maiden name
59. TV ET
60. Response to an online joke
61. Bauxite, e.g.

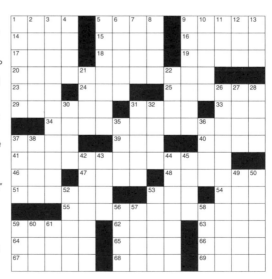

by Edgar Fontaine

ACROSS

1 Schmooze
5 Tanning lotion letters
8 Discombobulates
13 Bum
14 Chimney feature
16 Praise to the skies
17 1922 Willa Cather novel that won a Pulitzer
19 Email option
20 Prefix with lateral
21 "___, With Love"
23 Jazz instrument
24 Next-to-last Greek letter
25 Bridge or Scrabble need
28 Classic pop brand
30 Darwin's "On the ___ of Species"
34 PC alternatives
36 Verdi's "Don Carlos," e.g.
40 Very much
41 University address ender
42 Class boosters, for short
43 Big attraction for bargain hunters
47 Site of an occasional outbreak in Sicily
48 Musical incompetence
49 Light and breezy
51 Some school exams
55 Mrs., in Monterrey
58 With 35-Down, a court game
61 Discover
62 Innocent ones
64 Texas monument, with "the"
66 Maximum loads of hay or vegetables
68 B-ball player
69 Worry, worry, worry
70 Word with family or shoe

71 Speed units for seafarers
72 Flamenco shout
73 A really long time

DOWN

1 Bite from Pac-Man
2 Baseball Hall-of-Famer Wagner, one of the first five inductees
3 Prez who delivered a famous address on Nov. 19, 1863
4 Blow a whistle
5 Bay Area airport, briefly
6 Dwarf planet whose moons include Charon and 12-Down
7 Big to-do
8 Mondale's 1984 running mate

9 Log cutter
10 Hits with a Taser
11 Fitzgerald who sang duets with Louis Armstrong
12 Moon of 6-Down named for a mythological river
15 To be, to Tiberius
18 Take the bait?
22 Music lover's carry-along
26 Short smoke?
27 Big ___ (group of stars in Ursa Major)
29 High regard
31 Where 3-Down's address was delivered
32 1979 revolution site
33 2011 launcher of Curiosity
34 Crow's-nest site
35 See 58-Across

37 Sun. sermonizer
38 Summer cooler
39 One with a regular habit?
44 Seafarers
45 Our planet, to a German
46 Seafarer, informally
50 Library ID
52 Swerves at sea
53 Muse of poetry
54 Anaheim ballplayer
56 31-Down general's signature
57 Complete jerks
58 Hike, with "up"
59 Country singer Jackson
60 Shakespearean villain
63 Shaving lotion brand
65 Came across
67 Have creditors

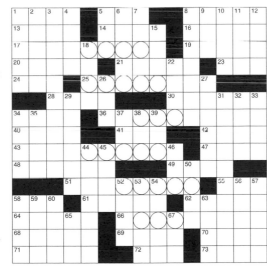

by David J. Kahn

ACROSS

1 Remarks not made seriously
6 Tiny arachnid . . . or tiny amount
10 Greek letters resembling tridents
14 Hawaiian greeting
15 Wild mountain goat
16 ___ trap (part of a dryer)
17 Italian city with a semiannual fashion week
18 Big jump
19 ___ Krabappel of "The Simpsons"
20 Start of a bumper sticker that may end with one's favorite vacation spot
23 Spanish hero El ___
26 ___ Xing (street sign)
27 Cheer for a torero
28 Mattress site
29 Start of a bumper sticker that may end with one's favorite hobby
33 Expect
34 Employ
35 Pens' contents
38 Condé ___ (magazine company)
39 Penalized for a driving violation, say
41 Slugger Carlos
42 Buzzing pest
43 Chapel Hill sch.
44 Prove appropriate for
45 Start of a bumper sticker that may end with one's favorite (usually expensive) vehicle
49 Piece of stage equipment

51 Wish undone
52 Possessed
53 "Love ___ neighbor . . ."
54 Start of a bumper sticker that may end with one's favorite attraction
58 Where Tibet is
59 Madison and Fifth, e.g.: Abbr.
60 College student's concentration
64 Casino game with numbered balls
65 Restaurant window display
66 Circumvent
67 Small fractions of joules
68 Tiny colony dwellers
69 Geeklike

DOWN

1 Alternative to jelly
2 Inventor Whitney
3 Note after fa
4 Spicy ethnic food
5 Hole dug on a beach
6 Term of address for a noblewoman
7 Sarcastic reply
8 Place to sip oolong
9 Kicked out
10 Commoner
11 Secondary advantage
12 Concave belly button
13 Be upright
21 Hoops official
22 Vintage car inits.
23 Former tennis pro Michael
24 Des Moines native
25 Gathering of biological evidence after an arrest

30 Poker pot
31 ¹⁄₁₆ of a pound
32 Venomous snake
36 Jewish turnover
37 4-Down skewered meat dish
39 Comedy Central cartoon set in the year 3000
40 Beyond elated
44 Troubling sign of things to come
46 Celestial body
47 ___ monkey
48 Half-___ (latte order)
49 No longer sleeping
50 Stingy sort
55 Vientiane's land
56 Clark ___, alter ego of Superman
57 Four-star review
61 Jelly container
62 Strange
63 King: Sp.

by Kevin G. Der

ACROSS

1 Decree
6 Paths of lobs
10 Basic quatrain scheme
14 "Hawaii Five-O" nickname
15 French 4 + 4
16 Olin of "Chocolat"
17 Hiker's snack
19 "It must be something ___"
20 European peak
21 What's being discussed in the National Enquirer or Globe
23 Mete out
25 Quick wit
26 Airhead
28 Willow twig
31 Matter of law
34 Adams in a bar
38 Winter woe
39 Provision in many a construction contract
42 Asian language with no plural form
43 "We're on!"
44 Said "Guilty" or "Not guilty," say
45 "Live long and prosper" speaker
47 "Suis" is part of its conjugation
49 Cranapple juice and others
53 Modern home of the ancient Zapotec civilization
57 Poor weight loss practice
60 Buns, e.g.
61 Winds up
62 Intellectual property protection . . . or what the starts of 17-, 21-, 39- and 57-Across once were
64 Siouan tribe
65 Jannings who won the first Best Actor Oscar
66 Didn't go out for dinner
67 Covered club, usually
68 Fit to be tried
69 Neck parts

DOWN

1 Mystery prize
2 Friend of Porky and Spanky
3 Unsuited
4 Fox News rival
5 Pretentious, informally
6 Starbuck's boss
7 Change in Russia
8 Bye lines?
9 "Dilbert" or "Doonesbury"
10 Cover stories
11 Stunning
12 Animated bug film
13 Singer of many Dylan songs
18 Imager of the earth's surface
22 Waggish
24 Inkling
27 17-Across ingredients, often
29 Otherwise
30 Lamented
31 Ones drawn to film?
32 "Hurry!"
33 Shaggy's dog
35 Extinct ostrichlike bird
36 Impulse
37 Transitional zone between plant communities
40 Fancied
41 Zenith
46 After-hours shop sign
48 Seller of cloth scraps
50 Casual evenings?
51 Skin: Prefix
52 Blotch
54 One with space to sell, for short
55 NPR news analyst Roberts
56 Professional grps.
57 "That hurts!"
58 Wise about
59 Thumb-twiddling
63 ___ glance

by Don Gagliardo and Zhouqin Burnikel

18 ⭐

ACROSS

1 Villain in the tale named by the starts of 20-, 32-, 41- and 52-Across
5 Chicago air hub
10 Letterman of late-night
14 Cleveland's lake
15 Forty-___ (California Gold Rush participant)
16 Grandson of Eve
17 Sound signaling the start and end of class
18 Flared dress type
19 Pants fillers
20 "The Bad News Bears" activity
23 Includes in an emailing
26 ___ Moines, Iowa
27 Scuba tank content
28 Colored part of the iris
30 Judges levy them
32 Supposed hints that mislead
34 With 61-Down, description of the 1-Across
37 Eve's mate
38 Number before dos and tres
39 Musical ending
40 Elephant's weight unit
41 Lawn tractor
45 Orange traffic markers
46 Staggered
47 Disco light
50 Caribbean ___
51 NNW's opposite
52 Jaguar on the front of a Jaguar, e.g.
56 Slightly
57 Part of a carpenter's joint
58 Spirited horse
62 Malden or Marx
63 Steaming mad

64 "Come to ___"
65 In other ways
66 Following
67 Took a gander at

DOWN

1 What a spider spins
2 Valuable rock
3 "___ Abner"
4 Cut down, as a tree
5 Running wild
6 Sword handles
7 Indigo dye
8 Actress Russo
9 Soon, old-style
10 Airport woes, as due to bad weather
11 Lay ___ (bomb)
12 Style
13 City on the Ruhr
21 Nothing doing?
22 Former spouses
23 Diamond unit

24 The Golden Rule is a good one
25 Alternative to a station wagon
29 George with a physics law
30 The end
31 Hip to
33 Like talking during a movie, e.g.
34 Soup holders
35 Notions: Fr.
36 En ___ (fencer's cry)
39 College in Iowa
41 Movie lead-in to Cop
42 Subject of Newton's first law of motion
43 Like the grass on the other side, in a saying
44 Be defined as
45 Treat like a baby
47 Drink that may be ordered with a burger

48 Completely wreck
49 Sounds heard at the start of MGM movies
50 Struck down, biblically
53 Soft ball material
54 Med. school subj.
55 Adhesive
59 Sunbeam
60 Copy
61 See 34-Across

by Adam G. Perl

ACROSS

1 Latch (onto)
5 Shin-related
11 "Mad Men" output
14 Premium brand of the Volkswagen Group
15 National color of the Netherlands
16 Blow away
17 Bobbysoxer's footwear
19 Presidential nickname
20 Made a perfect engine sound
21 Draw a breath
23 Toledo Mud Hens' class
24 Sleeveless garment
26 "I had not thought death had undone so ___": "The Waste Land"
28 Mater ___ (the Virgin Mary)
29 Hindu honorific
30 The S.E.C. regulates it
31 Goes fast
33 Gapes
37 Impromptu
40 Bone: Prefix
41 Wished
42 Cliff ___, 2008 Cy Young Award winner
43 U.P.S. unit: Abbr.
45 One likely to go [hic!]
46 ___ Kudiddlehopper (Red Skelton character)
47 Nestlé bar
51 ___ alai
52 Trap
53 Bad serves
56 Cubs' and Eagles' org.
57 The signs in the movie "Signs"
60 Contraction in "The Star-Spangled Banner"
61 Allude to

62 Modern prefix meaning "super"
63 Score tally: Abbr.
64 Much H. L. Mencken output
65 Professional filibusterers: Abbr.

DOWN

1 Laceration
2 Pig-out party?
3 One that doesn't belong
4 When Armed Forces Day falls
5 Steel-___ boots
6 Bureau of the Dept. of the Treasury
7 "___, humbug!"
8 How French fries are fried
9 Some are secret, and some are special
10 One low in a pantheon
11 Anticipate
12 Certain guitar
13 Win four out of four, say
18 Meadow
22 King killed in the sack of Troy
24 Candy bar brand
25 Line to fill a line
26 Sushi bar soup
27 Computer downloads, informally
28 Rapper Mos ___
31 Odontalgia
32 India's ___ Rebellion, 1857–59
34 "Who'da thought?!"
35 Lower end of the strike zone
36 Mushroom piece
38 Scout's job, informally

39 ___ Life
44 N.H.L.'s James ___ Memorial Trophy
46 Political assembly
47 Some jazz
48 Many a map of Hawaii
49 Ivan IV and V
50 Old Dodge compacts
51 Shake
53 Conniptions
54 High schooler, typically
55 Ukr., Est. and Lith., once
58 Elhi support grp.
59 Small, low island

by Phil Ruzbarsky

ACROSS

1 ___, crackle, pop
5 When repeated, lucky lottery purchaser's cry
9 ___ Crunch (Quaker cereal)
13 Regretful one
14 Emperor at the Circus Maximus
15 Ho-ho-hoing
16 Coerce
18 1940s computer
19 Hitchcock roles, famously
20 Play-Doh, e.g.
21 "I tawt I taw a puddy ___"
22 Treeless plain
25 Perched on
27 Abbr. on a bottle of Courvoisier
29 Civic group with more than 45,000 affiliates
31 Font lines
34 Dairy Queen purchase
35 Martians, e.g., in brief
36 Like some broadcast frequencies
39 Admirals' org.
42 Mars's Greek counterpart
43 Moistens, as a turkey
47 Illicit Prohibition-era establishment
50 "How r u?," e.g.
51 River to the North Sea
52 Cast (off)
55 Jason Bourne, for one
56 Uncles' wives
58 "Pretty" thing to say, with a cherry on top?
60 The ___ Brothers (R&B group)
61 Where lifeboats are generally stored

64 Head, as a committee . . . or a word that can follow the ends of 16-, 29-, 36-, 47- and 61-Across
65 Nietzsche's "no"
66 Onetime Harper's Bazaar illustrator
67 Observed
68 Summers in St.-Tropez
69 Cape Canaveral acronym

DOWN

1 Sophs., in two years
2 Crackpot
3 Seltzer-making device
4 Dance for 1-Down
5 Gold bar
6 One that goes "pop" in a children's song
7 Rink star Bobby
8 ___ de plume
9 Popular cold and flu medicine
10 Somewhat
11 Develop in a particular way
12 The Big Apple: Abbr.
15 Game: Fr.
17 Super ___, old game console
20 Fountain head?
21 Some Sharp and Sony products
23 "Les Demoiselles d'Avignon" artist
24 Winnie-the-___
26 Airer of Masterpiece Classics
28 More, to a musician
30 ___ Genesis, old game console
32 Criticism, informally
33 Accent
37 Authentic

38 D.D.E.'s predecessor
39 Manipulate
40 Ostentatious
41 Interstellar clouds
44 Tile piece
45 Anticipates
46 Home in the mud
48 Epic tale that begins with the flight from Troy
49 Marketer's target, maybe
53 Small, secluded valleys
54 ___ Majesty the Queen
57 Mars's Norse counterpart
59 Yemeni port
60 Glacier, essentially
61 Article in Arles
62 Cat or gerbil, e.g.
63 Mauna ___ Observatories

by Nina Rulon-Miller

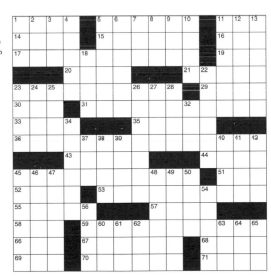

21

ACROSS

1 Czech or Pole
5 Make use of
11 Ring org.
14 Commercial prefix with postale
15 Pal of Pooh
16 Pipe joint with a 90-degree turn
17 Pen with a fat felt tip
19 Not firm ground to stand on
20 Weaver's apparatus
21 Come to pass
23 All-star lineups
29 Zap with light
30 Pal of Pooh
31 Aboriginal healers
33 Writer Quindlen
35 One barred from bars
36 Annual Vicksburg pageant
43 ___ worms
44 Board of directors hirees, for short
45 Band with the 2007 #1 album "We Were Dead Before the Ship Even Sank"
51 Rap's Dr. ___
52 Country subject to 2006 U.N. sanctions
53 Like Lombard Street in San Francisco
55 Plain or peanut candy
57 Suffer from
58 Company name ending
59 Pooh-bah
66 Certain special FX
67 What Darth Vader serves, with "the"
68 "Let us ___"
69 See 65-Down: Abbr.
70 Showed mercy to
71 Cashier's tray

DOWN

1 Cooke of soul
2 Meadow
3 Evita's land: Abbr.
4 "Behold!"
5 Bump down
6 Really chewed out
7 Firth of Clyde port
8 Moo goo gai pan pan
9 Prospector's quest
10 Peter on a piano
11 Video chat necessity
12 Garment traditionally buttoned on the left side
13 Nelson who wrote "The Man With the Golden Arm"
18 Ways and Means, e.g.: Abbr.
22 White-collar job?
23 Apothecary unit
24 Rice-A-___
25 Many ages
26 Sets one's sights on
27 Early 12th-century year
28 50-Down and others
32 Prohibitions
34 Go up
37 More, in Madrid
38 Certain gridiron stats. Abbr.
39 Certain
40 Mani-___
41 NSFW material
42 Words often said with a nod
45 Apes
46 Actual color of an airplane's black box
47 1978 Bob Fosse musical
48 Higher calling?
49 Like fortunate subway riders
50 Green-eyed monster
54 Entice
56 Sras., across the Pyrenees
60 One behind home plate, informally
61 Balancing expert, in brief?
62 Aperitif with white wine
63 State sch. in the smallest state
64 Berkeley school, informally
65 Jon ___, former 69-Across from Arizona

by Bill Thompson

ACROSS

1. ___ lazuli
6. "Gotta go!"
10. Jabbers
14. Springtime of life
15. All roads lead to it, in a saying
16. Pitcher Hershiser
17. "I'm outta here!"
19. ___ Major (constellation)
20. Kind of band
21. Like a recently waxed floor
22. They connect cooling units to rooms, in brief
25. Unmemorable low-budget film
26. Beaches
27. ___ longue (daybed)
29. Snake's warning
30. Bent over, as from pain
33. Letter holder: Abbr.
34. This puzzle's theme
36. Brian who was a pioneer of ambient music
37. Locales for T-bars
39. Cleveland's lake
40. Infant's wear
41. Leprechaun, for Notre Dame
43. Bleachers
45. Bowling game
46. Vowel sound at the end of 39-Across
47. Deliberately gives wrong information
49. Elec. or water
50. "¡Adios, amigo!"
54. Marvin of Motown
55. Kuwaiti leader
56. Earl of ___, favorite of Elizabeth I
57. Chairmaker's strip
58. "Cheerio!"
59. Answer

DOWN

1. The Beatles' "Rubber Soul" and "Revolver"
2. "We ___ the Champions"
3. Quiche, for one
4. Candy heart sentiment
5. Event that might involve a Ouija board
6. Overpacks
7. Letter before kappa
8. "Praise be!"
9. "___ the ramparts we watched . . ."
10. Poor sport's taunt
11. "Godspeed, Bruno!"
12. Joe of "My Cousin Vinny"
13. Satisfy, as a thirst
18. Response to "Shall we?"
21. "Peace begins with a ___": Mother Teresa
22. Fireplace residue
23. Armor flaw
24. "Farewell, Vladimir!"
25. Infant
27. Computer programmer
28. Centers of wheels
30. Dummy
31. The "U" of U.S.S.R.
32. "Dead ___ Society"
34. Air freshener brand
35. "My bad!"
38. Wrestler's wear
39. Advocate
41. Small plateau
42. Weapon for a reindeer
43. Hits with the fist
44. Bottom line of an addition
45. Four: Prefix
47. Tibetan priest
48. "Really?"
50. Plenty worked (up)
51. Mind reader's inits.
52. Toothpaste form, often
53. Clearasil rival

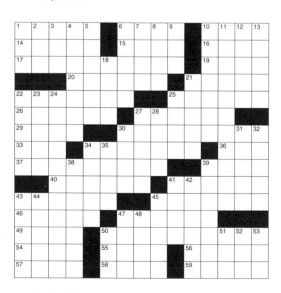

by Greg Johnson

ACROSS
1 "___ Poetica"
4 Alerts to cruisers, for short
8 Footlong sandwich maker
14 Fraternity T
15 In fashion
16 "Seinfeld" ex-girlfriend
17 *Sheriff's insignia, in old westerns
19 How to make money "the old-fashioned way"
20 Like trees during the spring
21 Privy to
23 Shot from an air gun
24 Burns black
25 L.B.J. or J.F.K., but not D.D.E.
26 Speak on the stump
28 Old coll. entrance hurdle
29 *Actor named in a "Six Degrees" game
31 Hemingway novel title location
33 Oaxaca uncle
34 Piece next to a bishop: Abbr.
35 Word with sister and story
36 Some appliances, for short
38 Alley ___ (hoops play)
41 "Nope, not interested"
43 Ironfisted ruler
46 *Tangy breakfast item
49 Stock exchange debuts, briefly
51 Author James
52 Sounds from Santa
53 Surgically implanted tube
54 Org. found in the answer to each asterisked clue

55 Swiss river
56 Italian granny
57 Supercute marsupials
59 *Packers' hometown
61 "Good enough for me"
62 ". . . happily ___ after"
63 Carbon-dating estimation
64 Have faith in
65 Shoulder muscle, for short
66 The "R" of Roy G. Biv

DOWN
1 Where webs may accumulate
2 Galoshes go-with
3 *Tanning method
4 Prep schools: Abbr.
5 M.A. follow-up, maybe
6 Grandiose proposal
7 Part of many a Shakespearean act
8 Observed
9 Suffix meaning "little one"
10 Singer Streisand
11 *Recover, as lost love
12 Jennifer of "Friends"
13 "Not ___" ("Be patient")
18 Puts underground
22 Neglect to mention
26 Wind instruments
27 "The Lord of the Rings" creature
29 Serving on a skewer
30 Bruce who played Dr. Watson
32 Bub
37 Show disdain for, in a way
38 "___-la-la!"
39 Lacking in variety

40 *Tommy's game in the Who's rock opera "Tommy"
42 Response to a wisecrack
43 Merit
44 *Feature of many a charity gala
45 Ship's carrying capacity
47 How some temperatures—and tests—are taken
48 Stuffed
50 Didn't go
53 "Hägar the Horrible" dog
55 "He's like ___ to me"
57 ___ Royale (cocktail)
58 Hubbub
60 Sinuous fish

by Paula Gamache

ACROSS

1 Coca-___
5 It represents a family on a coat of arms
10 Sound from Big Ben
14 Police action
15 ___ de Mayo (Mexican holiday)
16 Love: Lat.
17 Italian soup pasta
18 Mammal with the largest brain of any animal
20 Holy hymn
22 Thin-layered mineral
23 Complain, complain, complain
24 Riding on someone else's shoulders
28 Marsh gas
31 School for an English prince
32 Blood classification system
33 Opposite of fem.
35 44-Across, en español
39 "Believe you me!" . . . or what you can do with the start of 18-, 24-, 53- or 63-Across?
44 Peepers
45 Je ne sais ___
46 Xbox alternative
47 ___ & Chandon (Champagne)
51 Chicken pieces that aren't legs, thighs or wings
53 Young Indiana Jones portrayer
57 Street: Abbr.
58 Director Joel or Ethan
59 Hog sounds
63 Dry-ice contraption for theatrical effect
67 Squeal of delight
68 Trolley
69 Vietnam's capital
70 Produce
71 "Auld Lang ___"
72 Back of a boat
73 Like show horses' feet

DOWN

1 Corn, wheat or soybeans
2 Relatives of paddles
3 Multitalented Minnelli
4 Newspaperman Ochs
5 Hypodermic amts.
6 ___ Van Winkle
7 A Hatfield, to a McCoy
8 Professional writer
9 Philanderer, in slang
10 Cry before "humbug"
11 Fastballer Ryan
12 Muscat citizen
13 Allman brother who married Cher
19 Texas city on the Brazos
21 Home for the Dolphins
25 Flying pest
26 Heroic exploit
27 Old radio or TV part
28 Aussie's buddy
29 Online auction site
30 Puff from a joint
34 ___ au vin
36 1975 shark thriller
37 "You can count ___"
38 Equipment for schussing
40 Salinger's "For ___-With Love and Squalor"
41 London subway, with "the"
42 What Little Boy Blue blew
43 "Old MacDonald" refrain
48 Shamu, for one
49 Pleistocene and Eocene, for two
50 Something to pass at a fund-raiser
52 Self-evident truths
53 Whitewater transports
54 Piano key material, once
55 Eschewing both meat and dairy
56 Cat-___-tails (whip)
60 Ark builder
61 Executioner in "The Mikado"
62 What many furry animals do in the spring
64 Butterfly or Bovary: Abbr.
65 Neither's partner
66 German "a"

by Michael Blake and Andrea Carla Michaels

ACROSS

1 United rival, once
4 Large number
8 With 68-Across, prison where 36-Across spent 18 years
14 Enjoy a repast
15 Green land
16 Philippine seaport with a reduplicative name
17 Cockpit reading: Abbr.
18 With 60-Across, 1994–99 role for 36-Across
20 Yeats's "___ and the Swan"
22 Non-U.S. gas brand
23 "Oh no!"
24 Class of automobile inspired by the Ford Mustang
26 In the back, nautically speaking
28 Born: Fr.
29 Predecessor of 36-Across and sharer with him of the 1993 Nobel Peace Prize
31 Dog tail motions
33 Abbr. at the end of a French business name
34 Knot
35 Chicago White ___
36 Late political leader who wrote "Long Walk to Freedom"
42 "___ a living"
43 Hubbub
44 ___-advised
46 Father, in Xhosa, and a nickname for 36-Across
48 Bygone policy in 60-Across
51 Boycott
52 Vote for
54 Reads carefully
55 River that can be seen from the Uffizi Gallery

57 Geezer
59 Zero ___ (near)
60 See 18-Across
63 Acid holder
65 Rubbernecker
66 Glitch
67 Flight board posting, for short
68 See 8-Across
69 Watch like a wolf
70 "Oedipus ___"

DOWN

1 Kind of party
2 Be immersed by
3 Barack or Michelle Obama, at the memorial service for 36-Across
4 Prepare to travel again
5 Make known
6 Unlimited latitude
7 "___ of the D'Urbervilles"
8 Finished with
9 Corrida cry
10 Skeletal
11 Harsh, as winter winds
12 Runs off, as Romeo with Juliet
13 Checking account come-on
19 Author Dinesen
21 L'Oréal product
24 Enlistee with a chevron above an arc: Abbr.
25 Some horns
27 Having no depth, briefly
30 Draw up new boundaries for
32 Log chopper
35 Saw logs
37 Illuminated

38 "Don't go anywhere"
39 Evolving
40 Covers
41 Estrange
45 Mormons: Abbr.
46 Fortunetelling decks
47 Like many physicals
48 Beginning
49 Battlefield procedure
50 Part of Attila's legion
51 Low voices
53 Online greeting
56 Other, in Oaxaca
58 Approximately
61 Rooster's mate
62 Low-___ (for weight-watchers)
64 Strain

by David J. Kahn

ACROSS

1 Bird's "arm"
5 Pasta often baked with tomato sauce
9 Place to live
14 Birthright seller in the Bible
15 Mimicked
16 U.C.L.A. athlete
17 ___ of one's existence
18 In some common women's office attire
20 Embarrass
22 Lexicographer Webster
23 Good name for a garage mechanic?
24 What may lead to an emotional explosion
27 Command opposite to "gee"
28 Blood component
29 News, Post, Tribune, etc.
31 Basketball officials, informally
35 NW Indiana city
36 Half-quart container
40 Sit for a painting, say
41 L. Frank Baum princess
42 "Like I care!"
44 Gentlemen: Abbr.
50 Unlock, in poetry
51 Creamy French cheese
55 Trac II successor
57 ___ Bora (former Taliban stronghold)
58 Dutch-speaking isle in the Caribbean
59 Gridiron runback
62 Lab container
63 Pass, as a law
64 "Green-eyed monster"
65 Villa d'___
66 Seized vehicles
67 Card game played without twos through sixes
68 Protected, as horses' hooves

DOWN

1 Google Calendar, e.g., informally
2 Novelist Allende
3 Refrain syllables
4 Whom hosts host
5 Electrocute
6 Classic toothpaste brand
7 Carpentry piece inserted into a mortise
8 Dog collar add-on
9 ___ Dhabi
10 Verve
11 Highly unconventional
12 Related to food intake
13 Provides money for, as a scholarship
19 Generic collie name
21 Beehive sound
25 Role
26 Pasta sauce brand
30 Score between a birdie and a bogey
32 Comedian Philips
33 Hat with a tassel
34 "Uncle ___ wants you"
36 Afternoon office pick-me-up
37 Ending like -like
38 ___ tide
39 Identical
40 Candidate for the Top 40
42 Daytime drama, informally
43 Schlep
45 Actress Mendes
46 Starts of tennis rallies
47 Step on, as a bug
48 Fluctuation of musical tempo
49 Like an envelope that's ready to be mailed
52 Memoranda
53 Front of an elephant or back of a car
54 Caterpillar stage, for example
56 Classic record label
60 N.F.L. linemen: Abbr.
61 W.S.J. rival

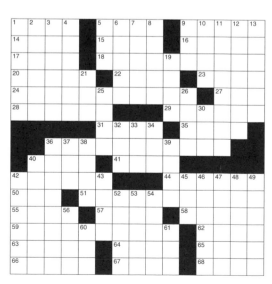

by David Steinberg

ACROSS

1 Insurance giant with a duck in its ads
6 "I messed up!"
11 Food preservative, for short
14 Pack animal
15 Eagle's nest
16 Big name in jeans
17 Being extravagant and self-indulgent
19 Comfort ___
20 Place to relax
21 Baseball count
22 North American finch
24 "Ragged Dick" author
27 Site of Kubla Khan's "pleasure dome"
30 ___ terrier
31 Pirouette
32 Barbershop symbol
34 Pocket watch accessory
37 Illumination in "The Star-Spangled Banner"
41 Adam's ___ (water)
42 Gorgons
43 One of Spain's Balearics
44 "Survivor" immunity token
46 King Arthur's resting place
47 All-malt beer
52 Jeweler's eyepiece
53 Feminine name suffix
54 Terrier's bark
57 Cause of inflation?
58 Scotch whisky brand
62 Mop & ___ (floor cleaner)
63 "Raw" or "burnt" color
64 It's moving at the movies
65 Lombard Street feature

66 "The Wrestler" actress Marisa
67 Blender setting

DOWN

1 "___ right with the world"
2 1960s hairstyle
3 Volcanic emission
4 Bordeaux buddy
5 Be lovey-dovey
6 Valletta is its capital
7 It's not used to make matzo
8 "It's c-c-cold!"
9 2008 U.S. govt. bailout recipient
10 Record spinner
11 Fancy gold jewelry, e.g.
12 Ergo
13 Opera's Mario Lanza, for one
18 Expert

23 Suffix with glob
24 "Listen up!," old-stylo
25 Archipelago parts
26 Green lighted
27 Bonus, in ads
28 Barracks no-show
29 "Good job!"
32 "The Lord is my shepherd . . . ," e.g.
33 Assn. or grp.
34 Not make the grade?
35 Rice-shaped pasta
36 Noggin
38 G
39 Be concerned, slangily
40 Letter-shaped shelf support
44 Jackanapes
45 Like most jigsaw puzzles
46 I.R.S. employees: Abbr.

47 French beach
48 Stirs up
49 Continental cash
50 Flood barrier
51 Creator of the game Missile Command
54 Petri dish gel
55 Storm
56 Hightail it away
59 Managed care plan, for short
60 Co. with the motto "Think"
61 Australia's national bird

by Tracy Gray

ACROSS

1 Follows orders
6 Be a passenger
10 Hop, ___ and a jump
14 Mass destruction
15 Ruler of Dubai
16 Small plateau
17 *"The Sixth Sense" director
20 Actress Ward of "CSI: NY"
21 Recent: Prefix
22 Apportion
23 *1988 Best Play Tony winner inspired by Puccini
27 Kiddie racer
30 Gift upon arriving in Honolulu
31 Bit of cheesecake
34 California's Santa ___ racetrack
35 Girl in Byron's "Don Juan"
37 Upstate N.Y. campus
38 TV hookups
39 *Craft knife brand
40 Duck or one of its colors
41 Antlered animal
42 Two-lanes-into-one highway sign
43 "Voilà!"
44 Chicken drumstick
45 ___ nutshell
46 More than enough
47 *2007 Stephen Colbert satirical book
51 Mosey along
53 Holder of sale goods
54 Praise
58 *22nd in a Sue Grafton series
62 "The Time Machine" people
63 Puts on TV
64 Actor Hirsch of "Into the Wild"
65 Philosopher Descartes

66 Information on a boarding pass or stadium ticket
67 ___ numerals (what the initial letters of the answers to the five starred clues all are)

DOWN

1 ___ law (electricity principle)
2 Source of misery
3 Diabolical
4 They may be unrolled before meditation
5 Acad. or univ.
6 Button putting everything back to zero
7 Declaration while perspiring
8 Handyman's inits.
9 Gay Nineties, e.g.
10 Wee
11 Good color for St. Patrick's Day
12 Golfer Aoki
13 Huff and puff
18 Letter-shaped bolt fastener
19 "The Sopranos" subject
24 Garment under a blouse
25 Best of the best
26 Move, to a real estate agent
27 It helps call a meeting to order
28 "Mon ___" (Jacques Tati film)
29 Dodgers slugger who was the 1988 N.L. M.V.P.
32 In pieces
33 "Wrecking Ball" singer Cyrus
35 Former West Coast N.F.L.'er
36 Heart chart: Abbr.
39 TV's "warrior princess"
40 Something to remember in San Antonio?
42 Old copy machine
43 "Here Comes Honey Boo Boo" channel
46 ___-Pong
48 "What's it all about, ___?"
49 Late critic Roger
50 Light wash
51 State forcefully
52 1/500 of the Indianapolis 500
55 Lively, on scores: Abbr.
56 Its fight song is "The Mighty Bruins"
57 TV chef Paula
59 Cleaning cloth
60 By way of
61 Always, in odes

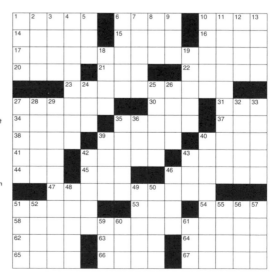

by Zhouqin Burnikel

ACROSS

1 Anatomical pouches
5 Rocker Hendrix
9 Ingredient in a screwdriver
14 Online source for TV shows
15 Dos you don't want to sit behind at movies
16 "Let ___!" ("Full speed ahead!")
17 Norse war god
18 Aggressive swarms
20 Glittery stone
22 Headline event in India in 1974 and '98
23 ___-pitch softball
24 Facilities with padded walls
27 And more, in brief
28 Neighbor of Hung.
30 Hitter's stat
33 Square root symbol
39 Florence's river
41 Complete makeovers
42 Pinza of "South Pacific"
43 One of two figures in "The Wizard of Oz"
46 Eastern newt
47 Spoil
48 Like some baseball teams and batteries
50 1969 platinum record for Creedence Clearwater Revival
58 Feathered stole
60 Joyful cry
61 Equestrian, e.g.
62 Question posed while pulling leftovers from the fridge . . . or a query about the initial words of 18-, 24-, 33-, 43- or 50-Across?
65 Suffix with concession
66 Boxer's bane
67 Mixed bag
68 Stellar phenomenon
69 "Chicago" director/choreographer
70 Surrealist played by Adrien Brody in "Midnight in Paris"
71 Editor's retraction

DOWN

1 Japanese chess
2 "In Memory of W. B. Yeats" poet
3 Ad awards
4 It may have a cherry on top
5 Alternative to Newark or La Guardia
6 One of Chekhov's "Three Sisters"
7 Sloughs off
8 R&B's ___ Brothers
9 Almost real
10 Place to put down stakes?: Abbr.
11 Number at a bridal boutique
12 German city on a canal of the same name
13 Lhasa ___ (dog)
19 Adult ed course, often
21 ___ 'acte
25 Greeting that saves postage
26 Calliope or Euterpe
29 End-of-week cry
30 Damp and chilly
31 One loyal to the Union Jack, informally
32 Sits on to keep warm, say
34 Mountain ___
35 Despot Amin
36 Infirmary sight
37 Leave ___ (do permanent damage)
38 Excluding
40 Some pods
44 How sausage links are connected
45 Locks
49 About 60% of the world's inhabitants
51 More, in Madrid
52 "My heavens, no!"
53 "Alley Oop" woman
54 Dieter's salad request
55 Bonehead
56 "You have some ___!"
57 Distinguished
58 Son of Willy Loman
59 Capital near the 60th parallel
63 Suffers from
64 "___ Hear a Waltz?"

by Mark Bickham

ACROSS
1 Bid
6 +
10 Police officer
13 Actor Nick
14 Countless centuries
15 Arrow-shooting Greek god
17 Buy a meal for
18 An operator may help place one
20 Hem and ___
21 Letter after theta
23 Luxurious country house
24 Suffix with shepherd
25 Wine-producing area of SE France
28 Pokes in the rear
30 Assistance
31 Fabric amts.
32 Exclusively
33 1, 1, 2, 3, 5, 8, 13, 21, 34, . . . e.g.
36 Flown into a rage
41 In a composed manner
42 Historical periods
44 Distant
47 Cry loudly
48 Widespread food shortage
50 Refused to cooperate
54 Savor, as fine wine
55 Marisa of "Anger Managem~ ..
56 Anise-flavored liqueur
57 President before D.D.E.
58 Everybody . . . or part of the contents of 18-, 25-, 36- and 50-Across
61 Adhesive
63 Go separate ways
64 Rights group, for short
65 Message in 140 or fewer characters

66 British bathroom
67 "Porgy and ___"
68 ___, Roebuck and Co.

DOWN
1 Always rushing, rushing, rushing
2 Very inexpensively
3 Went without a copilot
4 When a plane is due in, for short
5 Stop working at 65, say
6 ___-Bismol
7 "Freaky Friday" actress Lindsay
8 First numero
9 Nine-digit fig.
10 Filmmaker ___ B. DeMille
11 Through word of mouth

12 Surveyed, as before an election
16 Leaves rolling in the aisles
19 Avoids, as capture
22 Noncommittal replies
26 Late's opposite
27 Britain's last King Henry
29 In ___ (working harmoniously)
33 Rio carnival dance
34 Building wing
35 Flower's support
37 Enter gently
38 Hard hit
39 Isle of Man's locale
40 Flour or sugar container
43 Groups like Disney's dwarfs
44 Camera setting
45 Lacking a key, musically

46 Cesar who played the Joker
48 Turkish topper
49 Accepts formally, as a resolution
51 "Cool!"
52 Lies languidly
53 Real doozies
59 Apply lightly, with "on"
60 Snoopy, in his dreams
62 Stupefaction

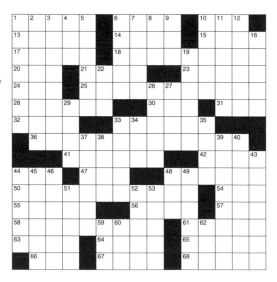

by Lynn Lempel

ACROSS

1 Nonsense
5 Nonsense
9 Nonsense
14 "California ___ Alles" (classic punk rock song)
15 James who wrote "A Death in the Family"
16 Car with a stylized caliper in its logo
17 Target of NASA's Rover mission
18 B&Bs
19 Clear of vermin à la the Pied Piper
20 Nonsense
22 Nonsense
24 Near-prime seating
26 Overseer of N.Y.C. subways
27 Nonsense
31 "Didn't you leave out something . . . ?"
33 Emulates Jay Z and Master P
37 Score before a service break, maybe
38 Windshield material
40 ___ King Cole
41 Nonsense
42 Nonsense
43 Nonsense
45 "Well, ___ be!"
46 River crossed by the Pont d'Avignon
48 Kingly
49 "Sax on the Beach" musician John
51 '50s presidential nickname
52 Nonsense
53 "Thumbs up" response
55 Sailor's tale
57 Nonsense
61 Nonsense
66 Some jabs and turns
67 "Right back ___!"
69 Second hearing?
70 Skylit rooms

71 Tiny bit of time: Abbr.
72 Thin Russian pancake
73 Nonsense
74 Nonsense
75 Nonsense

DOWN

1 Hurdle
2 Certain metal beam
3 Wang of fashion
4 Long ago, once
5 Turnkey
6 Nixon's number two
7 Kind of state that's peaceful
8 Piquancy
9 Attacked
10 Brand of mops and brooms
11 Member of a Turkish minority
12 Russia's ___ Mountains
13 Australian pal
21 More hackneyed
23 Iraq war concerns, for short
25 Nonsense
27 Chewing one's nails, e.g.
28 The black swan in "Swan Lake"
29 E-ZPass charges
30 Follower of Jul.
32 Silver of fivethirtyeight.com
34 Near, poetically
35 Fruit also known as a prairie banana
36 Inscribed stone slab
38 Understand, informally
39 Drawn (out)
44 Lo-___ (not so clear)
47 Shout after a series of numbers
50 McDaniel of "Gone With the Wind"

52 Bring up, as a subject
54 "Can you see" preceder
56 "Sure, I remember!"
57 Shrug-worthy
58 Actor Jared of "My So-Called Life"
59 Do that may have a pick
60 Tirade
62 Jimmy who wrote "Galveston" and "MacArthur Park"
63 Rights org.
64 Leg part
65 Beep
68 General on a menu

ACROSS

1 Modern set in the family room
5 Family name of Henry VIII
10 Canine newborns
14 Suffix with buck
15 Tehran native
16 Samoa's capital
17 Site of a 1963 speech by 38-Across
20 Asparagus unit
21 Matchmaker's match-ups
22 George Eliot's "Adam ___"
25 Allow
26 Boston ___ Party
27 Boeing 747, e.g.
30 Cause associated with 38-Across
33 Docs' org.
34 Enthusiastic
35 Actress Saldana of "Avatar"
36 "Morning Joe" co-host Brzezinski
38 Annual Jan. honoree
41 Vampire's bedtime
44 When a plane is due to take off: Abbr.
46 Long narrative poem
48 Three on a grandfather clock
49 Repeated phrase in 38-Across's speech at the 17-Across
53 Genetic stuff
54 Super ___ (game console)
55 Employ
56 Seize
58 Aggressive campaign TV spot
61 New arrangement of tracks on a recording
65 Famous closing words of the 49-Across speech
68 "Rule, Britannia" composer Thomas

69 Muscat citizen
70 Poet ___ Khayyám
71 "Star Wars" sage
72 Pulls apart
73 Muted trumpet sound

DOWN

1 Dutch old master Frans
2 Burning candle feature
3 Voice inflection
4 Words, informally
5 "___ Death" (2000s Fox sitcom)
6 Large container of coffee
7 Moist
8 Tie score early in a game, maybe
9 Covered with more frost
10 ___-mutuel betting
11 Still undecided

12 Luxury watch brand
13 Does a Latin dance
18 Vacuum cleaner brand
19 David ___, baseball's Big Papi
23 Per ___ (by the day: Lat.)
24 Stuntman Knievel
27 Smucker's product
28 Former owner of Capitol Records
29 Get off the fence?
31 Print shop device
32 "In ___ We Trust"
37 Dunes transport, briefly
39 Emailed pic, often
40 Niagara Falls sound
42 Take home the gold
43 Actress Long of "Boyz N the Hood"
45 Score before ad in or ad out

47 Brainy
49 More or less
50 Prefix with sexual
51 Request
52 "My goodness!"
57 Under
59 Zone
60 College adviser
62 Papa's mate
63 What "vidi" means in "Veni, vidi, vici"
64 Bonus, in commercial lingo
66 Conclusion
67 "___ for apple"

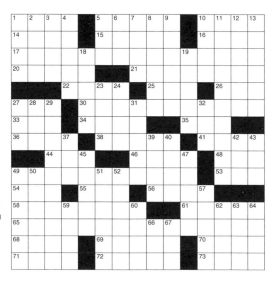

by Elizabeth C. Gorski

33

ACROSS

1 With 72-Across, what the answers on this puzzle's perimeter form
5 Beech and birch
9 "Yay!," in a text message
13 Drink served either hot or cold
14 Qualified
15 Iberian river
16 Any hit by the Everly Brothers, e.g.
17 Swarm (with)
18 Brief reminder
19 Performs, as historical scenes
21 Turkish hospice
23 Taunt
24 Moved smoothly
26 Fictional Flanders and Plimpton
28 Not worthy of
32 Hack's vehicle
35 Nancy Reagan's maiden name
37 2007 documentary about the health care system
38 Wilson of "The Life Aquatic With Steve Zissou"
40 Put back to zero, say
42 Latin musician Puente
43 Celebrate noisily
45 Inspiration for Old Major of "Animal Farm"
47 Summer clock observance: Abbr.
48 Florida home for Hemingway
50 Caddie's pocketful
52 Brew, as tea
54 Indonesian currency
58 Certain paint protector
61 Heed
63 Curve in a crown molding

64 Dress ___ (impersonate)
66 Nostalgic style
67 Writer Sarah ___ Jewett
68 Ski resort in Salt Lake County
69 Leaking, as a faucet
70 Nutcase
71 Take a gander
72 See 1-Across

DOWN

1 ___ Coyote (toon)
2 More bizarre
3 Control, as costs
4 Like calls from bill collectors, typically
5 Unit of power
6 Way overweight
7 Cheer in Chihuahua
8 Death
9 Cry upon arrival

10 High, in German names
11 "Coffee, Tea ___?" (1960s best seller)
12 Beep
13 Telephone attachment
20 Chest material
22 ___ Health magazine
25 Part of AWOL
27 Gracefully thin
29 ___ wash jeans
30 Times Square booth sign
31 Knee-slapper
32 One may pop on New Year's Eve
33 Bide-___
34 Group of beauties
36 Ending with advert
39 Magazine launch of 1933 with a hyphen in its name
41 Wedding cake parts

44 "___ thousand flowers bloom"
46 Car gear
49 ___ relations
51 Suit company founded in Australia
53 Student of Socrates
55 Emcee's delivery
56 Take ___ (travel)
57 Basketball target
58 Diner employee
59 Farming: Prefix
60 City NNE of Tahoe
62 "Babette's Feast" author Dinesen
65 Mideast grp.

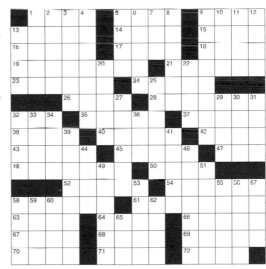

by Todd Gross

ACROSS

1 Attack with a knife
5 "Oops-a-daisy"
9 Hypermasculine
14 See 2-Down
15 Duet minus one
16 Patriot Ethan of the Revolutionary War
17 *Flying
19 "Silly" birds
20 Renter's document
21 "No idea"
23 Mormons, in brief
24 *One placed between warring parties
29 Ivy League school in Philly
30 Encountered
31 Docs' grp.
32 *Contestant's help on "Who Wants to Be a Millionaire"
36 Like some cereals
38 Colored part of the eye
39 Softly, in music
42 Born and ___
43 Serving on a skewer
45 *King, queen or jack
47 Brian who composed "Music for Airports"
48 The "L" of L.A.
51 Squabbles
52 *Piece of furniture that might be under a chandelier
55 "There ___ is, Miss America"
58 Epic work by Virgil
59 Quick
61 Hybrid kind of battery
63 Vacation lodging purchase . . . or an arrangement between the two halves of the answer to each starred clue?

66 Desert flora
67 Battery
68 Port of Yemen
69 "America's Finest News Source," with "The"
70 Car parts that have caps
71 Hotel and hospital features

DOWN

1 Shower unit
2 ___ and 14-Across (reliable)
3 Surrounding glows
4 Risks
5 It's between Can. and Mex.
6 ___ lane
7 Kind of acid in soapmaking
8 World Series of Poker game

9 X-Men villain
10 Coeur d'___, Idaho
11 1963 Elizabeth Taylor role
12 Guys
13 First number dialed when calling long distance
18 Push back, as an attack
22 Hawaiian strings, for short
25 "Idylls of the King" lady
26 ___ Domini
27 Mideast bigwig: Var.
28 Early stage of industrial work, for short
29 Mexican money
32 Had a crush on
33 Resident of Tehran

34 Eponym of a number series that begins 1, 1, 2, 3, 5, 8, . . .
35 Munchkin
37 Kindergarten basics
40 Bit of pasta, for short
41 Green science: Abbr.
44 Not be conspicuous
46 Pitchers
49 Mined metal
50 Hilarious person, in slang
53 "Far out!"
54 Fond farewell
55 Digging tool
56 Put on the payroll
57 Perfect places
60 Ill-fated captain
61 Sgt., e.g.
62 Suffix with Dickens
64 Cubs and White Sox org.
65 Windy City trains

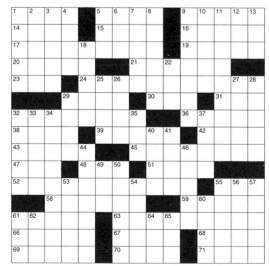

by James Tuttle

ACROSS

1 Stern's opposite
5 Varieties
9 Exercise unit
14 One of the Smurfs
15 Father of Ham
16 Monastery wear
17 ___ rock
18 Fit ___ king
19 Archaeological site
20 Celebration dance after a goal?
23 Sr.'s challenge
24 "Stop!"
25 Oodles
27 Combat engineer
30 Separated, as a couple
33 Degree in math?
34 Get through to
37 Part of a drum kit
38 Many millennia
40 Sag
42 They're tapped
43 Like many traffic violators in court
45 E.M.T.'s cry before using a defibrillator
47 Network that airs the Soul Train Music Awards
48 Find, as at an archaeological site
50 Hardships
52 Stuff in a muffin
53 Goddess of the hunt
55 Letter before omega
57 Punched out a Disney elephant?
62 Ration out
64 Slender reed
65 It may be checked, in more ways than one
66 "Fiddler on the Roof" character
67 Rural route
68 Politico Gary
69 Impassive
70 It's just one thing after another
71 Not duped by

DOWN

1 Relaxing spots
2 Crunchy sandwich
3 Vast
4 Like the Marx Brothers
5 Like some vision
6 Tapestry-making aids
7 Gold standard
8 Its appearance is deceiving
9 Torahs, for example
10 Marker letters
11 Aerobics done to Chubby Checker music?
12 Forearm bone
13 Head-turner
21 Eternally
22 Like Jimmy Carter and Bill Clinton, religiously: Abbr.
26 Farm sound
27 Real mix-up
28 Didn't go anywhere for dinner
29 Give a hobbit a ring?
30 It's about a foot
31 Prompter
32 Raid targets
35 Eyebrow shape
36 Rank above maj.
39 In the vicinity
41 One known for talking back?
44 Extreme, as measures
46 Orange exterior
49 Channel with the catchword "Drama"
51 South American cowboy
53 Home of the Burj Khalifa, the world's tallest building
54 Desktop pictures
55 Fours on a course, often
56 Thin strip
58 Cinnabon purchase
59 Haunted house sound
60 Former baseball commissioner Giamatti
61 Comics canine
63 Kimono sash

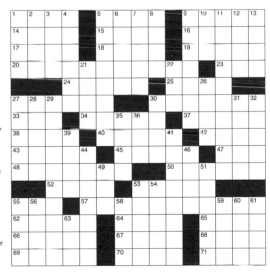

by Jeff Stillman

ACROSS

1 ___ of the Apostles
5 Gentleman's partner
9 Veranda
14 Circle
15 "Essays of ___" (1823 volume)
16 French farewell
17 Leader of Qatar
18 Run ___ (go wild)
19 Mechanical man
20 January 1 to December 31
23 Chicago trains
24 Tack on
25 Little devil
28 Texter's "If you ask me . . ."
31 First pilot to travel faster than the speed of sound
35 Florida city between Tampa and Fort Myers
37 Egyptian peninsula
38 Curves
39 Evening news hour
42 Snorkasaurus of toondom
43 Contents of some urns
45 Line across a circle
47 Area around a henhouse
50 Hosp. areas
51 Barrett of Pink Floyd
52 Slip of paper in a poker pot
53 Recipe meas.
55 Bright color
61 Everglades critter
64 Black: Fr.
65 Prefix with dynamic
66 Chicago airport
67 Deal (with)
68 Burrito alternative
69 Cold-weather jacket
70 Squeezed (out)
71 Spoken

DOWN

1 Baldwin of "30 Rock"
2 Result of a concussion, maybe
3 "Double, double, ___ and trouble"
4 Binge
5 Air rifle pellets
6 ___ mater
7 Fashionable Christian
8 Gab and gab some more
9 Fourth of July and Veterans Day events
10 Aroma
11 Tidbit often served barbecue-style
12 Co. head
13 Thatch-roofed dwelling, maybe
21 Pennant race inits.
22 Big name in ice cream
25 Set on fire
26 More cruel
27 Rap sheet listings
28 "Inside Llewyn Davis" actor Oscar and others
29 Like wetland
30 Common corsage flower
32 Member of a Western tribe
33 Checkout counter staple . . . or, when read as three words, what 20-, 31-, 47- and 55-Across have in common
34 Helper
36 "Hold on ___!"
40 Zadora of "Santa Claus Conquers the Martians"
41 Like Joan of Arc
44 Vail in the winter, e.g.
46 Goods: Abbr.
48 Seeming eternity
49 Subtlety
54 Philosopher who said "Writing is the geometry of the soul"
55 Popped topper
56 Corner piece in chess
57 "Eek!"
58 Shakespearean king
59 Killer whale
60 Winter wear material
61 Republicans, for short
62 "Oh, I see!"
63 Paving material

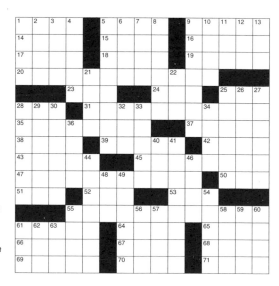

by Sean Dobbin

ACROSS

1 Coal carriers
5 Take pleasure, as in one's glory
9 One-named singer with the 2006 hit "Too Little Too Late"
13 Soon, quaintly
14 Tennis's Nastase
15 "Same with me"
17 Author of the best-selling book series in history
19 ___ buddy
20 Founder of U.S. Steel
21 "Thank you," in Hawaii
22 Actress Caldwell and others
23 Instant
24 Office PC hookup
25 Joe Namath or Mark Gastineau
28 Actress Christine of "Funny About Love"
30 Wall St. operator
31 Eschews takeout, say
35 A deadly sin
38 Means of a castaway's escape, maybe
40 Early bloomers
41 "Inside the Company: C.I.A. Diary" author Philip
42 Vocalist Lovett
43 Itch (for)
45 R.N. workplaces
46 Take pleasure in
48 The "A" of James A. Garfield
50 Stew holder
52 "___ Boys" (Louisa May Alcott novel)
53 "___ Lisa"
55 HOW THIS CLUE IS WRITTEN
57 "Peter Pan" author
61 Kind of jacket
62 Dagwood Bumstead's boss
63 Campaign sign directive
64 On task
65 Exclude
66 Josip ___ Tito, Yugoslav statesman
67 Egyptian goddess whose headdress was shaped like a throne
68 A model strikes one

DOWN

1 Muslim's trek
2 Cleaning a mess, maybe
3 Quad quarters
4 Alarm clock button
5 Baloney
6 Name after "a.k.a."
7 ___ Féin (Irish political party)
8 "Animal House" party fixture
9 "The Well-Tempered Clavier" composer
10 "I'm intrigued!"
11 Reclusive best-selling novelist
12 Alley Oop's girl
16 "That was my cue"
18 Composed, as an email
21 Villain
23 Like pomaded hair
25 Viscount's superior
26 Word with tube or vision
27 Pen name for Angela Lansbury's character on "Murder, She Wrote"
29 Boston Harbor jetsam
32 They often elicit blessings
33 Photocopier parts
34 Holy Trinity member
36 Stylish Wang
37 Polite rural affirmative
39 Real hottie
44 Charged, as in battle
47 Arizona Diamondbacks pitcher who was a 2007 All-Star with Seattle
49 Drink a little here, drink a little there . . .
50 Woodsy odor
51 Candy bag wt., maybe
53 2,502, to ancient Romans
54 Newspaper part with mini-bios
56 With a bow, on a score
57 Hwy. crossings
58 San ___, Italy
59 Showy bloom
60 Villa d'___
62 ___ alai

by David Steinberg

ACROSS

1 Period just before dark
5 Sprint
9 Barnyard brayers
14 "Do ___ others as . . ."
15 ___ -bitty
16 Goes like a racecar
17 Item accompanying a pencil in miniature golf
19 Em and Jemima
20 Judging component at a beauty pageant
21 Face-to-face exams
23 Hurled weapon
24 Money available for nonessentials
28 Poet Ogden
30 Hawaiian medicine man
31 C.I.O.'s partner
34 Lifeguard areas
37 When flights are due in, for short
38 Food, warmth or a cozy bed
42 See 33-Down
43 Hotel robe material
44 Cloud's place
45 Samantha's mother on "Bewitched"
48 ___ of Sandwich
50 Stuffed figure in a cornfield
53 Make sport of
57 Native of 58-Across
58 The Last Frontier state
59 Beginning of a Flintstones cry
62 Gym locale . . . or feature of 17-, 24-, 38- and 50-Across
64 Premature
65 Elvis's middle name
66 Many a new driver
67 High heels, e.g.
68 It's often long at Disneyland
69 Dinner scraps

DOWN

1 Does some light housework
2 Take the lid off
3 Embezzled, e.g.
4 Like Hyundais or Kias
5 Place to find wds.
6 One thing ___ time
7 Barber's sharpener
8 Nine-headed serpent of myth
9 Red or pink bloom
10 Second-in-command in a kitchen
11 Junior, to Senior
12 CPR expert
13 Leaky tire sound
18 Mesmerized
22 Noah's construction
24 Position between second and third, informally
25 Hyundai and Kia
26 Cattiness
27 Quickly made, as a decision
29 Not worth a ___
31 Symptoms of rheumatism
32 Swiss currency
33 With 42-Across, help out
35 "To Kill a Mockingbird" author Harper
36 Item in the hardware department with a "+" or "−" on its head
39 So darned cute
40 ___ pro nobis
41 ___ Beach, S.C.
46 Pass-the-baton events
47 Fortunate card to have with a queen or king in blackjack
49 Makeshift shelter
51 Out of town?
52 Cheri formerly of "S.N.L."
54 Fall bloomer
55 Sport with clay pigeons
56 Makes, as wages
58 Proactiv target
59 "You betcha!"
60 Response to a massage
61 Preppy, party-loving, egotistical male, in modern lingo
63 Swindle

by C. W. Stewart

ACROSS

1 "___ be my pleasure"
4 Like some doughnuts
10 Sweets
13 ___ culpa
14 Ford featured on "The Waltons"
15 Piano, on a music score
16 3, 4 or 5 on a golf hole, typically
17 Say that neither side benefited
19 "___ stupid question . . ."
21 Mai ___
22 Año starter
23 Strand
27 Playwright O'Neill
28 Homer's father on "The Simpsons"
29 Pilot's announcement, for short
30 Exert, as energy
31 Monopoly square between Connecticut Avenue and St. Charles Place
33 Words of estimation
34 Start being printed
37 Early Ron Howard role
40 Hula dancers shake them
41 Edwards or Andrews: Abbr.
45 Coffee dispenser
46 ___ -X
47 Autonomous part of Ukraine
48 Join a community again
52 F.D.R.'s affliction
53 Bank offering with a pct. yield
54 Season to drink 58-Across
55 Extensive enumeration . . . or what's formed by the ends of 17-, 23-, 34- and 48-Across

58 See 54-Across
59 Shamu, for one
60 Be on the precipice
61 Pull (on)
62 Book after Ezra: Abbr.
63 Reason for an inquisition
64 Ave. crossers

DOWN

1 Stabs
2 Comb into a beehive, e.g.
3 Hardly a period of enlightenment
4 Maker of the Yukon S.U.V.
5 More than dislike
6 Two-time loser to Dwight
7 1983 Woody Allen mockumentary
8 Inventor Whitney
9 Suited to be a suitor
10 More than a pack rat
11 In a way
12 ___ degree
15 Nor. neighbor
18 Hathaway of "Les Misérables"
20 Take an eye for an eye for
24 Within: Prefix
25 Unpleasant discoveries in soup
26 Ming of the N.B.A.
31 31-Across, slangily
32 Form of many a modern game
33 Become inflexible
35 Civil War winning side
36 "You bet!"
37 Your and my
38 Make, as a meal
39 Connected with someone

42 Quantities
43 Left a military formation
44 No-goodniks
46 Electrical system
47 Goes after
49 Radius neighbor
50 Persian Gulf vessel
51 Too-often repeated
55 Chaney of the silents
56 "___ haw!"
57 Give it a go

by Matthew E. Paronto and Jeff Chen

ACROSS

1 Lose one's footing
5 Bruins' sch.
9 Sewing machine inventor Howe
14 Dialogue unit
15 Bridge
16 Lone Ranger's sidekick
17 1989 John Hughes movie starring John Candy
19 Concluding notations
20 Took to the slopes
21 Accepts punishment unflinchingly
23 Contains
24 "There, there . . . stop crying"
28 Vain person's problem
29 Letters before an alias
30 35, as a minimum to be U.S. president
31 "___ on your life!"
32 Belgrade resident
34 Volcanic debris
36 Many a dreadlocks wearer, informally
38 Paul McCartney/ Michael Jackson hit . . . or a hint to the starts of 17-, 24-. 57- and 65-Across
42 Like one's voice when one has a cold, maybe
45 Letter after ess
46 Biblical garden
50 "Incidentally," in a text
51 The "L" in 5-Across
54 Spinks foe
56 Gobbled up
57 Snack that leaves the fingers orange
60 Puppy's cry
61 1996 Mario Puzo novel, with "The"
62 Door fastener
64 Vice ___
65 "This is just ridiculous!"
68 Animal cavorting by a stream
69 "Mona ___"
70 Once again
71 Boxer Spinks and others
72 Tater
73 "Darn it all!"

DOWN

1 Fruit-flavored ice drinks
2 Connection
3 Front tooth
4 One-named soccer star
5 ___ port (computer feature)
6 Heart of a computer, for short
7 Milk: Prefix
8 Turkey's capital
9 And so on
10 Tight's opposite
11 Mumbai residents
12 With some speed
13 Emergency call
18 Poet ___ St. Vincent Millay
22 Frat party fixture
25 "Fine by me"
26 The "m" in $E = mc^2$
27 Train stop: Abbr.
33 Troop grp.
35 It may be tipped as a sign of respect
37 Captain's affirmative
39 Best of the best, sportswise
40 Calendar's scope
41 Buy's opposite
42 Jimmy Fallon's network
43 Olympian, e.g.
44 Solemnly affirm
47 Nascar race locale
48 Printout taken to the airport, maybe
49 Huey, Dewey and Louie, to Donald
52 Ref. with about 22,000 pages
53 Looks of displeasure
55 "La ___ Bonita" (1987 Madonna hit)
58 Ruhr Valley city
59 Not cool
63 Slightly open
64 Remote button abbr.
66 Sun Devils' sch.
67 Smidgen

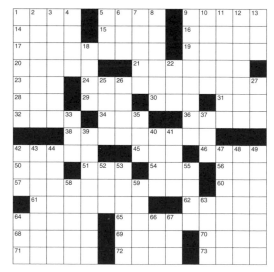

by David Gray

ACROSS

1 *Everything
5 "Yo mama" joke, e.g.
9 Hopeless case
14 Buffalo Bill's surname
15 *Rap devotee, slangily
16 University of Maine locale
17 "Gotcha, dude!"
18 *One who goes on and on
20 *"What should I ___?"
22 Lollapaloozas
23 "___ tu" (Verdi aria)
24 Run like the wind
26 "Am I nuts?"
28 Former Rocket Olajuwon
31 *Sarah Palin or Arnold Schwarzenegger, informally
33 "Vous êtes ___" (label on a French map)
34 In a crowd of
36 *Dish served with long-handled forks
40 *Part of Manhattan's Midtown West
44 *Football snaps
45 Robt. E. Lee, e.g.
46 Like a ___ to me
47 *Less welcoming
49 Bearlike
52 Yamaha products
55 In-law of Esau
56 1970s–'80s TV planet
57 Get extra value from, say
60 *2002 Denzel Washington drama
64 *Wood cutter?
67 Hawaiian do
68 Online line
69 *2014 TV retiree
70 Marriott alternative
71 Supped
72 James Patterson sleuth Cross
73 *Standard deviation deviates from it

DOWN

1 Trip provider?
2 Hullabaloo
3 Role in "Thor"
4 Fertilized egg
5 "Sherlock" and "EastEnders" network
6 Hate
7 Horse of a certain color
8 Small storage unit
9 Becomes less strict
10 Iceman Bobby
11 Casino pass?
12 Huge, in poetry
13 "Chicago" song
19 One of the Palins
21 Like some hours
25 "Walk Like ___" (1963 hit)
27 Composer Novello
28 Over the estimate
29 Healthful berry
30 "Star Trek" captain
31 What can get you down?
32 Marked, as a box
35 Loan insured by the F.H.A.: Abbr.
37 Not final, legally
38 Popular pesticide
39 Reader founder
41 Chow ___
42 Accompanied
43 Pivot on an axis
48 Therapist's words
50 Rule ending in 1947
51 Yiddish author Aleichem
52 Moseyed (along)
53 Ayatollah Khomeini, for one
54 Goodyear headquarters
55 Sierra ___
58 Pac-12 team
59 Children's author Silverstein
61 Brit of Fox News
62 "Peter Pan" dog
63 Christie's "The Mysterious Mr. ___"
65 Supped
66 Curse

by David Steinberg

42

ACROSS

1 Knocked off
6 Parsley bit
11 German auto known by its manufacturer's initials
14 Online publication
15 Maine university town
16 Vote for
17 Isn't serious
19 Hosp. areas for lifesaving operations
20 Suffix with lemon or orange
21 Pick up the tab for someone
22 News item of passing concern?
23 Compete
24 Computer memory unit
27 Weapons depot
31 French girlfriend
32 Cheech's partner in 1970s–'80s movies
33 Writer ___ Rogers St. Johns
36 Lucy of "Charlie's Angels," 2000
39 Author who created the characters named by the starts of 17-, 24-, 49- and 61-Across
42 Ensign's org.
43 Spittin' ___
44 Actor MacLeod of old TV
45 Romantic outing
47 Having sides of different lengths, as a triangle
49 Maryland home of the Walter Reed medical center
53 Mrs., in Marseille
54 Newswoman Logan
55 Three-time A.L. batting champion Tony

57 Not bright
60 Smart ___ whip
61 Chemical compound in "poppers"
64 Nov. follower
65 Centuries-old object
66 Roof overhangs
67 Antlered animal
68 Justice Kagan
69 Considers

DOWN

1 ___ vu
2 Sport shirt brand
3 It holds back the water in Holland
4 Suffix with serpent
5 Place to lay an egg
6 Peeved
7 Like some televised tourneys
8 What a travel planner plans
9 Quaint lodging
10 The Almighty
11 1957 Everly Brothers hit with the repeated lyric "Hello loneliness"
12 Deserve
13 Trash
18 Kind of rug or code
22 Geisha's sash
23 "___, vidi, vici"
25 Black-tie party
26 United, as corporations or labor unions
27 Rights org.
28 Greek R's
29 Film score
30 Dalai ___
34 ___ Hammarskjöld, former U.N. secretary general
35 Hurricane centers
37 "Put ___ writing!"

38 ___ Reader (alternative magazine)
40 Iowa State's home
41 Racer Yarborough
46 "I've got it!"
48 The year 906
49 Bit of grass
50 Artist's stand
51 Holmes's creator
52 Tuckered out
56 Ancient Peruvian
57 Action from a springboard
58 Thing
59 Pigsty
61 "What ___ the chances?"
62 Singer Tormé
63 "Norma ___"

by Adam G. Perl

ACROSS

1 Where Matisses hang in N.Y.C.
5 Sun and moon, poetically
9 Sacred Egyptian bird
13 Sarcasm, informally
15 Paper quantity
16 Madrid tidbit
17 John known as the "Teflon Don"
18 Big do
19 Med. student course
20 EPEE
23 Discourteous
26 Asian-American basketball sensation Jeremy
27 "Let's ___!"
28 ETUI
34 Foot-pound?
36 Remote button
37 Driver's license datum
38 Tomato and lettuce pickers' org.
39 ERNE
42 Energy
43 Computer-connecting system, for short
44 Wheel connector
45 Tortilla chip dip
47 EMIR
51 Barack's re-election opponent
52 Pirate's quaff
53 Makeshift shelters
55 What this puzzle's capitalized clues are, both by definition and pun
60 Jupiter, to the Greeks
61 Relative of a bassoon
62 N.B.A. Hall-of-Famer Thomas
66 Actress Hathaway
67 Guns, as an engine
68 Burn a bit
69 Reels' counterparts
70 Putin put-down?
71 Once more

DOWN

1 Abbr. on Chinese menus
2 Lennon's love
3 Gymnast's surface
4 Highbrow theater screening
5 Seer
6 New mortgage deal, informally
7 Place for an owl
8 What can take your breath away in L.A.?
9 Bold alternative
10 Fountain treat with cherries on top
11 Apple tablet
12 Fill to excess
14 Chicken ___
21 Diarist Anaïs
22 Runs, as a color
23 Bond girl Andress
24 Relatively near
25 Be a goof
29 Many a Persian Gulf war correspondent
30 It makes MADD mad
31 Photocopier setting: Abbr.
32 Takes care of
33 Yanks living abroad, e.g.
35 Sacred songs
40 Computer file extension
41 Pie ___ mode
46 Overused plot device in soaps
48 Hearty kisses
49 Firstborn
50 Riddle-me- ___
54 Yard sale caveat
55 Peter the Great or Ivan the Terrible
56 Clinton attorney general Janet
57 Threadbare
58 Follow orders
59 Wander about
63 Holiday ___
64 Grow long in the tooth
65 Chop

by Matthew E. Paronto and Jeff Chen

ACROSS

1 "America's Most Wanted" host John
6 Bedwear, informally
9 Meager
14 Prized violin
15 Triumphant cry
16 "Yup"
17 Operatic singer on a sofa?
19 "I ___ for animals" (bumper sticker)
20 Taken care of
21 Curved path
23 Mountain goat
24 Kooky
26 Ins' partner
28 Chitchat about a dressmaking template?
33 "May ___ excused?"
35 Former part of Portuguese India
36 Set of keys?
37 Complimentary road service in Sierra Leone's capital?
42 Like Dylan Thomas, by birth
43 Oozy stuff
44 180 degrees from WNW
45 Egg-hunting time in the Orient?
50 "___ Man," Emilio Estevez film
51 Former capital of Italy?
52 Pizazz
55 Many a C.E.O.'s deg.
57 Broadway's ___ O'Neill Theater
61 Sheriff's star
63 Memorize lines for a Shakespearean king?
65 Evil character in "Snow White"
66 Mess up
67 Superman's adoptive parents
68 "Pasted" or "wasted," for "drunk"
69 "Balderdash!"
70 Art Deco, for one

DOWN

1 Money rolls
2 Parisian girlfriend
3 Wash
4 Lyric unit
5 Insinuate
6 ___ Beta Kappa
7 Software platform suitable for Starbucks?
8 Actress Stone of "Casino"
9 Easily pranked teacher, maybe
10 New Jersey governor whose first name starts his last name
11 "Moby-Dick" captain
12 Zap in the microwave
13 TV's "___ Factor"
18 "Please stay!"
22 Quarter of a quart
25 "Man, that hurts!"
27 Reel-to-reel
28 Banana skins
29 Mountain chain
30 ___ Tots
31 Son of Seth
32 Investment firm T. ___ Price
33 "___ Never Meet Again" (Elvis song)
34 La ___ Tar Pits
38 Hormone in the pill
39 Quaker pronoun
40 Baby horse
41 More optimistic
46 33 1/3, for a record album: Abbr.
47 More high-minded
48 Elephants' feelers
49 "Bald" baby bird
52 Outdoor meals with hamburgers or hot dogs, say, in brief
53 Fidel Castro's brother and successor
54 Notion
56 Commercial prefix with postale
58 "___ meeny miney mo"
59 The "N" of N.A.A.C.P.: Abbr.
60 Scottish Gaelic
62 Coll. major of many writers
64 Paintings, sculptures, etc.

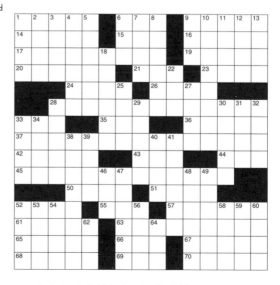

by Andrea Carla Michaels and Michael Blake

ACROSS

1 Archenemy of the Fantastic Four
7 Tech product introduced in '81
12 Rapper with the 2002 #1 hit "Always on Time"
13 Make into cornrows
14 Like 50/50 vis-à-vis 60/40
15 Merits
16 With 23-Down, what 27-Across/32-Down is often credited with
18 Song girl who's "sweet as apple cider"
21 Chicago-to-Tampa dir.
22 Sup
23 Coup d' ___
24 Yellowfin tuna, on menus
25 On vacation
26 Trumpet
27 With 32-Down, person associated with the scene depicted in this puzzle's grid
30 Silences
31 Added slyly, as a comment
32 Mink, e.g.
33 Young chap
34 What Command-P means on a Mac
35 With 44-Down, advice to 27-Across/32-Down?
38 Herringlike fish
39 Towel holders
43 Continental coin
44 "Absolutely right!"
45 "Yeah, right!"
46 Suffix with señor
47 Real stinker
48 Milan's La ___
49 Martial arts instructor
51 Veteran
53 Cope
54 Say wrongly
55 Military command
56 Precursor to talk shows for Jimmy Fallon and Seth Meyers, in short
57 River of W.W. I

DOWN

1 Provided the music for a party, informally
2 Enraptured
3 Order often "on the side"
4 Post office scale unit
5 Yellow spread
6 Game show maven Griffin
7 Spanish or Portuguese
8 Opposite of dense
9 River of W.W. I
10 Worrisome engine sound
11 Some 60-mo. investments
17 Buzz Aldrin's real first name
18 Writer Calvino
19 "Buffy the Vampire Slayer" girl
20 "This is only ___"
23 See 16-Across
24 $5 bill, informally
25 Surrounded by
26 Seriously overcook
28 Dessert brand once pitched by Bill Cosby
29 The Beatles' "___ in the Life"
30 British pound, informally
32 See 27-Across
34 Sports wonders, say
35 Dancer in a kimono
36 Best in an annual Nathan's contest, say
37 Site of 27-Across/32-Down's ambassadorship
38 The Mustangs of the American Athletic Conf.
40 2000s White House family
41 Remove, as spam
42 One not blinking, perhaps
44 See 35-Across
47 Dos x tres
48 A, B and F, e.g., in D.C.
50 Jamaican music genre
52 Fast way to connect, briefly

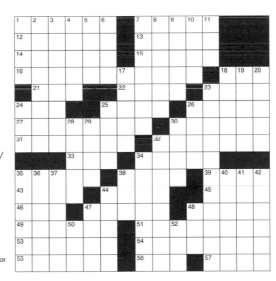

by Bruce Haight and Peter A. Collins

ACROSS

1 Mr. ___ (handyman)
6 Geishas' sashes
10 Amo, amas, ___
14 Nicholas Gage memoir
15 Speedy
16 Coin with F.D.R.'s image
17 One-by-one formation, as in walking
19 Similar (to)
20 Sushi fish
21 Perfect diving score
22 Briefest of kisses
23 "Rule, Britannia" composer
25 "Yeah? Try and do better!"
27 It stinks
30 See 34-Across
32 Latina lass: Abbr.
33 Solo of "Star Wars"
34 With 30-Across, black writing fluid
36 Extra energy
39 Mel of the Giants
40 Handyman's tote
42 Stooge with bangs
43 Big laughs
45 With magnanimity
46 Muff one
47 Stately shaders
49 Turf
50 Vicinity
51 "Swan Lake" and others
54 Skill needed when being asked "Does this dress make me look fat?"
56 Barely got, with "out"
57 Marker in a poker pot
59 Bing competitor
63 One way to record a show
64 Manicurist's target
66 Bygone British gun

67 Toss, as a coin
68 Belly button
69 New Haven school
70 Concordes
71 Goes downhill in the winter

DOWN

1 Admit, with "up"
2 Nastase of tennis
3 TV's Warrior Princess
4 Engaged, as a transmission
5 Flooring installer
6 Insect repellent brand
7 Worm on a hook, e.g.
8 Spot of land in the ocean
9 Dictation takers of years past
10 Get comfortable with, as new conditions

11 Spillane detective
12 ___ curiae (friends of the court)
13 Marathon warm-up races
18 Pacific weather phenomenon
24 ___ a happy note
26 Authorized substitute
27 "I almost forgot . . . !"
28 Numerical info
29 Honest
31 Weights of some contraband
34 Informal response to "Who's there?"
35 Monk's superior
37 Skin opening
38 Wife of Zeus
41 The golden years
44 "There, finished!"
48 Doesn't leave a tip
50 Lacking a key, musically

51 Ross the flagmaker
52 Large Japanese dog
53 Dirties
55 Foot woes
58 Condo, e.g.
60 Donated
61 Didn't tell the truth
62 Right-angle bends
65 Auto accessory often mounted on the windshield, for short

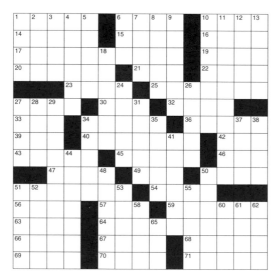

by Kelly Clark

ACROSS

1 Like yesterday's news
6 "Must be done NOW!"
10 Reduce to a pulp
14 Lugs
15 Latvia's capital
16 It may be just a hunch
17 Underway
18 Blend
19 Boxers Muhammad and Laila
20 Idles
22 Fey of "30 Rock"
23 Souvenir of Maui, maybe
24 How money may be won or lost
26 Like windows
30 Window segment
32 Monday, in Madrid
33 Allied supply route to China during W.W. II
38 Olympic skating champ Kulik
39 Physics Nobelist of 1903 and Chemistry Nobelist of 1911
40 Toasted waffle
41 Having a rounded end, as pliers
43 Tête topper
44 Big name in audio speakers
45 Fracases
46 Minor improvement in the Dow
50 Shout of inspiration
51 Thomas who wrote "Death in Venice"
52 Sycamore tree
59 "No ___" (reassuring words)
60 Spanish eight
61 Tolkien's ring bearer
62 Caesar's rebuke to Brutus

63 Lena of "Chocolat"
64 Supply, as a new ingredient
65 Like Easter eggs
66 "Citizen" of film
67 They return north in the spring

DOWN

1 Blind guess
2 Protein source for vegetarians
3 Tiny bit
4 Some summer babies
5 Topics for probate courts
6 Flaming felony
7 In ___ (undisturbed)
8 Opposed to, to Li'l Abner
9 "Scusi"
10 Autodom's MX-5
11 Wing it

12 What the Left Bank is a bank of
13 Attacks with vigor
21 "Far out, man!"
25 Three R's org.
26 Smooth-talking
27 She's back in town, in a Fats Waller song
28 Blue dye source
29 Fervor
30 Baby food, typically
31 Like much of the Southwest
33 Smooch
34 Recite quickly, with "off"
35 Brute
36 James who wrote "Let Us Now Praise Famous Men"
37 "i" and "j" tops
39 Volume that requires lots of preparations to compile?

42 "Parks and Recreation" network
43 Casual type of chair
45 Unit of electrical conductance
46 Made calls, in baseball
47 New Year's Eve staple
48 Federal security, for short
49 About to bloom . . . or a hint to 20-, 33-, 41- and 52-Across
50 Observe Yom Kippur
53 Pac-12 basketball powerhouse
54 Slender
55 Broad
56 Ye ___ Shoppe
57 Kimono securers
58 Puzzle solver's happy shout

by Mel Rosen

ACROSS

1 Ace of spades, e.g.
5 Room under the roof
10 Old Russian autocrat
14 Lothario's look
15 The middle Corleone brother
16 Six: Prefix
17 "Dies ___" (Latin hymn)
18 Poacher's nemesis
20 Guitarist Lofgren of the E Street Band
21 With it
22 In ___ of
23 Idaho's nickname
25 Muslim pilgrim's destination
28 Pringles container
29 Witness
31 Young 'un
32 College concentration
35 Request for some skin
38 Gung-ho
39 Regulations
40 Streets: Abbr.
41 Mayberry resident who became a Marine
43 Lifeless
44 Beat by a hair
45 Old what's-___-name
46 Picnic pest
47 Hersey's "A Bell for ___"
49 Round candies in a vending machine
54 Stow, as cargo
56 Burma's first prime minister
57 Campbell's product
58 Sport that includes the pommel horse and parallel bars
61 "Assuming that's true . . ."
62 Round hammer part
63 Most accessible seating choice
64 Grub

65 Out of kilter
66 "___ Gold" (Peter Fonda film)
67 Eye woe

DOWN

1 Hold on (to)
2 Eagle's nest
3 Domain
4 Casual Friday relaxes it
5 Kabul native
6 Characteristic
7 City near Phoenix
8 Suffix with sulf-
9 Monk's hood
10 Number of Scrabble points for a B, C, M or P
11 Alluring
12 Lumberjack's tool
13 Moved fast
19 "Save Me" singer Mann

24 Cigarette substance
26 Report on, as a news story
27 1945 Alamogordo event, informally
29 Captain Hook henchman
30 Ambulance letters
32 ___ Carta
33 Steer clear of
34 Orioles Hall-of-Fame pitcher who modeled Jockey underwear
35 Fellas
36 Not well
37 Excursions to la-la land
39 School in Troy, N.Y.
42 "The Mary Tyler Moore Show" spinoff
43 Bach's "Mass ___ Minor"
46 Makes laugh

48 One minding the baby
49 False front
50 "I give up!"
51 Lite
52 Robust
53 "Assuming it's true . . .," informally
55 Jacob's twin
58 Transcript stat
59 Archery wood
60 Up to, briefly

by John Lieb

ACROSS

1 Corrupt
4 Outfielder Ty
8 Brainy
13 Amman's Queen ___ International Airport
15 Law office worker, for short
16 Talented newbie
17 Home-invading Gore?
19 Opera's birthplace
20 Response to "Are not!"
21 Señor chaser?
23 Elevator pioneer Elisha
24 Area for aristocrats?
28 Mistake
30 Bush's labor secretary
31 Eight fluid ounces
32 Retrovirus material
34 Obstructs, as a pipe
38 W.W. I novel hinted at by 17-, 24-, 52- and 64-Across
43 Liszt's "Consolation No. 3" is in it
44 Story of one's life
45 Irritating cry
46 Leading inits. in frozen desserts
49 Visual gag character of British TV
52 Exchange of vows again for the Grim Reaper?
56 Railroad chartered in 1832
57 Old Testament prophecy book: Abbr.
58 "X-Men" character with blue fur
62 Remove gradually
64 Emmy, Oscar and Grammy-winning reptile?
67 Dwelling changes, in Realtor-speak
68 "Don't take ___ seriously!"
69 Oscar nominee Garr
70 Neighbor of Minneapolis
71 Keep in check, with "in"
72 Explorer's aid

DOWN

1 Yeast cake made with rum
2 Eisenhower vis-à-vis West Point, informally
3 Malicious gossip
4 E-file preparer
5 Rower's need
6 Alternative to a ponytail
7 Like Latvia or Lithuania
8 Discovery Channel subj.
9 Razr maker
10 One instrumental in history?
11 Old object
12 Secret meeting
14 To the max, '60s-style
18 Editor Marshall of financial publications
22 Residue in a fireplace
25 Oslo's home: Abbr.
26 Hue
27 Burrito alternative
28 Yellow-brown color
29 Translucent gem
31 Heel
33 Edmonton's province: Abbr.
35 Whale of a movie?
36 Agent under Hoover, informally
37 Yemen-to-Zimbabwe dir.
39 Turned in, in a way
40 Help make an impression?
41 Exec's car, maybe
42 Star of "Fringe," Anna ___
47 Home of the Bahamas, once: Abbr.
48 Emphatic affirmative
50 Early film star Daniels
51 Put up
52 Caterpillar rival
53 Acted in a human way?
54 Need for some fish dishes
55 Beatrice's adorer
59 "Excuse me"
60 Lub fluids
61 Excursion
63 Finnish hockey star Tikkanen
65 "Try ___ might . . ."
66 ___ -Tiki

by David Kwong

ACROSS

1 What winds do
5 French goodbye
10 Troubles
14 Exercise in which you might sit cross-legged
15 Birds' homes
16 Rick's love in "Casablanca"
17 Not just well-off
19 Like Jack Sprat's diet
20 "Am not!" comeback
21 Where many digital files are now stored
23 "Curse you, ___ Baron!"
24 Film director Lee
26 "Excellent, dude!"
27 Low-class diners
33 Surrendered
36 Oktoberfest beverage holder
37 Kilmer of "The Doors"
38 Word after eye or makeup
39 Give the cold shoulder
40 ___ Le Pew of cartoons
41 On fire
42 Belgian treaty city
43 Pimply
44 Window material in many cathedrals
47 Pop singer Carly ___ Jepsen
48 Suffix with east
49 When repeated, a ballroom dance
52 Kind of soup
57 Male or female
59 Some savings plans, in brief
60 Curses . . . or the starts of 17-, 27- and 44-Across?
62 Alternative to a man-to-man defense

63 Tatum of "Paper Moon"
64 Apple's apple, e.g.
65 Lambs' mothers
66 "Beau ___"
67 Sign for the superstitious

DOWN

1 Overwhelmingly
2 France's longest river
3 Girl-watched or boy-watched
4 Light bulb measure
5 "Do I have a volunteer?"
6 German "the"
7 "What time ___?"
8 Write permanently
9 Welcomes at the door, say
10 "O.K., I'm on it!"
11 Margarine
12 Older son of Isaac
13 Hourglass filler
18 Be a pack rat
22 Quaker's ___ Crunch
25 Said "Oh . . . my . . . God!," e.g.
27 Jewel
28 Attacked by bees
29 Dr. Seuss's turtle
30 Pizzeria fixture
31 Scruff of the neck
32 Iditarod vehicle
33 Disney Store collectibles
34 Way out
35 Facts and figures
39 Border collie, for one
40 Mac alternatives
42 Pesky insect
43 Good ___ (completely reconditioned)
45 Purple spring bloomers

46 Diamond-shaped stocking design
49 Electronic storage medium
50 Word before "fund" or "one's bets"
51 Burning issue?
52 Regular or large
53 Nose of a ship
54 Lois of the Daily Planet
55 Mozart's "___ kleine Nachtmusik"
56 Olympian war god
58 ___ contendere (court plea)
61 Body art, in slang

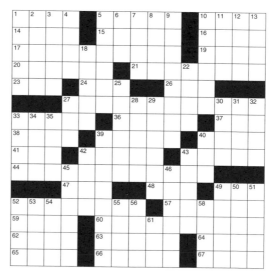

by Tom Pepper

ACROSS

1 Rainbow maker
6 Bad-mouth
10 Cereal word after Rice, Wheat or Corn
14 An Obama girl
15 Frisco's state
16 Like unwashed hair
17 With 57-Across, a diehard's statement
20 Somewhat, informally
21 TV's "___ Edition"
22 In a mischievous manner
25 Smucker's container
26 President pro ___
27 Hit that proves 17-/57-Across
31 Award for Best New American Play
32 Designer Cassini
33 Heart of the matter
36 ___ of God (epithet for Jesus)
37 Makeup for the cheeks
39 "Jolly old" fellow
41 Lipton selection
43 City on Utah Lake
44 "___, boy!" (cry to Rover)
45 Shot that proves 17-/57-Across
48 Film noir weather condition
51 ___ of the land
52 Access to a highway
53 More than just a five o'clock shadow
55 Overhauled
57 See 17-Across
62 Chips Ahoy! alternative
63 Smidgen
64 Perjurers
65 Tamed animals
66 Glitz
67 Swiss peak in an Eastwood title

DOWN

1 The Beatles' "___ Love You"
2 Fink
3 "Rhythm ___ Dancer" (1992 hit by Snap!)
4 Serving with a skewer
5 Shoe designer Blahnik
6 Sean Connery, for one
7 Mauna Kea emission
8 Sam Adams product
9 Moses' sister
10 Not pros
11 Show-starting words
12 Skip, like the H's in "'enry 'iggins"
13 Plant tissue
18 Go after
19 General Assembly participant, for short
22 Baselessly off-base?
23 Capital of Morocco
24 The Arctic, for one
25 Pedometer wearer, maybe
28 Roxie in "Chicago," e.g.
29 1/24 of un jour
30 Shakespeare character who says "I have set my life upon a cast"
34 Certain sorority woman
35 Setting for Scheherazade
38 Personify
40 Suspect, in police lingo
42 Certain bacteria fighting drug
46 Pleasingly plump
47 Strand, in a way
48 Aperture setting
49 Yellowish hue
50 Shake hands with, say
54 ETs pilot them
55 Pro ___ distribution
56 Big wheel in the cheese world?
58 Online chuckle
59 Pester
60 Test for future Ph.D.'s
61 Moldavia, e.g.: Abbr.

by David Woolf

ACROSS

1 Dress that falls between the knee and ankle
5 Nature walks, e.g.
10 Droid
13 Comment to a card dealer
14 Triangular chip
15 I.R.S. filing time: Abbr.
16 *Where Romeo and Juliet meet
19 Dick, to Liz, twice
20 Hank Aaron finished his career with 2,297 of them, in brief
21 Schooling: Abbr.
22 Pour, as wine from a bottle
24 *Often-seedy establishment
29 Brad of "Moneyball"
30 Wedding vows
31 Antlered animal
34 Kerfuffle
35 Rural couple . . . or what the respective halves of the answers to the four starred clues start with
38 Gift that may be presented with an "Aloha!"
39 ___ Lingus
40 Bushy hairdo
41 Actor Arkin
42 *1978 #1 Donna Summer hit that covered a 1968 #2 hit by Richard Harris
47 Pop artist Johns
49 Take ___ (catch some Z's)
50 Together, musically
51 The handle of the Big Dipper is its tail
56 *New Orleans event with floats
59 Yolk's place

60 Car famously available in any color, as long as it was black
61 Like 2, 4, 6, 8 . . .
62 Visualize
63 Drunkard
64 Like this clue among all the Acrosses

DOWN

1 Silent performer
2 Big-screen format
3 Food serving
4 Official investigation
5 "Ars Poetica" poet
6 Tehran's land
7 N.B.A. player-turned-coach Jason
8 Summer in France
9 Soak (up)
10 1968 Jane Fonda sci-fi film
11 Choose to participate

12 Meeting at a no-tell motel
14 Fix, as a computer program
17 Org. that rates meat "Choice" or "Prime"
18 West Coast gas chain
22 Plunge
23 "Born Free" lioness
24 Film-rating grp.
25 Adviser, for one
26 Rise of seawater that might accompany a hurricane
27 ___ noir (red wine)
28 Tack (on)
32 Shakespearean king
33 Twist, as in a chain
35 Attacker repellent
36 Many miles off
37 Opposite of "Dep." on a flight board

41 Clothing
43 Parroted
44 Big inconvenience
45 Not fitting
46 "___ Lama Ding Dong" (1961 hit)
47 King ___ Bible
48 Proverb
51 Language in Lahore
52 Actress Charlotte and explorer John
53 Jakarta's island
54 Poems by 5-Down
55 Landlord's income
57 Chats online, for short
58 When repeated, early baby sounds

by Robert Cirillo

ACROSS

1 Award-winning 2012 film about a fake film
5 Game with a 32-card deck
9 AK-47, e.g.
14 Desktops' desktop accessories
16 The Hunter constellation
17 With 56-Across, common format for a wager
18 Handle wrongly
19 Suffix with cartoon
20 Marijuana plant
21 Clobbers
22 The "E" of Q.E.D.
23 Opposite of WSW
24 Bring down
28 Sun-Maid dried fruit
31 Princeton and Yale
32 Peak in Greek myth
34 Holder of corn kernels
36 Queue cue
37 Winner of the wager in 17-/56-Across, depending on how you fill the circled squares in this puzzle
38 Old Italian money
39 Upsilon preceder
40 Nick who was named People's Sexiest Man Alive in 1992
41 ___ Python
42 AT&T competitor
44 Throat clearers
45 Had a bite
46 Blast
48 What scratch-and-sniff stickers emit
51 German automaker
52 Jiffy
55 Opera singer in an opera
56 See 17-Across

58 Remove, as a boutonniere
59 Not using Obamacare, say
60 Like some straws
61 GPS recommendations: Abbr.
62 Number of holes in a half-round of golf

DOWN

1 Prefix with -dextrous
2 Caviars
3 Sudden outburst
4 German direction
5 Globe
6 "Instant ___!" (John Lennon hit)
7 Highly capable
8 Mao ___-tung
9 Bucharest's land
10 Eye parts

11 It may be landed with a hook
12 It may have gold in them thar hills
13 Officer on TV's "The Dukes of Hazzard"
15 Roosevelt and Kennedy
21 Abacus row
24 Bit of color
25 Eye parts
26 Shuffle
27 Wager
28 Antagonize
29 It might read "Happy Birthday!"
30 Robb Stark's realm in "Game of Thrones," with "the"
32 Diner menu item
33 Part of retribution, in a phrase
35 Howls at the moon

37 Improves, in a way
38 "Skip to My ___"
40 Penn State's ___ Lions
41 Recurring themes
43 Nasty-smelling
44 Genetic sequence groups
46 Plague
47 Certain navel
48 Concert souvenir
49 Dunce cap shape
50 Channel with postgame analysis
52 Apple genius?
53 Equitable
54 Surrender
56 The "O" of SOS, supposedly
57 Band with the 2012 #1 hit "We Are Young"

by Andrew Reynolds

54

ACROSS

1 Couple
5 Spider's production
8 Having a couple of elements
12 ___ Domini
13 "Hell if I know" gesture
15 Initial money for the pot
16 High-stakes wager
19 Simple country person
20 ___ Canals, Michigan/Ontario separator
21 Overly
22 ___ out a living
23 Kimono, e.g.
26 Medical practitioners: Abbr.
28 See 68-Across
29 Gossipy sort
32 Arkansas town where Bill Clinton was born
35 Female deer
36 Traveling performers
38 Complete lawlessness
40 Fainted, as in rapture
41 Small fight
42 Letter after pi
43 One minus one
44 Stainless ___
45 One of a couple in a 767
47 Jabber
48 "You are so-o-o funny"
49 A sleeve covers it
52 Droop
55 By way of
57 Impossible to see through
59 Boeing 767, for one
63 Encourage
64 Canis, for dogs
65 Wading bird
66 Couple

67 Used a chair
68 One of a couple for the Roman god 28-Across

DOWN

1 San Diego baseballer
2 Actress Aimée
3 Occupied, as a restroom
4 Gen. ___ E. Lee
5 First of a journalist's five W's
6 Flub
7 Hot dog holders
8 "Zip-a-Dee-Doo-___"
9 The "U" of B.T.U.
10 ". . . ___ cost to you!"
11 Toy brick maker
13 More, at a meal
14 Someone who's so nice you almost want to smack him

17 Old Italian money
18 Matador
24 Floating marker for a sailor
25 WNW's opposite
27 Nap
28 Article of sports attire with a number
30 Something to whistle
31 Mimic
32 Broadbrim, for one
33 Burden
34 Future's opposite
37 Old name for Tokyo
39 Split with an ax
40 Actor LaBeouf
42 Stadium cheer
46 Northern Scandinavian
49 Jordanian port
50 Like Old Norse writing
51 Reagan attorney general Edwin

52 Macho guy
53 Wonky
54 Prefix with watt
56 Puts on years
58 First Arabic letter
60 Beatty of "Superman"
61 All ___ day's work
62 Pecan or cashew

by Douglas Taillon

ACROSS

1 Dashboard gauge, for short
5 Palindromic title
10 Jared of "Dallas Buyers Club"
14 Pretty agile for one's age
15 "+" terminal
16 Plow beasts
17 "That's enough!," to a hot dog-eating contestant?
19 Covet
20 Alfred Nobel and others
21 Doofus
23 "___-ching!" (cash register sound)
24 Full of nerve
25 "That's enough!," to a store clerk at Christmas?
27 Certain graph shape
28 Thin and graceful
31 Seeing red
32 Doc's "Now!"
34 Bit of intimate attire
35 Miracle-___
36 "That's enough!," to an assembly line worker?
40 Action verb that's also a Roman numeral
41 Org. for the Suns or the Heat
42 Beauty pageant wear
45 Soothes
48 Dutch cheese
50 Siren's place
51 "That's enough!," to a collagist?
53 Unexpected victory
55 Neighbor of Wash.
56 Singer DiFranco
57 I.R.S. inspections
59 Rich soil
61 "That's enough!," to a carnival thrower?
64 Singer Guthrie
65 Ghostly
66 Sports shoe brand
67 Dangerous slinger
68 Gridiron units
69 Tennis units

DOWN

1 Scolding sound
2 Jungle film attire
3 Unit involved in a shell game?
4 Overly promotes
5 Chess finale
6 &&&
7 Scooby-___
8 Program producing online pop-ups
9 Whiz group
10 Simmer setting
11 Two-horse wager
12 Drill sergeant's shout
13 Like books for long car rides, say
18 Bucolic verse
22 Vice president Agnew
24 Rental car add-on, in brief
25 Miscellaneous things
26 Gets wrinkles out
29 Mountain goat
30 A "T" in TNT
33 Marisa of "Crazy, Stupid, Love"
35 Pleased
37 View from a lookout
38 ___ Dhabi
39 Appliance with a pilot
43 Deems it O.K.
44 Deerstalker, e.g.
45 Body of environmental regulations
46 Dawn goddess
47 Super buys
48 ___ pig
49 "Truth in engineering" sloganeer
52 Well-pitched
54 Falafel holders
57 The "A" in RNA
58 Island music makers, for short
60 Cleaning tool
62 Boston #4 in years past
63 Musical notes after mis

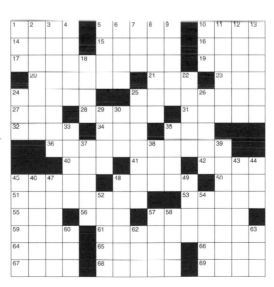

by Ian Livengood

ACROSS

1 Eve's mate
5 Bucket
9 Atmosphere of despondency
14 Launcher of the Curiosity rover
15 Major League Baseball family name
16 Cuban dance
17 Famous debate words from Reagan to Carter
20 Extreme happiness
21 Money outlay
22 Boatload
24 Always, in poetry
25 Yacht club locale
29 Sunbeams
31 Cartographer's drawing
34 Not just overweight
35 Sported, as a sports jacket
36 Unconscious state
37 Churchill's description of the Royal Air Force during W.W. II
40 Deep-six
41 ___ Korbut, 1972 Olympic gymnastics star
42 Cycle after wash
43 Mined metal
44 Lavish affection (on)
45 Expired
46 Mattress site
47 Homeowner's proof
49 Caribbean island nation south of Martinique
53 May-December romance features
58 Endorsement from Tony the Tiger
60 Golfer Palmer, to his "army"
61 ___ of passage
62 Canal of song

63 "April Love" singer Pat
64 Yearn (for)
65 Wriggling bait

DOWN

1 Pay to play, as poker
2 Roald who wrote "James and the Giant Peach"
3 Sailing
4 Feature of many a gas station nowadays
5 D.J.'s bribe
6 "Home ___" (Macaulay Culkin film)
7 Gambler's note
8 Olympic sled
9 Vine fruits
10 German pistol
11 Gulf country

12 Geishas' sashes
13 What a lion has that a lioness lacks
18 Former Disney chief Michael
19 Some daisies
23 Treated badly
25 "Semper Fidelis," for the U.S. Marines
26 Hate, hate, hate
27 Witherspoon of "Legally Blonde"
28 Sister and wife of Osiris
30 Square footage
31 Mars's Phobos and Deimos
32 Tickle
33 Used a peeler on
35 Droop, as flowers
36 Word with potato or chocolate
38 Gourmet
39 Wall Street worker

44 Official proclamation
45 Simon of "Uncle Tom's Cabin"
46 Pay to play, as poker
48 Third rock from the sun
49 Assault with a knife
50 "Comin' ___ the Rye"
51 Recently retired Jay
52 Site of the Taj Mahal
54 Got bigger
55 Prefix with dynamic
56 Low poker holding
57 Bloom's support
59 Ocasek of the Cars

by Gareth Bain

ACROSS

1 Filled with freight
6 Freeway haulers
11 Kilmer of "Heat"
14 Together
15 Take in exchange
16 Dingo's avian prey
17 Grounds for impeachment
19 Wheel part
20 Music of Mumbai
21 ___ clef
22 Sidestep
24 TV show anchored by Bill O'Reilly from 1989 to 1995
27 Concise summary
29 Termite look-alike
30 "Dry clean only," e.g.
31 In the hub of
34 Fail to note
38 Gannett's ___ Today
39 Underhanded attack
42 Jungle swinger
43 Wise one
45 Mountaineer's goal
46 Palomino or pinto
48 Grabbed a bite
50 ___ of interest
51 Hundred-to-one odds, say
57 Was inquisitive
58 Dawdling
59 Old record player
62 Be bedridden
63 Batter's reward after pitches like those described at the starts of 17-, 24-, 39- and 51-Across
66 "Cool!," in surfer slang
67 ___ gas
68 Cashmere alternative
69 Word ignored in alphabetizing
70 Aquaria
71 Having a sure hand

DOWN

1 Cowardly Lion portrayer Bert
2 Where Kyrgyzstan is
3 Holder of tomorrow's lunch, maybe
4 Improve
5 Circus safeguard
6 Position
7 Take out
8 En ___ (as a whole)
9 Wedding words
10 Submit, as a résumé
11 "Rigoletto" composer
12 Pal in Peru
13 Unit of light
18 Hank Aaron's 2,297
23 Filmmaker Preminger
25 Place for a window box
26 Middle part of a pedestal
27 In addition to
28 Tabula ___
31 Reverential regard
32 Deg. held by Mitt Romney
33 Type
35 "The Count of Monte Cristo" setting
36 ___ facto
37 Archie, Betty or Veronica
40 ___ page
41 "___ pigs fly!"
44 Lack of difficulty
47 Orange source
49 Morsel
50 One of 16 in a chess set
51 Eye-catching works
52 ___ Heep
53 "Mañana" feature
54 W.W. II bomb site
55 Grocery worker
56 Sounds like an owl
60 Turkey
61 "___ it rich?"
64 Repeated request from an Alabama cheerleader
65 Slithering predator

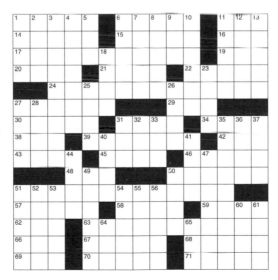

by Gary Cee

ACROSS

1 Small apartment
7 "And ___ makes three"
11 The "L" of U.N.L.V.
14 St. Francis's birthplace
15 Poker payment
16 Even so
17 Strike zone arbiter
20 Exam for an aspiring D.A.
21 Luau dish
22 Cubs legend Banks
23 George Bailey in "It's a Wonderful Life"
26 N.B.A. Hall-of-Famer Dennis
30 Going ___ (bickering)
31 Creme-filled cookies
32 "___ Dark Thirty"
34 Disaster aid org.
38 One getting hit in Vegas
41 Match up, as iPod and laptop files
42 Big heads
43 Warning
44 "The Thin Man" terrier
46 Spanish diacritical marks
47 Decennial official
52 Bubbling, as water
53 Fort ___, N.J.
54 Critic's high praise
58 They disprove claims . . . or 17-, 23-, 38- and 47-Across, in a way?
62 Lean-___ (simple shelters)
63 Asia's shrinking ___ Sea
64 War
65 "I Like ___" ('50s campaign slogan)
66 Back of the neck
67 At a reduced price

DOWN

1 Comedian Mort
2 General ___ chicken
3 West Point inits.
4 Cut down on calories
5 AOL or Comcast, for short
6 Crankcase reservoir
7 Tie-dye alternative
8 Hydrocarbon suffix
9 Air-conditioner output: Abbr.
10 Saudi neighbor
11 More than misleading
12 Eagle's nest
13 Navigate
18 ___ Center (Chicago skyscraper)
19 Buster Keaton specialty
23 Soak up the sun
24 A, B, C, D and F
25 Resting upon
26 Burgles

27 Air France destination
28 University official
29 Comfortable footwear
32 Restaurant guide name since 1979
33 "Foucault's Pendulum" author Umberto
35 Visually assessed
36 Trifling
37 ___ and Leisure
39 "West Side Story" gang
40 Den
45 Ottoman bigwig
46 Longtime sponsor of the Metropolitan Opera
47 Southwestern flora
48 Paperless reading
49 "It's ___!" (defeated cry)

50 Singer of "Skyfall," 2012 Oscar winner for Best Original Song
51 Second-oldest General Mills cereal
54 Turntable rates, for short
55 Jessica of "Sin City"
56 Calves' meat
57 Villa d'___
59 Bush ___ (early 2000s)
60 Genre of Macklemore and Master P
61 Tues. preceder

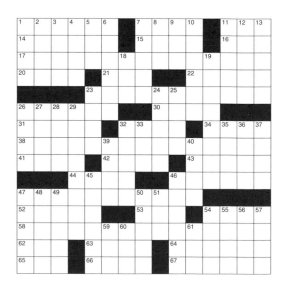

by John Lieb

ACROSS

1 Capital of Uganda
8 Radio operator
11 Syringe units, briefly
14 "Whoops!"
15 Peyton's QB brother
16 Chaney of horror films
17 ___ pink
18 Fruitcake
20 Where sailors go
21 Number pad locale, for short
22 Geometric calculation
23 It's not preferred for investors
27 Station on the Alaska Highway
31 Bather's exfoliant
32 Peeved
34 Clear the board
39 Full
40 Sweetheart
41 Full complement of dwarfs
42 1963 John Wayne comedy western
45 Chemical "twin"
47 Thumbs-up responses
48 Spot at the front of a theater
53 Bone below the elbow
54 SEAL's org.
55 ___ Murphy, W.W. II hero
60 It may be read to a miscreant
62 Half moon?
64 Odd or even, in roulette
65 Swelling reducer
66 Like some women's shoes
67 Praiseful verse
68 Palme ___ (Cannes award)
69 What a multiplex has a multiplicity of

DOWN

1 Smoky-voiced Eartha
2 Foreign exchange fee
3 Soft slip-ons
4 Dawdler
5 Insurer with a duck mascot
6 Tommy of Mötley Crüe
7 Do sums
8 Music critic Nat
9 Wellesley grad, e.g.
10 "Good Will Hunting" sch.
11 Mild cigar
12 Trig ratio
13 Act furtively
19 Feline
21 "I ___ the opinion . . ."
24 Ye ___ Shoppe
25 Cow's call
26 Charlie formerly of "Two and a Half Men"
27 Hot times in la cité
28 Reciprocal of 12-Down
29 Onetime "S.N.L."-type show
30 '30s migrant
33 He sings "Rubber Duckie, you're the one / You make bath time lots of fun"
35 Pro ___ (in proportion)
36 Suffix with buck
37 Down with the flu, say
38 Squeals of alarm
40 Gossip
42 Tony Soprano, for one
43 "Shake a leg!"
44 Lion constellation
46 Decorative wall coating
48 High-performance engine
49 Perjurer's admission
50 Bill worth 100 smackers
51 Kit ___ bar
52 Bigot, e.g.
56 ___ Reader (bimonthly magazine)
57 Be sweet (on)
58 :-), for one
59 Squeezes (out)
61 Help
62 Cow genus
63 Something a scanner scans, in brief

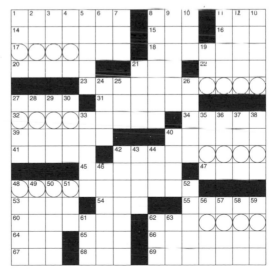

by Ed Sessa

ACROSS

1 Protein-rich food
5 Brand of instant coffee
10 Titles for attorneys: Abbr.
14 Mimicked
15 ___ terrier (dog breed)
16 Here: Sp.
17 Direct, as competition
19 Bankrupt
20 Newspaper advertising flier, e.g.
21 "___ Your Enthusiasm"
23 Snakelike fish
24 Four: Prefix
25 17-Across, literally: Fr.
27 Driver's licenses and such, for short
28 Co. bigwig
30 Flabbergasts
31 Italian ice cream
34 Sneakers since 1916
35 Star stand-ins . . . or a hint to 17-, 25, 48- and 58-Across?
38 ___ .45
40 Sleek fabric
41 Combination punch
44 M.A. or M.B.A.: Abbr.
45 Wide mouth
48 58-Across, literally: Sp.
51 Japanese cartoon art
53 Roush of the Baseball Hall of Fame
54 "Avatar" race
55 Filched
56 Crosby, Stills, ___ & Young
58 Direct, as combat
60 Redding of R&B
61 Winter pear
62 Memorial Day race, informally

63 Traveled
64 What a witness takes at a trial
65 Hurl

DOWN

1 Polynesian paradise
2 Made the first bid
3 Eats grandly
4 What a milking machine connects to
5 Many a person whose name starts "Mc-"
6 Reaction to a cold drink on a hot day
7 Aunt's girl
8 "Sauer" hot dog topping
9 Newswoman Mitchell
10 ___-piercing
11 Hugs tightly
12 Shushed

13 Immaculate
18 Followed back to its source, as a phone call
22 Collision sound
25 Ones with warts and all?
26 No longer available
29 English cathedral town
31 Reached
32 "Ode ___ Nightingale"
33 Best in competition
35 Is inconspicuous, say
36 Honey maker
37 In a smooth, flowing manner, in music
38 "Don't be absurd!"
39 Out with one's sweetie
42 Pale
43 Plains Indians

45 Certain Pepperidge Farm cookie
46 Changes, as the Constitution
47 Hamburger chain that offers the Baconator
49 ___-garde
50 Masked Japanese fighter
52 Perfect, as a pitcher's game
55 Hunky guy
57 F.D.R.'s successor
59 "___ we now our gay apparel"

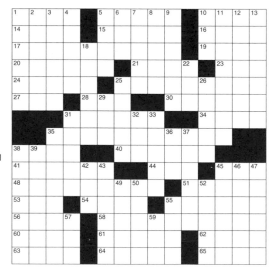

by Jim Modney

ACROSS

1 Long part of a lance
6 Radar screen dot
10 ___-à-porter
14 Actor Quinn
15 Charlie Chaplin's last wife
16 Singsong syllables
17 What Ali Baba found on the treasure in the cave?
20 In the mail
21 Heart of the matter
22 Simple
23 Not supportin'
25 Down Under runners
27 Sign of a failed practice?
33 Baseball exec Bud
34 ___ trap
35 Honour bestowed by Queen Elizabeth: Abbr.
36 Sch. near Beverly Hills
37 Letter closing
39 Bar from Mars
40 Avril follower
41 Grammy-winning blues guitarist Jonny
42 In need of some manscaping, say
43 Puzzles as gifts?
47 Web site that users themselves may revise
48 Many a Rolling Stone cover subject
49 You'll need to take steps to get to it
52 ___ sci
54 Lerner/Loewe musical set in Paris
58 Be startled by singing monks?
61 Suit to ___
62 ___ dire (court examination)
63 Seat for a stand-up
64 Coloratura's practice

65 1990s compacts
66 What a verb ending may indicate

DOWN

1 Suckers
2 Employ
3 Deuce follower
4 1940 Disney film
5 Big bang letters
6 Sound of disgust
7 Digs in an old warehouse, maybe
8 Prevalent, as a rumor
9 Sound of disgust
10 When repeated several times, child's entreaty
11 Sitar master Shankar
12 Stat for 26-Down: Abbr.
13 Stun with a charge

18 Option on "Wheel of Fortune"
19 Arctic language
24 Booking
26 Cascades, e.g.: Abbr.
27 Old Renault
28 Stan's film partner
29 Toupee alternative
30 Lose-lose
31 Car mentioned in the Beach Boys' "Fun, Fun, Fun"
32 Hot, like a hunk
33 Cesspool
37 American, in England
38 Moving stealthily
39 Party in the parking lot
41 Classic shooter
42 Doc bloc
44 Acquires with sticky fingers
45 Crude fleet

46 Guarantor of financial accts.
49 Open a crack
50 Hippo's wear in 4-Down
51 Eliot Ness and others
53 Home of Miami University
55 Wise to
56 Classic muscle cars
57 Archipelago part
59 "The whole family can watch" program rating
60 33rd president's monogram

by Paula Gamache

ACROSS

1 ___ skirt
5 "The Tao of Pooh" author Benjamin
9 One with ergophobia
14 "Look what I found!" cries
15 Kind of tradition
16 "___ talk?"
17 "Good thing I don't have the same problem!"
19 Following
20 River of film
21 1986 top-10 hit for Billy Idol
23 That's the point
24 Meal at which to drink four cups of wine
25 Part of a pickup line?
28 "___, boy!"
29 Earth goddess created by Chaos
33 Expanse
36 "Apparently"
38 What fell in the Fall
39 That is the question
41 Robert of "Quincy, M.E."
42 One who may need a shower?
44 Holder of a pair of queens
46 Shiner
47 Milk source.
49 N.B.A. Hall-of-Famer Walker
50 Belgian battleground during W.W. I
52 Letters in car ads
54 "Truthfully . . ."
57 Brought up to speed
61 Yokel, in slang
62 Classic rock song in "Easy Rider"
64 G.W. competitor
65 P.D.Q. Bach's "I'm the Village Idiot," e.g.
66 Rep. Darrell of California
67 Like the myth of Ragnarok
68 Luxury hotel name
69 Locale for a Village People hit, informally

DOWN

1 "Scrubs" locale: Abbr.
2 "Don't even think about it"
3 Bats
4 Showed politeness at the front door
5 Certain ring bearer
6 Relative of a gemsbok
7 ___ Schwarz
8 Fictional substance in a Disney film
9 Zodiac symbol
10 U.S.S. Enterprise chief engineer Geordi ___
11 Where reruns run
12 Overly precious
13 Mister, overseas
18 ___ Balls
22 Christmas hymn beginning
24 Events at which people are dead serious?
25 Some pyramids
26 In two, say
27 Ohio city WSW of Columbus
28 It's possessive
30 Some buggy drivers
31 Name on a bottle of Sensuous Nude perfume
32 Half of an old comedy team
34 Caen cleric
35 Butch Cassidy and the Sundance Kid, e.g.
37 Drifts away
40 Quaker product
43 Chardonnay feature
45 "Whatever!"
48 Fancy suite amenity
51 In and of itself
52 Ball mate
53 Mr. ___
54 What's not for big shots?
55 38-Across's genus
56 "Ah, my Beloved, fill the Cup that clears" poet
57 "I say" sayer
58 Menu section
59 Threat ender
60 Time of 1944's Operation Neptune
63 ". . . goes, ___ go!"

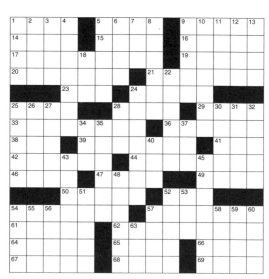

by Evan Birnholz

ACROSS

1 Exposure units
5 Like many a superhero
10 Cheater's sound, maybe
14 Biblical twin
15 First in a line of Russian grand princes
16 Jazzy James
17 & 20 Story by 42-Across on which the movie "Blade Runner" is based
21 Best-suited for a job
22 Kind of lily
23 Cold war foe, slangily
26 Cause of a dramatic death in Shakespeare
27 Go ballistic
28 Displace
31 Music magazine founded by Bob Guccione Jr.
35 Disloyal sort
36 Like bits of old music in some new music
39 Keats creation
40 One going for a little bite?
42 Author Philip K. ___
43 XXX
45 Cleanse
47 Auctioned investments, in brief
48 Affright
51 Eat, eat, eat
54 & 59 Story by 42-Across on which the movie "Total Recall" is based
60 Together, in Toulouse
61 Swiss miss of fiction
62 African antelope
63 "Shane" star Alan
64 Put back in the fold
65 "Gnarly!"

DOWN

1 Request after a failure, sometimes
2 Since
3 Christine ___, heroine of "The Phantom of the Opera"
4 Light that darkens
5 Club
6 "Let's take ___"
7 Competition category in bridge and skating
8 Break off a relationship
9 Kind of brake
10 Noncommittal response
11 Andrew Carnegie's industry
12 Author Madame de ___
13 Home of the N.H.L.'s Lightning

18 Accountants put them on the left
19 Mil. awards
23 Humorist Bennett
24 Like some contraceptives
25 Remote button
26 Bruiser
28 ASCAP rival
29 It's scanned in a store, for short
30 U2 song paying tribute to an American icon
32 Sulk
33 Run while standing still
34 Takes home
37 Throw in
38 View from Budapest
41 Ready for battle
44 Cares for maybe too much
46 "___ expert, but . . ."

47 "One ringy-dingy" comic
48 Ghastly
49 "Bleeding Love" singer Lewis
50 Astringent
51 Bird that's as small as it sounds
52 Beatnik's "gotcha"
53 Sparkly rock
55 Essen's river
56 Like hurricanes in January
57 Three-time N.H.L. All-Star Kovalchuk
58 "u r so funny . . . lmao," e.g.

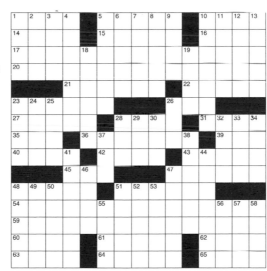

by Jason Flinn

ACROSS

1 Full of tears, say
4 Thanksgiving song
9 Behind
13 Name that's one syllable in English, two syllables in Japanese
14 Sister of Melpomene
15 Copy, briefly
16 "Was ist ___?"
17 Custodial tool
19 Put out
20 Literary March
21 Comic Meadows formerly of "S.N.L."
22 "___ to Apollo"
23 Needed
25 Basic process of genetics
28 Keenly awaiting
29 Currency superseded by the euro
30 Actor McShane
31 Some keep waiting for them
32 "Listen, ___ the sound be fled": Longfellow
33 "Phooey!"
35 Abbr. at the bottom of a letter
36 All the time?: Abbr.
39 Prefix with week
41 Rapper ___-E
43 Repetitive inits.?
44 Dweller in ancient Persepolis
45 Clover locale
46 Self-titled platinum album of 1986
47 Eligible to be called up
48 Like many breakfast cereals
51 Oxygen's electrons, e.g.
52 Cousin
53 Relative of Mme.
54 Global economic org.

56 Tie one on at dinner, maybe
57 Inconceivable
60 Spanish bear
61 Singer Rimes
62 Lycée attendee
63 Traditional
64 Constellation next to Hercules
65 The hare, notably
66 G, e.g.

DOWN

1 Show eager anticipation
2 Native
3 Common site for 36-Across
4 Brake, e.g.
5 ___ lily
6 Noël Coward play
7 Football stat.
8 Cosa ___
9 Nectar detector
10 Common site for 36-Across
11 Inscription on stained glass, maybe
12 "The New Yorker" cartoonist Ed
15 Doesn't leave
18 Xbox competitor
24 Some legal bigwigs: Abbr.
26 "Anything else that you require?"
27 Leader of ancient Troy?
29 It may leave a sour taste in your mouth
34 Peripheral basilica feature
36 Revered Chinese figure
37 Athenian general who wrote "History of the Peloponnesian War"

38 2002 Salma Hayek film or its title role
40 Nonspeaking role on "CSI"
42 Last of 26
44 Comfy footwear, briefly
46 Paint type
48 Halloween prop
49 Like some fancy sauces
50 Procter & Gamble brand
51 Tender
55 "Gangway!"
58 Chain in biology
59 Band with the '79 album "Discovery"

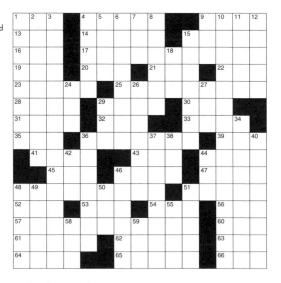

by Jeffrey Wechsler

☆ ☆ **65**

ACROSS

1 Creator of Fearless Fosdick
7 "This is bad"
11 Word part: Abbr.
14 Kind of pork on a Chinese menu
15 What's to eat
16 Cedar Rapids college
17 Blow away singer Johnny?
19 National Dog Day mo.
20 Navigational aid
21 Name on some euros
22 Mountain goat's perch
23 Boars?
27 "In the end the pressure got to me"
30 Bluffer's words
31 What may precede one
32 "You wish!"
33 Sounds of relief
35 Call it quits . . . with a hint to 17-, 23-, 48 and 56-Across
40 Western treaty grp.
41 First Chinese dynasty
42 Inspiration for a "Jackass" stunt, maybe
43 "No acting up!"
45 Ticked off
48 Sala?
50 Salt Lake City athletes
51 Zwei cubed
52 Bub
55 "Jeez Louise!"
56 Toddler raised on chocolate?
60 Slip-___ (some shoes)
61 Removal from harm's way, for short
62 Hotelier Helmsley and others
63 Hwy.

64 Warrior princess of TV
65 J.F.K.'s W.W. II craft

DOWN

1 Like most car radios
2 Showgirl in the song "Copacabana"
3 Many a city dwelling
4 Volcano on Kyushu
5 Telephone system hacker
6 Rock that may float
7 End of a lame pickup line
8 "You wish!"
9 Med. scan
10 Cry that may accompany fist-pumping
11 Frightens off
12 Words on a 20-Across at a mall
13 Hosiery brand that sponsored women-only 10K races
18 Biogenesis scandal nickname
22 Hellenic X
23 U2's frontman
24 Shore dinner entree
25 Indy racer Luyendyk
26 Ex-president who swore in President Hoover
27 Digging, so to speak
28 One sharing living space
29 Practical smarts
32 One-time link
34 Anchorage-to-Nome racer
36 "Hang on a sec!"
37 Currently airs
38 Spiders' nests
39 Lamar who married a Kardashian
44 Navigational aid, for short
45 Angel or enemy preceder
46 Totally useless
47 "Give me a sec"
48 Bookstore section
49 First to stab Caesar
52 Ranchero's hand
53 Simple quatrain form
54 Dermatologist's concern
56 Put the whammy on
57 Time to revel
58 Sought office
59 Go for apples

by Samuel A. Donaldson

ACROSS

1 Z3 maker
4 Onetime N.F.L. star nicknamed Joe Willie
10 Challenge in "Legally Blonde," for short
14 "Phooey!"
15 San ___, Argentina
16 D-Day objective
17 Distance at St. Andrews golf course?
20 Org. of which 18 U.S. presidents have been members
21 Hindu life lesson
22 Base figs.
23 Cost of mail from Manhattan?
27 Statue in the Parthenon
28 Itching
29 "___ Nature, red in tooth and claw . . .": Tennyson
30 Arcturus, e.g., spectrally
34 Places docs wear smocks
35 Wing, e.g. . . . or a hint to answering 17-, 23-, 49- and 56-Across
38 White House fiscal grp.
40 Stuffed animal option
41 "The Beverly Hillbillies" dad
44 One way to play something
47 One on a Facebook News Feed
49 First-aid supply for Springsteen?
53 Morsel
54 Summer camp sight
55 Aunt in "Bambi"
56 Top-secret proverb?
61 Drain
62 Actor Martin of 1960s–70s TV

63 "___, non verba" (Latin proverb)
64 Vase handle
65 Looks bad?
66 Forerunner of Bach?

DOWN

1 Shot from a certain gun
2 Source of the line "Something wicked this way comes"
3 Elite group
4 Zip
5 "___ reminder . . ."
6 Capital whose main street is Nezavisimosti
7 Tally
8 "___ Remember"
9 Like a speaker with a 25-Down
10 Trip inits.
11 Reel

12 Locale of a 1956 fight for independence
13 Low digits
18 Diggs of "Rent"
19 Pro ___
23 Writer Hentoff
24 Like a private peeling potatoes
25 See 9-Down
26 Pulitzer winner James
31 William Shatner's sci-fi drug
32 Year abroad
33 Dietary std.
35 Aid in a scam, e.g.
36 ___ Romeo
37 Only U.S. senator with a unit of measure named after him
38 Noted Ohio conservatory
39 "Good heavens!"

41 Dada pioneer
42 Listening, say
43 Onetime White House inits.
45 Slow pitches have them
46 Adjusts one's sights
48 Picked out of a lineup
50 In conclusion, in Cannes
51 Decorative fabric
52 Designer Geoffrey
53 Numerical prefix
57 One of two possibilities to Paul Revere
58 German article
59 "___ Poetica"
60 Abbr. after some professionals' names

by Gary J. Whitehead

ACROSS

1 Keystone place
5 Some vacation spots
10 Uttered, as a farewell
14 Carnaby Street's locale
15 Brown, in a way
16 Gershwin's "Summertime" is one
17 Tornado monitors?
20 AOL or MSN
21 Like Mao's "little" book
22 Tito, the King of Latin Music
23 Deg. from M.I.T. Sloan
25 Note in a poker pot
28 Cafeteria stack
29 What the only detective on a case has?
33 "It ___ over till . . ."
34 Improve, as one's manners
35 Prefix with classical
38 What a bouncer may confiscate
40 Makes tough
42 Medevac destinations, briefly
43 New British royal of 2013
47 Smelling salts holder
48 What a remorseful Iago might have said?
50 Send as payment
53 Classic car whose name is a monogram
54 ___ Antigua
55 Draw out
57 Get into
59 Wash. neighbor
62 Doubleheader . . . or what 17-, 29- and 48-Across are?
66 To be, to Béatrice
67 Make blond, maybe

68 Primordial ___
69 Spanish province or its capital
70 Fraternity letter
71 Band with the 1987 hit "Need You Tonight"

DOWN

1 Sparkling Italian export
2 Toils on a trireme
3 High-pitched group with a 1958 #1 hit, with "the"
4 Yuletide interjections
5 "Point taken"
6 Rush-hour subway rider, metaphorically
7 Director Jean-___ Godard
8 Ordinal suffix
9 Flow slowly

10 Business with an enticing aroma
11 Fight site
12 Like some looks and laundry
13 Slacks off
18 Disneyland vehicle
19 Often-breaded piece of meat
24 ___ noire
26 Shot-to-the-solar-plexus sound
27 Reuters alternative
29 It may have outdoor seating
30 "That is so not true!"
31 Happy Meal with a Sprite, e.g.
32 Beginning
35 "Lost in Yonkers" playwright
36 Airline that doesn't fly on the Sabbath

37 Kon-Tiki Museum city
39 Outfielder's cry
41 In perpetuum
44 Legendary Boston Garden skater
45 Part of a Reuben
46 Half a police interrogation team, maybe
48 Make queasy
49 Pend
50 Revolting sort
51 Make up?
52 Prefix with brewery
56 Clock sound
58 Gumbo need
60 Pierre's pair
61 Deadly snakes
63 Deadly snake
64 Peak next to a glacier, maybe
65 "Just ___ suspected"

by Robyn Weintraub

ACROSS

1 Become comfortable with
8 Spots for dipping, once
15 Bought more Time?
16 Reads with effort
17 Danced to Julio Sosa music, say
18 One-third of a French revolutionary's cry
19 She who says "sí": Abbr.
20 QB targets
21 Like the women in a famous Rubens painting
22 Hepster
23 QB goals
24 Investment house employee
28 Trap
32 Either of two N.F.L. coaches named Jim
33 Lift
35 One vote in Vichy
36 Unwelcome reversal . . . or a title for this puzzle?
40 It might come after sex
41 Singer/actress Lenya
42 "This guy walks into ___ . . ."
43 China collections
45 What the Beatles had but Wings didn't?
48 Actress Gardner
49 Flotsam or Jetsam in "The Little Mermaid"
50 Blazing
53 Nasdaq unit: Abbr.
54 Prefix with color
57 Contemptuous one
58 Bridge type
60 Uranium-235, e.g.
61 Chenoweth of Broadway's "Wicked"
62 Some slow dances
63 Necessitates

DOWN

1 Field of many nonprofits
2 Prayer starter, often
3 Karina in many a Jean-Luc Godard film
4 Square ___
5 & 6 Mutual relationship
7 Track figures
8 Dangerous time
9 & 10 Critical comments
11 Shoe shiner
12 Asgard ruler
13 Head of the Seine?
14 Green Bay-to-Greenville dir.
22 Paella ingredient, perhaps
24 Scope
25 Prop for many a western
26 Something made in a chocolate factory?
27 "___ life"
28 ___-day calendar
29 End of an era?
30 What pulls out all the stops?
31 ___ nous
34 Tinnitus treater: Abbr.
37 & 38 One who may give you a lift
39 Bomb
44 Pay tribute to
46 & 47 Means of getting home, maybe
50 To boot
51 Dupe
52 "___ Tu" (1974 hit)
53 Benefit
54 New World monkey
55 Churn
56 Sights at many interstate exits
57 Small story
59 LAX patrollers

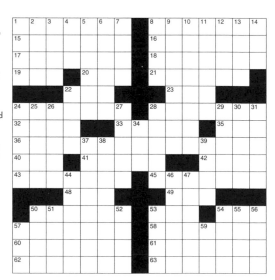

by Peter A. Collins

ACROSS

1 What quoth the raven?
4 Moving well for one's age
8 1988 Salt-N-Pepa hit
14 Washington in D.C., e.g.
15 Idiot
16 Country on el Mediterráneo
17 Coastal inlet
18 Part of a Halloween dinner?
20 Girl in tartan
22 Moisten, in a way
23 Upstate N.Y. college
24 Soft-shell clam
27 "Prince Igor" composer
29 Part of a Halloween dinner?
31 "Me neither"
32 Ways to go: Abbr.
33 Breathtaking creatures?
34 Checks out
35 Part of a Halloween dinner?
38 Pricey violin
41 Icicle site
42 ___ salad
45 Bed size
46 Part of a Halloween dinner?
49 One pushing the envelope?
51 Something found on a chemist's table
52 Certain Halloween costumes, for short
53 "Battling Bella" of '70s politics
55 State
56 Part of a Halloween dinner?
60 Man's name that's another man's name backward
61 Recruit
62 Stagehand

63 Part of the alloy britannium
64 ___ Peanut Butter Cups
65 What a colon represents in an emoticon
66 Heart chart: Abbr.

DOWN

1 Fast-food chain with a smiling star in its logo
2 Flew
3 Deceitful sorts
4 Part of GPS: Abbr.
5 Punch line?
6 Deli loaf
7 Jedi Council leader
8 Basil-based sauces
9 Walk down the aisle
10 Lotion inits.
11 Bob and others
12 Give rise to

13 Pastes used in Middle Eastern cuisine
19 Publisher's ID
21 Pizzeria owner in "Do the Right Thing"
25 "Whoops"
26 Jet
28 ___ impulse
30 Heretofore
34 Thick, sweet liqueur
35 Tilt
36 "Jeopardy!" column
37 42-Across shape
38 First pope
39 Black and blue, say
40 Savory deep-fried pastry
42 Lift
43 Not brand-name
44 Spare wear
46 Nuns' wear
47 Dix + 1
48 Org. with a snake in its logo

50 Billiards trick shot
54 Impulse
57 "___ So Sweet to Trust in Jesus"
58 Say "I do" when you don't?
59 Groovy music?

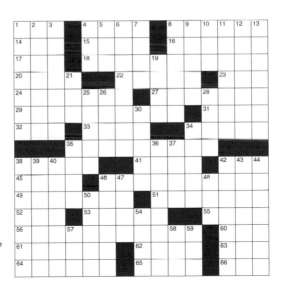

by Joel Fagliano

ACROSS

1 Universal Studios role of 1941
8 1-Across, in 23-Down
15 Not yet delivered
16 Thank you, in Tokyo
17 Universal Studios role of 1931
18 17-Across, in 23-Down
19 Gas grade
20 D.C. baseballer
21 Young socialite
22 Rapscallion
23 Clusterfist
25 Carnivorous fish
28 Through
29 "I beg to differ"
33 Shetland Islands sight
34 Unsettle
35 "St. Matthew Passion" composer, for short
36 Bit of chicken feed
37 What some hotel balconies overlook
39 Low reef
40 Like patent leather
43 Moon, e.g., to a poet
44 A, in Austria
45 Genesis wife
46 Genesis craft
47 Green touches?
48 Calls
50 Show age, in a way
51 U. of Miami's athletic org.
54 "Aladdin" monkey
55 Some bait
59 Universal Studios role of 1925
61 59-Across, in 23-Down
62 Starts gently
63 Comic strip infant
64 Universal Studios role of 1931
65 64-Across, in 23-Down

DOWN

1 Namby-pamby
2 ___ about (approximately)
3 Crescent shape
4 Second-largest city in Ark.
5 Period of focusing on oneself
6 "Your 15 minutes of fame ___!"
7 An I.Q. of about 100, e.g.
8 C. S. Lewis setting
9 Fields
10 Nickname for a 2012 presidential candidate
11 Ends of some close N.F.L. games: Abbr.
12 Secure, as a contract
13 Plains native
14 Development site
23 Things worth looking into?
24 Hold up
25 Trudges (through)
26 Furry folivore
27 Phoenix or Washington
28 Brewery fixture
30 Implied
31 Meager
32 "That's for sure!"
34 Crested bird
35 One-two part
38 Peeve
41 Glum
42 Acupressure technique
44 Pacific Northwest city
46 Barnard grad, e.g.
47 Stickum
49 Intensely stirred up
50 Winter forecast
51 Made like
52 Scorch
53 La mía es la tuya, they say
55 Some online communications, briefly
56 Part of graduation attire
57 Start of 19 John Grisham novel titles
58 Place to be pampered
60 Asian electronics giant

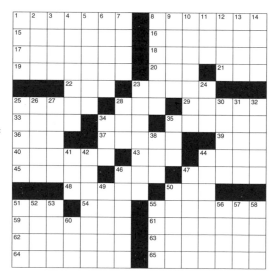

by David Kwong

ACROSS

1 Bust targets
6 Rumple
10 Group that inspired "Mamma Mia!"
14 Time for vampires
15 [gasp!]
16 Johnny Unitas, for most of his career
17 Can't take
18 "Don't put words in my mouth!"
20 Requests a dog treat, maybe
22 Hustler's card game
23 "I wasn't born yesterday!"
26 Special Forces wear
27 Gives a stemwinder
28 Part of "snafu"
29 "Sesame Street" viewer
30 Soup with sushi
31 Fleet
34 "Let this be our little secret" . . . with a hint to 18-, 23-, 50- or 54-Across
40 Edict locale of 1598
41 Contract period, often
42 Monopoly token
45 A.P.O. addressees
46 1966 answer to the Mustang
48 Warren Report name
50 "Wanna start somethin'?"
52 Swallower of Pinocchio
53 Take up residence
54 "Ooh, I'm shaking in my boots!"
56 Lead-in to fan or jet
60 Best Picture of 2012
61 Go a few rounds
62 Gaming pioneer

63 Big name in 59-Down exploration
64 Like a spent briquette
65 George of "Just Shoot Me!"

DOWN

1 Kind of fingerprinting
2 Slab unit, on a menu
3 "Ewww, gross!"
4 Tumbleweed locale, stereotypically
5 Bitter conflict
6 Rapid, in music
7 Relo rental, perhaps
8 Salon sound
9 Landscaper's purchase
10 John Wilkes Booth, e.g.
11 Easter wear
12 Stewed to the gills

13 Bear witness (to)
19 Former Philippine first lady ___ Marcos
21 How-___
23 Tangle untangler
24 Indy racer Luyendyk
25 Tammany tiger creator
26 Danube's color, to a Berliner
28 "Famous" cookie man
31 Small soldiers
32 Loaf with caraway seeds, maybe
33 Very soon
35 Most holes in ones
36 Camelot lady
37 Admissions honcho
38 Five-and-ten, e.g.
39 Suffix with switch
42 Elephant rider's seat

43 How driftwood may end up
44 Banjo sounds
46 The Cavs, on scoreboards
47 Japanese police dogs
49 Some saxes
50 Ark contents
51 Animator Tex
53 Treasure-hunters' aids
55 Former pres. Tyler sided with it
57 Dirt-dishing newspaper
58 It can leave a tan line
59 Texas tea

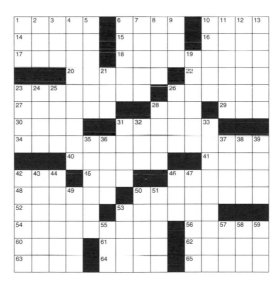

by Jacob McDermott

ACROSS

1 They're thrown from horses
7 Fake
11 "The Silence of the Lambs" org.
14 Join the game, in a way
15 Spun
16 TV ET
17 The "you" in "you caught my eye" in a 1965 #1 hit
18 Casino sights
20 It flows in the Loire
21 Pasta name suffix
23 Boss of TV's Mork
24 Small-time thieves
27 Johannes : German :: ___ : Scottish
28 O'Hare or Newark Liberty
29 Totally awesome
31 One usually buys a round one
35 Olympian Ohno
37 Some archaeological finds
39 Author of "The Prague Cemetery"
40 "Hawaii ___"
41 Suffix with drunk
42 Schleppers' aids
44 Relative of a tank top
45 "Roots" surname
47 Slip past
48 Touchdowns: Abbr.
50 Antibloating brand
51 It can cause bloating
52 German word that's 67-Across spelled backward
54 Con game
58 Glove material
60 Fool
61 It may be topped with an angel
62 What an intersection may have
65 Excavation

67 German word that's 52-Across spelled backward
68 Parthian predecessor
69 City north of Lisbon
70 Butt
71 Setting for a fall
72 Minimum

DOWN

1 Dish with melted cheese
2 Occupy
3 Just above
4 + 6
5 Some commuter "reading"
6 Joe of "NCIS"
7 Overran
8 Tramp
9 Shylock trait
10 Sharp circle?
11 Willingly, old-style
12 Nonkosher sandwich

13 Uncertainties
19 Discouraging advice
22 Japanese flower-arranging art
25 Line at a stationery store?
26 Topps collectible
30 Cataloging things
32 Fight back
33 Whacked
34 Vogue on a dance floor
35 Shaving brand
36 Place to get a bite?
38 Certain heat conduit
43 Mishmash
46 Lit
49 Ship's route
53 Familiar phone conversation starter
55 Common spice in Indian food
56 Shades
57 Cereal killer

58 Went to and fro
59 Convergent point
62 Oscar-winning John
63 Entry
64 Fence (in)
66 Word before rain, heat and gloom

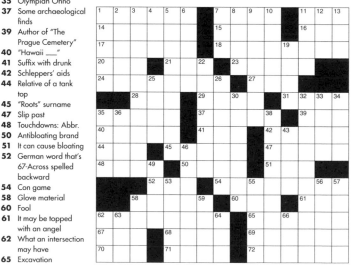

by Alan Derkazarian

ACROSS

1 Beverages in the a.m.
4 9-Across buy
9 Company founded by a 17-year-old Swede
13 Young boxer
14 Cry of fear or hilarity
15 House cat's perch
16 Foofaraw
17 Recipe instruction #1
19 Slips and such
21 Tony of "Taxi"
22 Recipe instruction #2
25 Owners of an infamous cow
27 Banshee's cry
28 Slaps the cuffs on
29 Number of pecks in a 34-Down
30 U.K. bestowal
33 Recipe instruction #3
38 Tarzan creator's monogram
39 Bell Labs operating system
40 Nifty
41 Seller's caveat
42 Renaissance, literally
45 Recipe instruction #4
49 Tilter's weapon
50 Renders unnecessary
53 Recipe instruction #5
56 An ex of Frank
57 Painter Mondrian
58 Term of address for a nobleman
59 Altoids container
60 Impersonal letter starter
61 What you get when you blend the results of this puzzle's recipe instructions
62 Bugling beast

DOWN

1 Gem of a girl?
2 Dench who played Elizabeth I
3 Squarish TV toon
4 Minimum age for a U.S. senator
5 ___ Army (golf fans of old)
6 Muscle strengthened by curls, informally
7 Van Cleef of "High Noon"
8 Heart test letters
9 Lost Tribes' land
10 Ceramists' fixtures
11 Pupil of 'enry 'iggins
12 ___ Highway (historic route to Delta Junction)
14 Lipstick slip
18 Be a fan of
20 Get, as a concept
23 Mil. truant
24 Brother of Fidel
25 As soon as
26 Cowardly Lion portrayer
29 Tough spot
30 Fudge, say
31 Patrolman's rounds
32 O.T. book read during Purim
34 Farmer's basketful, maybe
35 Have ___ (surreptitiously imbibe)
36 Emphatic assent, in Baja
37 "The Red Tent" author Diamant
41 Items at a haberdashery
42 PC start-over
43 "Green," in product names
44 Physique
45 Sounds of appreciation
46 Pizza cuts, essentially
47 Hypnotized
48 Year-end airs
51 Bad to the bone
52 Put in the cup, as a golf ball
54 Mischievous sort
55 Contend

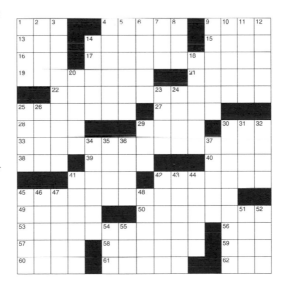

by Jean O'Conor

74 ⭐⭐

ACROSS

1. Ersatz cocoa
6. Works as an agent (for)
10. It may run during a campaign
14. Slack-jawed
15. The yoke's on them
16. Trek
17. Signal converter
18. Dole (out)
19. Eponymic Dutch city
20. Like 20-Across
23. Start of the names of three of the 10 most populous U.S. cities
24. Something often guessed
25. Island that's home to the world's largest lizard
28. Like 28-Across
31. 007, e.g.
34. Cowboy's charge
35. Part of a common Latin conjugation
36. Johnnycake
37. Wharves
39. Sidetrack?
40. Favorite
41. "One of ___" (1923 Pulitzer-winning novel by Willa Cather)
42. Levels
43. Like 43-Across
47. October event, informally, with "the"
48. Obituary listing: Abbr.
49. Kind of moment
52. Like 52-Across
56. Contained
58. Troubles
59. "___ we all?"
60. Quod ___ demonstrandum
61. Cool
62. "Gimme it!"
63. Spread out in the kitchen?
64. Sparklers
65. PowerPoint pointer

DOWN

1. Roughs it, say
2. Greek marketplace
3. Home inspector's concern
4. Dentist's request
5. Laments
6. 2012 newsmaker
7. High-up in a corp.
8. Officemate of Don and Peggy on "Mad Men"
9. Jordans, e.g.
10. Pat Nixon's given name
11. Outmoded rental
12. Otherwise called
13. Blue: Abbr.
21. Big thumbs-down
22. 007
26. Show reluctance
27. Some trails
28. OPEC member: Abbr.
29. Stage
30. "What's the big idea?!"
31. Meetings entered in P.D.A.'s: Abbr.
32. Lerner's partner on Broadway
33. Reciprocal action and reaction
37. Knight's activity
38. Site sight
39. Knight
41. Rack locale
42. Extremely juicy
44. Misled
45. Meetings probably not entered in P.D.A.'s
46. ___ no.
49. Assists, in a way
50. Bit of hardware
51. Shakespeare, at times
53. Sheltered
54. Dis
55. Ground
56. Box (in)
57. Century 21 competitor

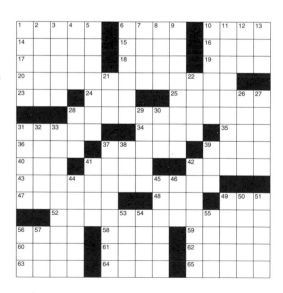

by Tom McCoy

ACROSS

1 Leading
6 Class-ranking stat
9 N.C.A.A. part: Abbr.
14 Ravel's "La ___"
15 Designer's major
16 Lincoln Center's Alice ___ Hall
17 Division signs
18 Chaotic scene
19 Valerie Harper title role
20 W.W. II female
21 "No kidding!"
23 Islands finger food
25 Chicago Cubs' station
26 Have in mind
28 Third-largest city in Italia
30 Stereotypical Mensan
31 Most athletes are in it
35 "And giving ___, up the chimney . . ."
36 Privateer's potation
37 Boot one
38 To be, in Québec
39 Org. criticized in "Sicko"
40 Software package medium
42 Owing the pot
44 Direction indicator
46 Like some checking accounts
49 Typical prerequisite to geom.
51 Celebrity groom in '68 headlines
52 Blue Jays, on scoreboards
53 Put into play
55 & 57 1977 Jackson Browne album . . . or a hint to what's depicted in this puzzle's grid
59 Hightails it
60 Like eggs in omelets
61 Pete Rose's 4,256
62 Mental picture

66 Many hands may be found on it
67 Tending to the matter
68 Someone born on Columbus Day, e.g.
69 Chain that sells Borgsjö bookcases
70 P.I.'s
71 Casey with a countdown
72 "___ Flux" (Charlize Theron movie)

DOWN

1 Stating firmly
2 Cuban dance
3 Kind of force that affects charged particles
4 Handy way of communicating?: Abbr.
5 Lower oneself
6 Steady look
7 Moneymaker?
8 On
9 Lobbies with trees, maybe
10 Ndamukong ___, 2010 N.F.L. Defensive Rookie of the Year
11 A bit dense
12 American flag
13 Poison pill contents
22 Mag. staffers
24 Number on a foam finger
27 Musician Johnny Winter's musician brother
29 Bel ___ cheese
32 Harry Potter's owl
33 Opposite of dep.
34 On the double
40 Shucker's debris
41 Night ray
43 Eavesdropping distance

45 A bust may come of it
47 Not busy
48 1965 Physics Nobelist Richard
50 Wolflike
54 LP introduction of 1957
56 Exterminators' targets
58 Omertà group
63 Unaccounted for, briefly
64 Six-pack ___
65 College sr.'s test

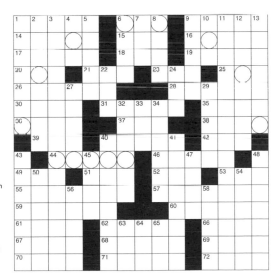

by Peter A. Collins

ACROSS

1 Pen denizen
4 Go ballistic?
7 In
13 Employee insurance plan, for short
14 Makeup of one of the homes of the Three Little Pigs
16 Isn't piglike
17 One putting out feelers
18 Wacko
19 Rug fibers
20 Commencement, e.g.
22 John who wrote "The French Lieutenant's Woman"
24 Formerly
25 People for whom "tena koe" means "hello"
27 401(k) employer matching contributions, e.g.
29 Card
30 Like CH₃CO₂H
31 Nicktoons character
34 Rigans, e.g.
38 Onetime Mideast org.
39 Cheese selection
40 Quite familiar
41 Some records
43 To-do
45 PC file suffix
46 Rustic poems
47 Make some travel plans
49 On
51 Holy ___
52 Ready for publication
55 Trypanosome carrier
58 Red Cross letters
59 Guideposts
61 Cager who retired in 2011
62 Jumps
64 Gad about

66 Part of the Australian coat of arms
67 Hosts
68 Her "birthday" is Oct. 4, 2011
69 Louis XIV, e.g.
70 Much of Mauritania
71 Acid
72 Head-to-head contact, for short?

DOWN

1 Mojo
2 ___ vincit amor
3 [ ]
4 Cobbler's tool
5 Skyline sights
6 O'Brien's Team ___
7 Say so
8 [ ]
9 Eats
10 Malay for "human"
11 Fray
12 Bookends on shelves?

15 Some bedcovers . . . or, literally, what the four unclued answers are
21 The Emerald Isle
23 Harvard University Press's ___ Classical Library
26 [ ]
28 Killed, as a test
30 Bygone hoops org.
31 Muslim mystic
32 Accountant's stamp
33 MS. recipients
35 [ ]
36 Fleet vehicle
37 Stride
40 Iowa's state tree
42 Do in, so to speak
44 El Al hub city
47 ___ Capital
48 Athletic supporters?
50 Black Sea port
52 Cries uncle

53 President whose initials "stink"
54 Tobacco holder
55 Several Peters
56 Aegean island
57 Furnish
60 Labor
63 Rustic locale
65 Prefix with century

by Jules P. Markey

ACROSS

1 One of the Obama girls
6 Like
9 Kindergarten stuff
13 Huskies' sch.
14 Heavy work
16 Word before income or exhaust
17 Source of easy money
19 Cube . . . or certain cubes
20 Certain
21 Salon supplies
23 "Evita" character
24 One of a pair in a court
27 Prickly one
30 Plains Indians
31 Suffix meaning "approximately"
32 Author Calvino
36 Hardly Mr. Cool
39 Setting for the starts of 17-, 24-, 51- and 64-Across
43 Brontë title heroine
44 Cartoon genre
45 Not miss a thing on
46 Lisa with the 1997 hit "I Do"
49 Short-sheeting and such
51 Locale for a big mirror
56 Director Anderson
57 Officers above sarges
58 Noodles in Japanese cookery
62 Suffix with Rock
64 Old ragtime dance
66 God with a quiver
67 Stake on a table
68 Many an aria singer, informally
69 Fillet
70 Short
71 "That threw me for ___"

DOWN

1 Makes faces
2 Onset of phobia?
3 Soil sort
4 Stockbroker's advice
5 "___ news?"
6 Parts of hearts
7 Bank department
8 Plain folk
9 Make sense, with "up"
10 LaCrosse, for one
11 Hidden store
12 Cold fall
15 Warm month in South America
18 They may be blind
22 Calendar abbr.
25 Old Nestlé brand
26 Viet ___
27 Footnote, perhaps
28 Wan

29 Dance from which the Lindy Hop developed
33 Muslim general
34 Jeremy of the N.B.A.
35 Egg: Prefix
37 Pool need
38 Salon supplies
40 Modernists, informally
41 Obtrude
42 "I, Claudius" role
47 Subj. for many newcomers
48 Fauna and flora
50 Brand from Holland
51 Hardly Mr. Cool
52 Like the Deco look, now
53 Nuts and bolts, e.g.
54 Body measurement
55 Enter again, as text
59 Rice-size pasta

60 Lamebrain
61 Opposite of under
63 Charlottesville-to-Richmond dir.
65 Sumac native to Peru

by Jules P. Markey

ACROSS

1 Not for the Parti Québécois?
4 Comcast and CenturyLink, in brief
8 Terminal info
12 Words of praise
13 Org. that fought Napster
14 Hook's place
15 Joe Louis, to fans
18 Kind of bean
19 Out, in a way
20 For instance
21 Flower feature
23 Anti-apartheid activist Steve
25 Base of a certain pole, figuratively
27 Grate
31 Some radios
34 One interested in current affairs?
36 Host of the 1972 Winter Olympics
38 ___ it all
39 Stowed stuff
40 Isn't content with the status quo, say
42 Gang Green member
45 Some TV drama settings, for short
46 ___ in progress (iPhone phrase)
47 Cottonwoods
49 Tennis's Mandlikova
51 Classic toothpaste name
54 "Gross!"
57 Recipe instruction
59 Door fixture
61 Cult classic whose title is depicted four times in this puzzle
64 Beaker material
65 Mrs. James Joyce
66 Toon's place
67 Positive principle
68 Mother of Nike, in Greek myth
69 Historic leader?

DOWN

1 They may be cast-iron
2 For a specific purpose
3 "I'm outta here!"
4 Like some verbs: Abbr.
5 Little Bighorn conflict
6 Future queen, maybe
7 Balloon ballast
8 Street shader
9 Keep ___ on
10 Lost
11 Nimble
14 Blarney Castle's county
16 Cinderella's soiree
17 Human ___
22 Chant from a 32-Down, maybe
24 Small antelope
26 6 letters
28 Hold dear
29 Cut
30 Voice mail imperative
31 Orgs.
32 See 22-Down
33 Offspring
35 Object of scrutiny at airport security
37 Outwit, in a way, with "out"
40 Horror film director Alexandre ___
41 School at which students are collared?
43 Some queens
44 "Ah-OO-gah!" horns
48 Canadian-born comedian once featured on the cover of Time
50 Kind of card
52 Antidiscrimination grp.
53 Ed of "Up"
54 Spot
55 "A Day Without Rain" singer
56 Tip off
58 Playing longer than expected, for short
60 One-named sports star who was once the highest-paid athlete in the world
62 Party congregation site, maybe
63 Bellum's opposite

by Loren Muse Smith and Jeff Chen

ACROSS

1 Lithium or iridium
6 Math subj. with proofs
10 W.C.'s
14 En masse
15 Area jiggled while twerking
16 Touched down
17 Food critic's assessments of calamari?
19 Brilliant 13-Down
20 Disbursed
21 Part of a Holmes comment to Watson
23 Nintendo's Super ___
24 Tony-nominated musical based on a 1992 Disney movie
27 Maneuver on a chessboard?
32 Ones coming on board
35 Biblical verb ending
36 River under the Ponte Vecchio
37 Steinway offering
38 ___ Cruces, N.M.
39 Follow-the-leader sorts
40 Identifies, on Facebook
41 One seeing pink elephants
42 Kosygin of Russia
43 Rug rat pursuer?
46 Believers in one god
47 Elvis's label
50 Stallone's genre
53 The last 30 seconds of many TV shows
56 Talk show physician
57 Outstanding posture for a catcher?
60 AT&T Stadium feature
61 Antidiscrimination org.
62 Horse with a patchy coat
63 Floored it
64 Long and lean
65 Elvis's trademark look

DOWN

1 Perry who's on the case
2 Ending like "-like"
3 Sellers of tips
4 Dye-yielding shrub
5 Helen of Troy's mother
6 Dairy aisle rating
7 Suffix with sonnet
8 Symbol of strength
9 James Stewart title role
10 Topiary pro
11 Burn application
12 Cheer starter
13 Southern Cross unit
18 Drawback
22 One on the first side to vote, usually
25 Year-end decorations
26 Collections
27 Made more aware
28 Proof finale letters
29 Cloned menace of film
30 About, on memos
31 "___ Fan Tutte"
32 Elevs.
33 "The Hurt Locker" setting
34 Prego competitor
38 Centers of attention
39 The "A" of I.P.A.
41 Baseball's Old Professor
42 Strong point
44 P on campus
45 Battle cry
47 Attend a homecoming, say
48 Jalopy
49 Tycoon on the Titanic
50 Puts in
51 Trim, as a photo
52 "The Complete Works of Shakespeare," e.g.
54 Cobras of Egypt
55 Newspaper ad meas.
58 Mens ___ (criminal intent)
59 Proterozoic ___

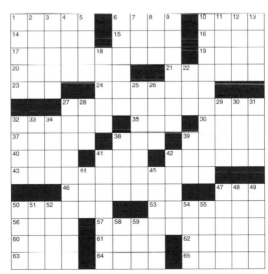

by Daniel Raymon

ACROSS
1 Like a satellite dish
5 Court disaster?
10 Call or email
14 Pac-12 team
15 Like the characters in "Angela's Ashes"
16 Vol. 1 of a four-volume encyclopedia, maybe
17 Unwind
18 Secure, in a way
20 Criticizes
21 Real conclusion?
22 In stitches
23 What a yeanling may grow up to be
24 Clarke who played the bride of Frankenstein
25 "O Tannenbaum" subject
26 Hot blood
27 Seekers of drug stores?
29 Technical writer's target
31 Holyfield rival
32 Shade of green
33 Classic Ford
34 Puzzlement . . . or a hint to getting the 10 words on the perimeter of this puzzle
38 Counterpart of paleo-
40 Word with wheel or deal
41 Did some surgery on, as an eye
45 Coke source
47 King of pop music
48 Early 10th-century year
49 Fingers
50 Glimmer
51 Anatomical foot
52 Kidding type
54 Give a whuppin'
55 Bric-a-___
56 Out to lunch
58 Unwind
59 Duke, e.g.
60 Like some errors
61 "___ unrelated matter . . ."
62 Pageant, e.g.
63 Repentant
64 Peace

DOWN
1 Simultaneous
2 Eroded
3 Evening service
4 Back-of-the-envelope figs.
5 Leg bones
6 Backspace, maybe
7 2012 political chant
8 West Coast setting: Abbr.
9 Locale of long-running Mideast conflict
10 "Voilà!"
11 Democritus or Leucippus, philosophically
12 Shrank
13 Title seeker
19 Napoleon Dynamite, e.g.
24 One to start?
25 Charges
28 ___ butter
30 Kind of nerve
32 Bulldog-like toy
35 June event televised by ESPN
36 Half-sawbucks
37 Cosmetics brand
38 Name in an envelope
39 Food
42 Member of a 2000s TV family
43 Nephew of Moses
44 Be patronizing
45 Call up
46 Sky: Fr.
47 Lightheaded one?
50 Stormed
53 One of Homer's greatest creations?
54 "Mon Oncle" star
55 Tea Party, e.g.
57 Choreographer Lubovitch

by Dan Schoenholz

ACROSS

1 Become inedible
6 Pull together
11 Big mouth
14 Start to type?
15 Nile Valley region
16 Org. with a noted journal
17 Classic Fender guitar, for short
18 Start of a quote about creativity by 58-Across/39-Down
20 Did some woolgathering
22 Body of 100
23 Quote, part 2
26 One on "Judge Judy"
27 Home of the Brave?: Abbr.
28 Cyberaddress: Abbr.
29 In the manner of a milquetoast
32 Bagel and lox purveyor
34 Mark down, perhaps
35 Quote, part 3
41 Quench
42 Level
44 Bygone Japanese camera brand
47 Shipping letters
50 Biomedical research org.
51 "Agreed!"
52 Quote, part 4
55 High-ranking noncom: Abbr.
58 With 39-Down, speaker of this puzzle's quote
59 End of the quote
61 Boos
64 "Bambi" deer
65 "Not ___ know of"
66 OH- or Cl-, chemically
67 Susan of "L.A. Law"

68 Shenanigan
69 Cross-dressing role for Streisand

DOWN

1 Many 16-Across members
2 Food scrap
3 Red light locale
4 Asteroids game maker
5 End of an academic 28-Across
6 Kid's cracker shape
7 G.I.'s civvies
8 Org. for D.A.'s
9 Serves on a panel
10 Opposite of out
11 Pillage
12 Dutch brew
13 Weak, as a brew
19 Deep perception
21 Gaseous prefix
23 Smidgen

24 Coordinate in the game Battleship
25 Suffix with hip or hoop
30 "___ be an honor"
31 Doorstep item
33 "Got it covered!"
34 Wish undone
36 "___ done!"
37 Be up
38 Trick-taking game
39 See 58-Across
40 Deutsch denial
43 Plato's P
44 Like the potatoes in shepherd's pie
45 "See ya!"
46 What's taken home
47 Larry Bird, during his playing days
48 Object in the right hand of the king of clubs
49 Wedding hiree

53 Port-au-Prince's land
54 Pax's Greek counterpart
56 Aqua Velva competitor
57 Lav
60 Turncoat
62 Become inedible
63 NBC show since '75

by Steve Savoy

ACROSS

1 Letter attachment?
8 Boomer born in 1961
15 Operate like a fan
16 Borg contemporary
17 Stroll
18 Kind of ray
19 Rapa ___ (Easter Island)
20 A long time past
22 Sanctioned
23 W alternative
25 Missouri's ___ River
26 Sounds from kids
27 Town in England or Nevada
28 Friday's preceder?
29 Rolling Stone co-founder Wenner
30 Energy-filled chargers
33 Tearjerkers?
35 Flashlight light
37 Maurice Chevalier musical
38 Want selfishly
40 "Explanation" that may follow "because"
44 Kind of tie
45 Make breathless
47 Saxophonist Al
48 Impact result
49 Tricot and others
51 Seek damages
52 Butt
53 Dish garnished with a lime wedge
55 Jeremy of the N.B.A.
56 Swellhead's trait
58 Awabi, at a sushi bar
60 Bath locale
61 They're unbeatable
62 ___ analysis
63 Moderates

DOWN

1 Scoop holders
2 Military attachment
3 "Samson and Delilah" director
4 Schubert's Symphony No. 8 ___ Minor ("Unfinished Symphony")
5 1970 hit about a girl with "a dark brown voice"
6 Later, to Luis
7 Banned event, informally
8 Attractive
9 Wise
10 Golfer Aoki
11 Kale source?
12 Subjects of Margaret Mead study
13 Certain bullet train rider
14 Relatives of Teddy's?
21 Pudding starch
24 Fastener with a ring-shaped head
26 Whack jobs
29 Nudges
31 Band parodied by Weird Al Yankovic's "Dare to Be Stupid"
32 Enclosure to an ed.
34 Britain's last King Richard
36 Munchies from Mars
38 Ski resort rentals
39 Chucklehead
41 Coin flipper's declaration
42 Excel
43 Concord
44 Joint application, maybe
46 Gas with or without an "m"
48 Judges
49 Casey of radio countdowns
50 "¿Quién ___?"
53 Itch (for)
54 "___ Rock"
57 Half of an exchange
59 Article in French papers

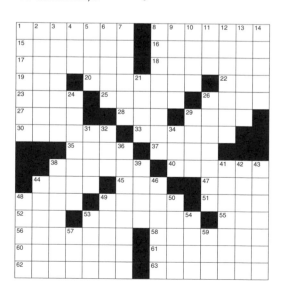

by David Steinberg

ACROSS

1 Good ol' boy
6 Airport security worker's device
10 Black, to a bard
14 Composer Copland
15 Outermost Aleutian island
16 Went like heck
17 Plaque from a governor?
20 Dredge, say
21 Can't deal with
22 "Downton Abbey" airer
24 Title for U2's Bono
25 Brit. military honor
27 Psych 101 topic
28 Sounds from saunas
30 It's tested in a fire drill
33 Blob, e.g.
35 Phrase before a future date
36 Mime's motto?
41 Machine that "nothing runs like"
42 Certain dupe
44 "Something is rotten in Denmark"
49 Drought-ridden
50 What Charlie rides, in a 1959 hit
51 Capp and Capone
52 Double-decker, e.g.
54 Municipal grid: Abbr.
55 Trims
57 Targets of sutures
59 Arrive via a red-eye?
64 Clark's Smallville crush
65 "Of wrath," in a hymn title
66 Longhorn's grid rival
67 Like centenarians
68 Adopt-a-thon adoptees
69 Like the sound of bagpipes

DOWN

1 Lea call
2 Detroit labor org.
3 Carrie on "Sex and the City"
4 Tiresome sort
5 Condor's habitat
6 Symbols of thinness
7 Envelope abbr.
8 Vowelless word
9 Scheduled to deliver (on)
10 ___ James (Beyoncé role)
11 Floating accommodations
12 Brand of taco sauce and shells
13 Liam of "Michael Collins"
18 Satellite radio's "The ___ & Anthony Show"
19 Baseball card collection holder, maybe
22 Sources of announcements, for short
23 ___ Men ("Who Let the Dogs Out" group)
25 Track event
26 Throw off
29 Trench maker's tool
31 More cuddly, say
32 Funeral flames
34 Narrowest of margins
37 Wishing site
38 Portfolio parts, briefly
39 Equestrian training
40 Ilk
43 Marks of illiteracy
44 Serengeti speedster
45 "Hogan's Heroes" setting
46 One of "the Few, the Proud"
47 Dies down
48 Keister
53 Do a shepherd's task
56 "OMG!," old-style
57 Wee pest
58 Leg up
60 Informer's info
61 Tee off
62 Empty (of)
63 A cipher needs one

by Ed Sessa

ACROSS

1 Cool dude
4 Woo
11 A train?
14 Times column: Abbr.
15 Canceled
16 Falstaff's quaff
17 Org. that usually meets in the evening
18 Living room fixture since the '50s
19 Born
20 Food wrap
22 Light for Aladdin
24 Asks in public, say
27 Flight simulator
29 Makeup of les Caraïbes
30 Extreme
32 A pride of lions?
33 Great finish?
34 Chicken for dinner
35 Founded: Abbr.
36 Incompatible
39 Cow, perhaps
40 Together
41 Sch. with a campus in Providence
42 Shrinking
43 Soother of an aching joint
44 Computer key
45 It may come in loose-leaf form
46 Poetic paean
47 Alfred Hitchcock title
48 Env. contents
49 Quarter or half
51 "L'chaim," literally
53 1960s British P.M. ___ Douglas-Home
54 Either the top or bottom half of this puzzle, figuratively speaking
58 Taking care of business
59 Kind of wave
60 Send

61 Sold (for)
62 Brine
63 Bulldozed
64 Wakeboard relative

DOWN

1 ___ America / Final maneuver
2 It gives Congress the power to declare war / Cyclist's stunt
3 Séance phenomena / Seattle Center Coliseum, since 1995
4 Jumps back
5 Tic-tac-toe loser
6 Blanc who voiced Bugs Bunny
7 Foofaraw
8 King Harald's land: Abbr.
9 Director's cry
10 Cry at an unveiling
11 Fruit or nuts / Silhouettes
12 Fourth pope / Snitch
13 Crimson / Opera texts
21 "All That Jazz" director
23 Treated, in a way, as a lawn
25 Big band member / Wee one
26 Camera type, briefly / London gallery
27 Numero di R's in "arrivederci" / Razzes
28 ___ avis / Two- or four-seater, maybe
31 Lightly scented perfume
37 Rebel yell
38 Rio ___ (Amazon feeder)
50 Restaurant freebie

52 Ideal condition in which to ford a stream
55 Yellowhammer State: Abbr.
56 Longtime Red Sox nickname
57 Somme summer

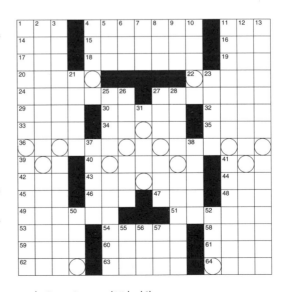

by George Barany and Michael Shteyman

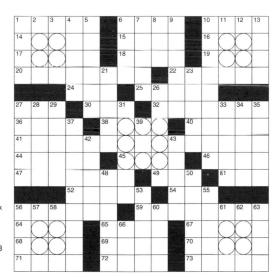

85

ACROSS

1 Punched-out parts of paper ballots
6 It's difficult to see through
10 Writes as a postscript, say
14 Monsieur ___ (Jacques Tati role)
15 It's east of Europe
16 Quite an achievement
17 Cara of "Fame"
18 Senseless
19 Prefix with present
20 Stronger and harder
22 Hullabaloo
24 Common desk shape
25 Tea type
27 Barn ___
30 Locale for an ibex
32 Error
36 "___ is not a lasting teacher of duty": Cicero
38 Senseless
40 ___ vie
41 One set of gifts in "The 12 Days of Christmas" . . . as suggested by the circled squares?
44 Hint
45 Ukraine and others, once: Abbr.
46 Nuts and fruit, in part, for squirrels
47 Rebellious region of the Caucasus
49 Method: Abbr.
51 Sellout sign
52 Via ___ (main street of ancient Rome)
54 The Big Apple, for short
56 Second-highest peak in the Cascades
59 Sport not played officially in the Olympics since 1908
64 "Me neither"
65 Devastation
67 Fuming
68 "Yikes!"
69 Not new
70 Christmas tree decoration
71 Godsend
72 Memory Stick manufacturer
73 Anatomical sacs

DOWN

1 X X X
2 Offended
3 Sheltered, at sea
4 Gift recipient
5 ___ Artois (beer)
6 Shock of hair
7 Seize
8 Backboard attachment
9 Japanese dance-drama
10 Raised above?
11 Infomercial part
12 ___ Perino, George W. Bush's last press secretary
13 Kool-Aid instruction
21 "___ Anything" (1994 Nick Nolte/Albert Brooks film)
23 Baffling problem
26 Poker targets?
27 Leaving for
28 Small dams
29 Aa and pahoehoe
31 Distant radiation source
33 North African capital
34 Lawn tool
35 Sauce made with pine nuts
37 Downturn
39 E.R. figures
42 Suggest
43 "This I Promise You" group, 2000
48 Hubristic flier of myth
50 Ancient Mideast language
53 Bizarre
55 Not subtle, as humor
56 Hardly the hoi polloi type
57 Syllables from Santa
58 Florence's river
60 Humorist Rooney
61 Downturns
62 Typesetting direction
63 Sushi fish
66 Tour grp.

by Jacob Stulberg

ACROSS

1 Some tubers
7 Anyway
15 Unqualified
16 Jamaican rum liqueur
17 Many a Manhattan Project worker
19 Search for, in a way
20 Undiluted
21 Brown shade
24 Toward safety
25 One on One: ___ vs. Larry Bird (old video game)
28 Growth on wet rocks or the surface of stagnant water
31 Pre-Susan B. Anthony dollar coins, informally
33 Bygone Brazilian airline
34 What a coiled spring or charged battery has, in physics
41 Public, as dirty laundry
42 Skinny
43 Targeted area?
48 Hit with an electric bolt
49 Silents sex symbol
50 Bogged down
52 Animated greetings
55 Oscillates
58 Chaos . . . or a hint to the contents of 17-, 28-, 34- and 43-Across
62 Dubai-based airline
63 California's ___ National Forest
64 Private dining area?
65 Maxim

DOWN

1 Golfer Baker-Finch, winner of the 1991 British Open
2 Sedate, say
3 Using the bow, in music
4 Purity rings?
5 Old iPod Nano capacity
6 More rough around the edges, perhaps
7 Partook of
8 End of a French film
9 Auto necessities
10 Discharge
11 Completely tuckered out
12 Site of some piercings
13 Name on a property deed, maybe
14 Brobdingnagian
18 Surrealist Magritte
22 Silver Stater
23 Fastidious to a fault
25 Skinny-___
26 1929's "Street Girl" was its first official production
27 Deep black
29 "The Way I ___" (2007 Timbaland hit)
30 Architectural designer of New York's Museum for African Art
32 Vikings, e.g.
35 Zip
36 Nickname for a junior's junior
37 Yesterday: It.
38 Cartoonist Chast
39 1.0 is not a good one, in brief
40 "You betcha!"
43 Flower cluster on a single stem, as in the honey locust
44 Many Shiites
45 Language of Pandora
46 Richard ___, former chief of the N.Y.S.E.
47 Continental pass name
49 Embellish, in a way
51 Like chestnuts
53 Alternative to hell?
54 Be plenty good for
56 Slips
57 "The poet in my heart," per a Fleetwood Mac song
59 Sports anchor Berman
60 48 U.S. states observe it: Abbr.
61 Ship's departure?

by Tim Croce

ACROSS

1 Frank's partner in the funnies
7 Old ___ (London theater)
10 À la mode
14 Asian entertainer
15 Have a mortgage, say
16 ___ O'Neill
17 Tree with extra-large acorns
18 ___ Cob, Conn.
19 NASA component: Abbr.
20 Card holder: Abbr.
21 Eponymous sitcom star of the 2000s
23 After-dinner wine
25 Narrow inlet
26 Model Porizkova
28 Dine
29 Ad nauseam
31 Far sides of ranges
33 ___ King Cole
34 Actor McKellen and others
36 Hawaiian singer with many 1960s–'70s TV guest appearances
37 New Year's greeting
40 Spelunker
43 Sleek swimmers
44 N.Y.C. line
47 Teresa Heinz or Christina Onassis
49 Spartan
52 Roth ___
53 People of Rwanda and Burundi
55 K.G.B. rival
56 2000s TV drama set in the 1960s
58 Smile
59 Like some sale goods: Abbr.
60 Tailor's case
61 The White Stripes or OutKast
63 Declutter
65 The White Stripes' genre
66 Rap sheet letters
67 Little-known
68 Johnson of "Laugh-In"
69 Permit
70 Aslant

DOWN

1 First king of the English
2 After-school activity?
3 Band with the 10x platinum album "Nevermind"
4 That, in Toledo
5 Economics Nobelist William F. ___
6 Sample the hooch
7 Not shy about expressing opinions
8 ___ Jima
9 Business jet maker
10 Dunce cap shape
11 Make rough
12 "Actually . . ."
13 Afro-Caribbean music
22 Capital spanning the Danube
24 Achieved through difficulty
27 1971 #1 hit for Carole King
30 Alternative
32 "Try!"
35 Bill ___, the Science Guy
38 "___ there yet?"
39 Classic Stephen Foster song
40 Fire-breathing creature of myth
41 Faucet attachment
42 Span across a gorge, say
45 Soloist's performance
46 Persian Wars vessel
48 Bit of beachwear
50 San ___, Calif.
51 Took home
54 W.W. II menace
57 Love from the Beach Boys?
62 Instrument for 36-Across, informally
64 "Life of Pi" director Lee

by Peter A. Collins

ACROSS

1 Some support beams
6 100%
9 Key of Chopin's Polonaise No. 6
14 Hit the highlights
15 Husband and wife, e.g.
16 Sponge
17 Food or drink dispensers
19 ___ to the top
20 First word in the English lyrics of "Frère Jacques"
21 Nick of "The Deep"
22 Kind of cartridge
23 Burning the midnight oil
25 Like virtually all gold medalists in Olympic table tennis
27 Science of light
28 Lads
29 Performs, in the Bible
30 Shimmery silks
31 "You ___" (2011 Lady Gaga song)
32 Robert Frost poem that includes "Good fences make good neighbors"
33 Three-toed runners
37 Designed (for)
39 Yoga pose that strengthens the abs
40 Pope who declared "I am a sinner. This is the most accurate definition"
42 With skill and grace
43 Hog
44 Ignoring
45 Maid on "The Jetsons"
46 ___ squash
48 Sea eggs
50 Sci-fi novelist ___ Scott Card

51 Taking liberties
53 Mock attack
54 "Star Trek" prosthesis
55 Oceanward
56 Tour de France stage
57 Board member: Abbr.
58 Full of spunk

DOWN

1 "___ la Douce"
2 Relate to
3 Successful, as an applicant
4 Sound of support
5 Ingredient in Florentine dishes
6 "Someone Like You" singer
7 Hircosity
8 1968 #1 hit for the Supremes
9 Feeling romantic
10 Going without help

11 Car not in a garage
12 Gatekeeper's grant
13 "Voilà!"
18 Forget-me-___
24 Future court case
26 Mistreatment
27 ___ Mae ("Ghost" role)
28 Parts of clogs
30 Softened up, in a way
32 Where Snickers, Skittles and Starburst are manufactured
34 Crash pad?
35 Frees
36 It goes around the world
38 Diplomatic agreement
39 Inconsequential stuff
40 Little bloom
41 Don's place

42 Charlie Chan's creator Earl ___ Biggers
43 "Grand Canyon Suite" composer
44 Red Sox Hall-of-Famer Bobby
47 Tea type
49 Company with a 1998 Nasdaq I.P.O. that hired its first employee in 1996
52 Mauna ___

by Todd Gross

ACROSS

1 Message indicating "adult beverages not supplied"
5 Cowboy's prod
9 Analyze, as a sentence
14 Karl who advised Bush 43
15 Give the once-over
16 Amazon.com's line
17 [Attention, please . . .]
18 Tub accessory
20 Outfielder Hunter with nine Gold Gloves
22 Mob turncoat
23 European capital until 1990
24 Doohickey
28 Frequent hoax subj.
29 Latin lover's declaration
30 Manse occupant
32 Ear-related
35 Washing-up spot?
36 Channel for the character named by the ends of 18-, 24-, 52- and 59-Across
40 Morticia, to Fester, on "The Addams Family"
42 Mummy's place
43 Big Brother's creator
45 Be momentarily fazed by
51 Navigate a biathlon course, say
52 New Year's Eve hot spot
55 She, in Salerno
57 Lavatory sign
58 Throat bug, briefly
59 2011 Tina Fey autobiography
63 One of a jungle couple

64 Tickle
65 Occasion to eat poi
66 Great Plains tribe
67 Davis with a 1988 Oscar
68 "Omigosh!"
69 All of these may be off

DOWN

1 Like a spoiled kid
2 Start of a pirate's refrain
3 No longer bothered
4 Candy heart request
5 Melodramatic response
6 FedExCup org.
7 Michelob ___ (light brew)
8 Fix up, as a building
9 ___ rally
10 Tiny bit of progress
11 Left in the lurch

12 Accept officially, as a package
13 "Gee, I think you're swell" girl of a 1960s song
19 Knock off
21 Supermarket franchise chain
25 In a frenzy
26 Church choir song
27 Location in a game of tag
31 "Homeland" network, for short
33 U.N. workers' agcy.
34 Part makers
36 Initial public offering
37 Puck handler's surface
38 Bill Russell or Larry Bird, briefly
39 Some substantial hits: Abbr.

40 Feeder in a stable
41 Annoying
44 Evidence of an ankle sprain
46 Stanford-Binet figs.
47 Weirdo
48 Activity that includes roundhouse kicks
49 "Am too!" counter
50 Homes for the 66-Across
53 Like the consistency of an old apple
54 Yawn inducer
56 Part of 6-Down: Abbr.
60 Roll-call call
61 Keg feature
62 Drag to court

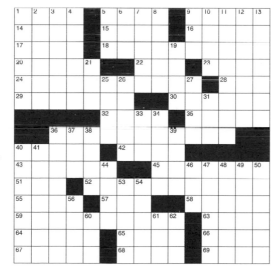

by Sam Ezersky and Victor Fleming

90 ⭐ ⭐

ACROSS

1 Flies (along)
5 Clutter
8 What spies collect
13 Voyaging
14 Flaming Gorge locale
16 Who has scored more than 850 points in an official Scrabble game
17 Frolic
18 "Beloved" author Morrison
19 Bagpipe music, maybe
20 Delt neighbor
21 You might slip on it
22 Fragrant compound
23 Lucy ___, title character in Sir Walter Scott's "The Bride of Lammermoor"
25 Security Council veto
27 Sure-___
29 Shellacs
31 First name in folk
32 ___ factor
37 Drippings, maybe
38 City in southern California
40 Unloading point
41 Food processor?
43 Overseas
44 Like some numbers and beef
45 Bill producers, for short
48 You might slip on it
51 Extemporizes
54 Theater's ___ Siddons Award
55 Assign stars to
57 Distillery sight
58 Prefix with type
59 Plaintiff
60 Agree
61 Western German city
62 Shade providers
63 Genesis locale
64 Big name in tractors

65 ___-square
66 Wallop

DOWN

1 Rock and Roll Hall of Fame inductee with only one Top 40 hit
2 British ___
3 Sign of puberty, maybe
4 For example
5 Certain horror film villain
6 Alma mater for David Cameron
7 Site of slippage . . . both geographically and in this puzzle
8 Thorough
9 "Make some ___!"
10 Calorie-heavy dessert
11 Richard ___, "War Zone Diary" journalist

12 What womanizers do
15 Glistening, as Christmas ornaments
21 Haunted house sounds
24 Actor Maguire
26 Lead-in to plane
28 Site of a piercing
29 Forest female
30 ___ Burgundy, the anchorman in "Anchorman"
33 Splenda competitor
34 Make pieces of pieces?
35 OPEC member: Abbr.
36 Barrett of Pink Floyd
38 ___ Israel Medical Center
39 Experiment site
42 The speed of sound
44 See 46-Down
46 With 44-Down, "key" invention of the 1830s

47 500 people?
48 Carefully examine
49 Appeared
50 Something to pare, informally
52 Genesis locale
53 Blocked vessel opener
54 Tore
56 Agenda part
60 One of the Bushes

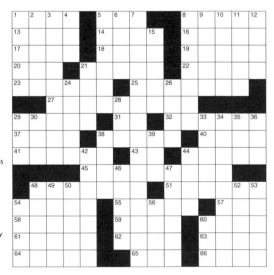

by Caleb Emmons

ACROSS

1 Furrier John ___ Astor
6 Musical closing
10 Rum-soaked cake
14 Bouquet
15 Request under deadline
16 Not many
17 It's all about location, location, location
19 Kansas City daily
20 Sustenance for aphids
21 Farm cry
22 Reverent quality
23 Narrow wood strip
24 Willow tree
26 Glowing coal
29 Admit
31 White House advisory grp.
34 Philosopher who wrote "It is difficult to free fools from the chains they revere"
36 "Angela's Ashes," for one
38 West of "Batman"
39 1955 hit for the Platters
41 Tops
42 Trickery
44 Pretends to be singing
46 Rocky Mountain ___
47 Insignia
49 Causes of glowers
50 Expunge
52 Wacko
54 Lobby
56 Inner circle
58 Pool tool
61 Neck and neck
62 Environs for Blackbeard
64 Hwy. safety org.
65 "Come ___!"
66 Have because of
67 Home of the Brenner Pass

68 Kind of party
69 Arc lamp gas

DOWN

1 Sprees
2 Vicinity
3 Chicken's place
4 "Horrors!," in texts
5 Newswoman Walters
6 Southern tip of South America
7 Factory-inspecting org.
8 City near Wright-Patterson Air Force Base
9 Manhunt letters
10 Count of music
11 Occasion for sandwiches and scones
12 Shellac
13 Off-balance

18 Cover girl Carol
22 Hookah, e.g.
23 "Step aside, I can handle this"
25 Recap
26 Circumvent
27 Poser
28 Soul food ingredient
30 "Hmm, imagine that!"
32 Inasmuch as
33 Salad green
35 Bits
37 Like some ancient pyramids
40 Soft to the touch
43 Building unit with flanges
45 Line of greeting cards billed as "a tiny little division of Hallmark"
48 Pour, as wine
51 Rips apart
53 Sphere

54 Org. that prepares flood maps
55 Elliptical
57 Andrea Bocelli offering
58 Battle of Normandy locale
59 Golden rule preposition
60 One of the social sciences, for short
62 N.Y.S.E. listings
63 21-Across crier

by Bernice Gordon

ACROSS

1 Harley, e.g.
4 First of all
8 Cartoonist who said "I don't read or watch TV to get ideas. My work is basically sitting down at the drawing table and getting silly"
14 Speaker's aid
16 "The Glass Menagerie" woman
17 Paddle pusher
18 Indulge
19 Grasped
20 Ball holder
21 Kitchen gizmos
22 Bartlett's, e.g.
24 Pet saying?
26 Coll. units
27 What a public scene may elicit
30 Gets ready to play, say, with "up"
33 Hunt's production
34 What some waiters never see?
35 Prepare to plant, perhaps
36 Lowercase letter illustrated six times in this puzzle?
38 Actor Stephen
41 Shoes and socks, typically
42 Start to take off one's pants, say
44 Girl's name meaning "beautiful"
45 Constituency
46 Lead
47 Slumber party togs
50 Rap's Dr. ___
51 Senility
54 ___ card
56 Newswoman Paula
59 Not shoot for the stars, to put it mildly
60 "I'm not the only one!"
62 River to the Missouri
63 Vitamin, e.g.
64 Some plasma TVs and digital cameras
65 Roman rebuke
66 Poor grade

DOWN

1 Break (into)
2 ___ incline (tilted)
3 Produce
4 Suffix with orange
5 "Go ahead!"
6 Flummoxed
7 Thing that might have a needle
8 "Charlie's Angels" actress
9 French mine?
10 Wheel with sloped teeth
11 Contemptuous responses
12 They may be picked up in a locker room
13 Indian breads
15 Crouches in fear
23 Like England in the Middle Ages
25 Arctic ice
27 Tech, e.g.: Abbr.
28 Subject of meditation
29 Turn
31 Make sense
32 Made up
34 Some sports cars
37 Part of a drain
38 Passed on, in a way
39 Bracket shape
40 Had
41 It's an imposition
43 Russian wolfhound
44 For whom Alfred Pennyworth is a butler
46 "Behold!"
48 Old-time actress Meadows
49 Corpulent
51 Fist-bumps
52 Attend
53 Female Cotswolds
55 Kennel Club reject, no doubt
57 Sharpen
58 ___ to self
61 "___ Hill," 1996 platinum album

by Elizabeth A. Long

ACROSS

1 Arcing shots
5 Liberal arts subj.
9 2010 Jennifer Aniston movie
14 Spread unit
15 Keen on
16 Drop off
17 "South Park" boy
18 "Where America's day begins"
19 "___ pray"
20 & 23 Giant in fairy tales
24 ___ Quimby of children's lit
27 Rock band named for an inventor
28 Do some diner work
29 Tough spot
30 Kicked to the curb
34 Ending with tea or cup
35 Story mapped out in this grid, from lower left to upper right
39 Much binary code
40 Flat takers
41 Music genre that influenced No Doubt
42 Top point value of a Scrabble tile
43 Debussy masterpiece
47 Purposely loses
49 View from a highway overlook
52 Publishers of 35-Across, with "the"
54 Hungry as ___
56 Trial fig.
57 Answer to "That so?"
58 Associate with
59 Like many highlighter colors
60 Where many Sargents hang, with "the"
61 Do-it-yourself libation

62 Ray of fast-food fame
63 Bad marks for a high schooler?

DOWN

1 Criticize severely
2 Pump figure
3 Ranch irons
4 Lacking reason
5 Weather map notations
6 Get used (to)
7 Woodworker's supply
8 Some cats
9 Actresses Shire and Balsam
10 Letter-shaped girder
11 Emulate Jack Sprat
12 Ungar of poker
13 Broomstick riders
21 Ache for

22 Walk through deep snow, say
25 Company endorsed by Tiger Woods
26 Relative of a lutz
28 Hospital count
31 Most cool, in slang
32 City east of St.-Lô
33 Weigh station wts.
34 Swiss "king of hoteliers"
35 Rio vis-à-vis the 2016 Olympics
36 Egyptian "key of life"
37 It has a low percentage of alcohol
38 Record again
42 Like some farm cultivators
44 Drink sometimes served in a hollowed-out pineapple

45 N.F.L. career rushing leader ___ Smith
46 One of 11 pharaohs
48 Provide an address?
49 Fizzle (out)
50 "Star Wars" droid
51 Justin Timberlake's former group
53 Hammerin' ___
54 In the house
55 Dribble catcher

by Jared Banta

ACROSS

1 Pudding flavor
4 Rapper Lil ___
7 Take on
13 Sea goddess who rescued Odysseus
14 "Mit," across the Rhine
16 Mixture of cement
17 "Deliver Us From ___" (2003 film)
18 Actress Rogers
19 Less loose
20 Member of a boy band with nine top 10 hits / Supply line cutter
23 Fatigue
24 Triple-platinum Sinatra album
25 Boundary river
26 Western actor Wooley
28 Move like goo
32 Invitation info
33 Top-heavy
34 Kitchen counter option / Some street gatherings
39 Befuddled
40 Jordan's only seaport
41 Color of el mar
42 Crescent
43 Enticed
47 Calrissian of "Star Wars" films
50 Expensive boot material
51 Bygone delivery / "Titanic" or "Avatar"
56 Daisy's love
57 "The Time Machine" people
58 Decline
59 Zenith
60 Blacken
61 Thrilla in Manila participant

62 Settings for some escape scenes
63 Ten Commandments keeper
64 Do-over

DOWN

1 Buffs
2 Flip
3 "Beat it!"
4 Pack tightly
5 Poet who wrote "If you want to be loved, be lovable"
6 Little ___ (early comic character)
7 ___ crow flies
8 Weather warning
9 Beach bag item / Represses, as bad memories
10 ___ Minor
11 Black-and-white horse?

12 "The ___ Affair" (Jasper Fforde novel)
15 Building unit / Set-off chunks of text
21 Puffed cereal
22 Angel food cake requirement
26 "___ Bop" (1984 hit)
27 Royal messengers
29 ___ Clean
30 Actress/model Kravitz
31 Rescue letters
32 "Huh?"
33 It might be under a tank
34 Barnyard cry
35 Snack brand represented by Sterling Cooper on "Mad Men"
36 Houston sch.

37 Cooler part / Obstruction
38 Fin
43 Its name may be written with an ampersand
44 Make plain
45 Food item
46 Smidgen
48 Less inept
49 The Graces in Raphael's "The Three Graces," e.g.
50 Smug look
51 One of the Argonauts
52 Deal
53 Sufficient, for Shakespeare
54 Zeno's home
55 Thunder

by Michael Hawkins

ACROSS

1 Part of una casa
5 Totally disgusted
10 Compressed pic, of a sort
14 Let off
15 Brief concession
16 Brewery fixture
17 Spa wear
18 See 22-Down
19 Hospital sticker
20 A general and his country
23 Loaded with substance
24 Title for a J.D. holder
25 Impossible point total in American pro football
28 Clandestine sort
32 Remove, as a corsage
34 Trigram on rotary phones
37 A hoops great and his league
40 Cake similar to a Yodel
42 Battle zone of 1956 and 1967
43 Baja resort area
44 A comic and his former show
47 Kobe cash
48 Cassette half
49 Soup alternative
51 Brian who's a self-professed "nonmusician"
52 Part of a bridle
55 Harem wear
59 A president and his conflict
64 Mazar of "Entourage"
66 What "-phage" means
67 Wear a long face
68 ___ ether
69 Final part of most Broadway musicals
70 Away from the wind

71 Like candy corn's texture
72 Woman's golf garment
73 Motorola phone brand

DOWN

1 Immunizing fluid
2 Whac-___ (carnival game)
3 Benghazi's land
4 Bikini atoll trials, informally
5 Word after "take" or "give me"
6 New Haven collegians
7 Fruity candy since 1945
8 Grammarian's concern
9 Exerters of pressure, maybe

10 W.C.
11 Ante up
12 Psychic's "gift," for short
13 Classic muscle car
21 1/1 title word
22 With 18-Across, an old term for brandy
26 Weeper of myth
27 Scandalous company with a tilted-E logo
29 Joy Adamson's big cat
30 Opposed to, in dialect
31 Classifications
33 View from Ft. Lee, N.J.
34 Thumb-sucking, e.g.
35 "The Kiss" sculptor
36 Spar with nobody
38 Simba's mate
39 Jessica of "7th Heaven"

41 Kipling's "Follow Me ___"
45 1988 N.L. Rookie of the Year Chris
46 Noted first name in raga
50 San Diego-area horse-racing venue
53 Bits of creativity
54 Follow, as a U.P.S. shipment
56 Sicilia, per esempio
57 "J to tha L-O!" artist
58 Smile like Snidely Whiplash
60 In need of a shampoo, say
61 German Expressionist ___ Dix
62 Small dam
63 Order in the court
64 It might get your feet wet
65 Bambi's aunt

by Michael Black

ACROSS

1 ___ Beach, city near San Luis Obispo
6 Hide
10 "It follows that . . ."
14 Totally stoked
15 Metro ___
16 Naughty look, maybe
17 With 27-Across, an old riddle
20 U.S. city known to some locals as Siqnazuaq
21 Girl's name that sounds like French for "she has it"
22 Microscopic, informally
23 Starting words at many a sporting event?
25 Rich soil
27 See 17-Across
32 "To Kill a Mockingbird" author
33 One on probation, maybe
34 In this matter
37 Key of Beethoven's Symphony No. 7: Abbr.
39 Flop
41 What lemon adds to a dish, in food lingo
42 "I won't miss it"
45 Take off
48 Kerfuffle
49 Answer to one spelling of the riddle
52 1998 Sarah McLachlan hit
53 Similar
54 Author of the quote "I am not what you call a civilized man!"
57 All the ___
59 Capital in 2004–'05's Orange Revolution
63 Answer to another spelling of the riddle

66 Locks in the stable?
67 Dark genre
68 Where Rosalind becomes Ganymede, in Shakespeare
69 Plunks (down)
70 Head-turning night fliers
71 Detroit's county

DOWN

1 Hostage
2 Modern "methinks"
3 Filter target
4 Luminary in a late-night show?
5 Has more than enough, briefly
6 Home is one corner in it
7 Russian river
8 Special election
9 Gab
10 Time-sensitive items
11 Santa's deer leader?
12 Savvies
13 ___-dokey
18 Like a rat's eyes
19 Drive drunkenly, say
24 Box ___
26 "Wow!"
27 One of the men on "Two and a Half Men"
28 Fictional character who says "I am not what you call a civilized man!"
29 Handled, with "with"
30 No-goodnik
31 Sports segment that often includes highlights
35 'Bama, with "the"
36 Cleaner's target
38 Artist Vermeer

40 Violet Crawley of "Downton Abbey," and others
43 Elvis's "Viva Las Vegas," recordwise
44 Fed. stipend
46 Established the price of
47 Sch. near Albany, N.Y.
50 Constrained
51 Site of the Museum of Anatolian Civilizations
54 Seductress
55 Genesis man
56 Little sucker?
58 Blue dye source
60 May race, informally
61 Genesis place
62 Weather indicator
64 Start for a Spanish count
65 Manhandle

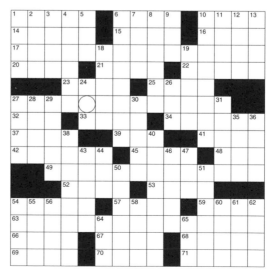

by Dan Schoenholz

ACROSS

1 Celebrity ribbing
6 Hissy fit
10 Urban housing option
14 Dazzling success
15 Practice
16 Con artist's mark
17 *Any foreseeable difficulty
20 Sitcom character from Melmac
21 Oom-___ (tuba sounds)
22 Falling-out result
23 Good economic news
25 *"Good night, John-Boy" series
29 ___ of Gibraltar
31 PC key below Home
32 Pay a call to
33 Lacrosse goalie's area
36 Do some leg-pulling
37 Breakfast cereal . . . or a hint to what's found in the answers to the four starred clues?
41 Mixed bag
42 "As I was saying . . ."
43 "Slung" stuff
44 Suffix with lion
46 Puts up
50 *Fearsome shark
54 Bit of harmless mischief
55 Official proceedings
56 Like a couch potato
58 Night on which "60 Minutes" originally aired: Abbr.
59 *"Why am I not surprised?"
63 Botanical wings
64 Gear-cutting tools
65 Yak, yak, yak
66 Specifications marked on 10-hole harmonicas

67 Knife of old
68 Quality that produces taste

DOWN

1 Fixes up, as a fixer-upper
2 Spotted wildcat
3 Totally in favor of
4 Mule of song
5 Muscle car roof option
6 "Quiet, please!"
7 It may elicit a 6-Down
8 Multinational bank that sponsored the New York City Marathon
9 "Reading Lolita in ___" (2003 best seller)
10 Make by hand
11 On a cruise
12 Knighthood letters

13 Unit pricing word
18 Squealed (on)
19 Like some Uno cards
24 Certain econ class
26 Needing hoeing, say
27 Leaves home?
28 Part of a gig
30 Tick off
34 Add ___ of salt
35 One in an upper chamber: Abbr.
36 Crown inset
37 Ethnic joke, often
38 Secluded spot
39 Huff and puff
40 Vert.'s opposite
41 Online "Yikes!"
44 James who was portrayed by Beyoncé
45 Mowers' paths
47 Catch a few Z's
48 Following, as one's beliefs

49 Shish kebab need
51 Analgesics' targets
52 "Well, ___!"
53 Café au lait holder
57 Puppy sounds
59 Cinch ___ (trash bag brand)
60 World Cup chant
61 Long, long time
62 Mexican Mrs.

by Tracy Gray

ACROSS

1 Report of a shooting
5 Brunch offerings, for short
8 Affected to a greater extent
14 Home of ancient Greek scholars
15 Google result
16 Civic alternatives
18 *Blubbered?
20 What a nod may mean
21 "Wouldn't miss it!"
22 Cone origin
23 Heartbreak, e.g.
24 Home of El Greco
25 *What happened after Mr. Onassis contacted A.A.A.?
27 Reputation, on the street
28 Kind of sum
30 Aero- completer
31 Washington ___ (N.Y.C. neighborhood)
32 "That can't be good!"
33 Maligned
35 *Imaginary overthrow of the government?
37 Robin Hood and others
40 "Mad Men" star Jon
41 Jim Bakker's ___ Club
44 Place to get clean
45 Title heroine described in the first lines of her novel as "handsome, clever and rich"
46 Not at all chipper
47 *Give a Dust Bowl migrant a ride?
50 Director Christopher and actor Lloyd
52 1998 Sarah McLachlan song
53 First name in ice cream

54 Bank numbers
55 Not mind
57 Language that gave us the words heard phonetically in the answers to the starred clues
58 Motivate
59 Back
60 Third person
61 Prepared for a long drive, with "up"
62 Part of a gym set
63 Roman foes

DOWN

1 Enchant
2 Gravely ill: Fr.
3 Gets snug
4 Ripped with a knife
5 "Here we go again!"
6 Agree
7 Messy spot
8 PC data format

9 Major alteration of a business structure, for short
10 Old cable inits.
11 Warning to the unwary
12 Kind of set
13 Quickly sought safety, in a way
17 Fretted
19 Multivolume set, for short
22 Get too much sun, colloquially
25 Condition treated with Adderall, in brief
26 Theater
29 Red state handouts?
32 Words always preceding a date
33 Source of ill-gotten gains
34 Kind of shop
35 Exodus figures
36 "Alas!"

37 Business establishment where customers can make a killing?
38 Something taken from a meter
39 Teacher/astronaut McAuliffe
41 Level off
42 Catches on the radio
43 Eases
45 One from Berlin
46 Boil for a short time
48 Extra-large
49 Typed (in)
51 ". . . ___ close second"
54 Zoo keeper?
56 Clear tables
57 Shock

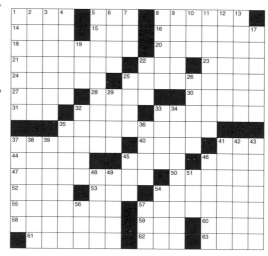

by Joe Krozel

ACROSS

1 Word of exasperation
7 Katmandu tongue
13 Wrinkly-skinned dog
14 One of the red Monopoly spaces
16 Triumphing
18 Open-house org.
19 ___ polloi
20 Lunes or martes
21 Ring decision, briefly
23 Matt who scored the only Jets touchdown in Super Bowl history
25 2B, SS or CF
26 ___ Stic (retractable Bic pen)
27 Comic Fields who was an Ed Sullivan regular
28 "Amores" poet
30 Designed to minimize wind resistance
31 Prepare, as some peanuts
32 Campbell of "Party of Five"
33 Traditional pre Christmas activity
36 Cartoon shriek
37 Roll-call call
38 Bub
41 The First State: Abbr.
43 Cry at the World Cup
44 Fleet member retired in '03
47 Place on a pedestal
49 Last book of the Old Testament
51 Element in chips
52 Became too old for foster care, say
53 Testifying accurately
55 Rare sight on casual Friday
56 Hawke of Hollywood
57 Buffalo's county
58 Marks of good bowlers

59 Surgical bypass
60 AOL alternative

DOWN

1 One operating a loom
2 End of Kurosawa's "Rashomon"?
3 Directional ending
4 Prefix with center
5 Nixon, e.g., for two yrs.
6 1952 Gary Cooper classic
7 Believer that life is meaningless
8 Suffix with acetyl
9 S.F. summer setting
10 It's about 1% argon
11 Had a break between flights
12 Clear and direct, as reporting

13 Common Nascar letters
15 Letters on a perp's record
17 Morgue ID
22 Christmas carol starter
23 They vary according to batters' heights
24 Poison gas, e.g
25 Florence's ___ Vecchio
26 Bopper
29 "___-lish!" ("Yum!")
34 Longtime Florentine ruling family
35 There might be one on the corner of a sail
38 Atomizer outputs
39 They're said at the end of a soirée
40 Dog that might be named Shep

42 Derby victory margin, maybe
43 Many an urban Cornhusker
44 Searches high and low
45 Quarantine, say
46 Dime-on-the-dollar donation
48 Happy tunes
50 To the point, in law
54 Day after hump day: Abbr.

by Peter A. Collins

ACROSS

1 One way to stand
7 Sources of wool
14 Come up again, as a web page
15 Statement preceding a blunt truth
16 Title girl in a children's book series set in Paris
17 Meter reading
18 Like the first two "Brandenburg" Concertos
19 City known as "Florence on the Elbe"
21 Prefix with form
22 Trim
24 Plotter's place
25 Sportscaster who lent his name to a popular video game series
26 Unconvincing
27 Fleet
28 Cinco follower
29 Wash. neighbor
30 One on the move
31 ___ the custom (traditionally)
32 1968 Beatles hit
35 Backs, as a front
37 Member of the familia
38 Big name in plastic
42 Almond ___ (candy brand)
43 Big hit
44 Earth sci.
45 What shouldn't follow you?
46 Macbeth or Macduff
47 Golfer ___ Pak
48 Woman
49 Ogle
52 Justice Dept. division
53 "Modern Family" actor
55 Boxster competitors

57 In situ, as stones
58 "Psst!" follower, perhaps
59 Sonnet enders
60 Corona alternative

DOWN

1 Carrier of plates?
2 Asset for a mimic
3 Notoriety
4 Cry of mock incredulity
5 Wedding staple
6 River through Pomerania
7 "Evangeline" locale
8 More easygoing
9 Nabokov novel after "Lolita"
10 Justice Dept. division
11 Italian actress Cardinale

12 Nickname for Michael Jordan, with "His"
13 Welcome to one's home
15 1963 movie with the tagline "Everybody who's ever been funny is in it!"
20 The Jetson boy
23 Disregard
25 Caused a stir
27 Added stipulations
28 Nine-digit ID
31 Flying without ___
33 ___ loss
34 Hold forth
35 Titian subject with Bacchus
36 Witticisms
39 Summer drink
40 Pitcher's woe
41 George Eliot and George Sand

43 Balance
45 Musical middle name
46 Time spent doing time, say
49 Dry
50 Marseille mates
51 "Glee" girl
54 Weirdo
56 Arabic name meaning "highly praised"

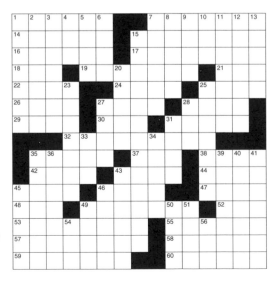

by Daniel Landman

ACROSS

1 Crumples (up)
5 Word of comparison
9 Destroy, as hopes
13 Drop
14 Relatives of Yodels
16 Object of ancient Egyptian veneration
17 Work written between "Typee" and "Mardi"
18 "Maria ___," 1941 #1 hit
19 Vivacious
20 Overly bold member of the "Little Women" family?
23 Salinger's "For ___- With Love and Squalor"
24 Granola bar ingredients
26 "No seats left," in short
29 Result of bankruptcy?
34 "Hungry hungry" game creatures
36 Schlep
37 Siouan tribe
38 Turn away
39 See 11-Down
40 Jewish deli offering
41 Thinker Descartes
42 Intellectual range
43 Nod's meaning, maybe
44 What blood donors do?
47 "___ fancy you consult, consult your purse": Franklin
48 Some summer wine
49 Dueling implement
51 Motivational words for a boss at layoff time?
57 "___ that sweet?"
60 Part of LED
61 One might run Lion or Leopard

62 Squeakers
63 Bob of "Full House"
64 Metaphor for punishment
65 Spur
66 Actor Coleman or Oldman
67 World's fair

DOWN

1 Pound sound
2 What might go on a belt
3 Parisian house of design
4 Vermont winter destination
5 Lunchbox accessory
6 Variety of poker
7 "Pardon the interruption . . ."
8 Singer Hendryx
9 "Oy" or "ow"

10 Japanese P.M. Shinzo ___
11 With 39-Across and 58-Down, response to a military command
12 F.D.R.'s third veep
15 Tahitian garb
21 Fancy necktie
22 Archipelago constituent, maybe
25 Much of "The Daily Show" and "The Colbert Report"
26 Quick
27 "Cry me a ___"
28 First game of the season
30 Joint assemblies
31 Vienna's land: Abbr.
32 Schlemiel
33 Titter
35 Like much media mail

39 "And ___ it moves" (what Galileo allegedly said in reference to the earth)
40 Casey of "American Top 40"
42 Works, as dough
43 Ungodly display
45 Suffix with many country names
46 Kindle or Nook
50 I.R.S. submission
52 TV meas.
53 What might get you through a quiet stretch?
54 Kind of screen
55 Potential flu symptom
56 Effect of a yodel, perhaps
57 Rapscallion
58 See 11-Down
59 Sgt., e.g.

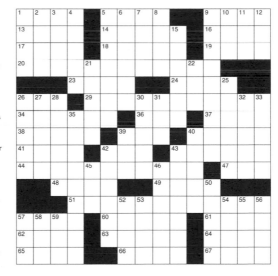

by Michael Dewey

ACROSS

1 One may follow a long drive
5 CNBC topic
10 Tidy sum
14 Subject of the 1994 best seller "The Late Shift"
15 Scoop
16 Flurries
17 Big mailer to the over-50 crowd
18 More than loud
19 Building often near a cafeteria
20 Rapacious
22 The Golf Channel co-founder, to fans
23 Ones getting a good licking?
24 Math subgroup
26 George Washington, for one
29 Do the trick
30 Trash collector
33 What un desierto lacks
34 First-aid kit staple
35 Article in Vogue Paris
36 Mug, e.g.
37 First name of a former president . . . or, read another way, what each of the circled lines is
39 Veer off course
40 ". . . ___ go!"
41 Reducing, after "on"
42 ___ die
43 "Phew!"
44 Empty talk
45 Patrol boat
47 Dictionary label
49 Gossipy Barrett
50 Cheerios
52 Things often left at copy shops
57 Kind of place
58 Dodge
59 Rice, for one
60 "The Grapes of Wrath" figure
61 Wyoming's ___ Range
62 Nude alternative
63 Reel in
64 Origami, e.g.
65 Drop, as pounds

DOWN

1 Make some noise
2 When repeated, "Amen!"
3 Latin phrase on a memo
4 Pink, e.g.
5 Laborer on an old roof, maybe
6 Island roots
7 Body ___
8 French Open feature
9 Flooey lead-in
10 One wearing a collar
11 "You failed to convince me"
12 Petty of "A League of Their Own"
13 Salinger girl
21 Hotshot
22 Out of kilter
25 Ricelike pasta
26 Ricochet
27 Old shopping locale
28 Polish-born musician who was awarded a Presidential Medal of Freedom
29 Got one's feet wet?
31 Harebrained
32 More current
34 Reviewing
37 Jazz trumpet sounds
38 God with two ravens on his shoulders
42 Golf fundamentals
45 Convincing, as an argument
46 Prefix with brow
48 Zapped, in a way
49 Through with
50 Drill, for one
51 Paul in the Songwriters Hall of Fame
53 Pro ___
54 Sole support?
55 Tales of old
56 Source of some carbs
58 . . . : Abbr.

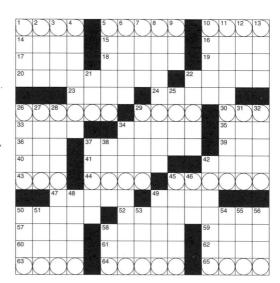

by Zhouqin Burnikel and Don Gagliardo

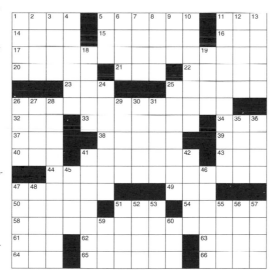

ACROSS

1 Fare in "blankets"
5 Do the Wright thing?
11 Half-___ (coffee order)
14 In a frenzy
15 Bahamas cruise stop
16 South American cruise stop, for short
17 Journalists covering abstract art?
20 Coriander, for one
21 Cry with a fist pump
22 Hill staffers
23 "Mob Wives" star Big ___
25 Aim high
26 Help from a jerk?
32 ". . . cup ___ cone?"
33 Model plane, e.g.
34 Like steak tartare
37 Letters on a radial
38 Sheer curtain fabric
39 Medium for short-lived sculptures
40 Ages and ages
41 Typists' copies, once
43 ___-devil
44 Canned tuna without mayo?
47 The Scourge of God
49 Like one texting :-(
50 Ill-humored
51 Shell carries it
54 Jump the shark, e.g.
58 Narcoleptics with string instruments?
61 Toledo-to-Pittsburgh dir.
62 Holding-hands-in-the-dark event
63 Gutter problem
64 Mike Tyson facial feature, for short
65 Guinness Book superlative
66 Equipment miniature-golf players don't need

DOWN

1 "Super" campaign orgs.
2 "You can stop trying to wake me now!"
3 Desert that occasionally gets snow
4 Winter topper
5 Hobby farm denizen
6 "Results may ___"
7 "Oh, O.K."
8 Hieroglyphics creatures
9 Chinese "way"
10 "1984" superstate
11 One unable to get a loan, say
12 TV station, e.g.
13 Bob who directed "Cabaret"
18 Mister in a sombrero
19 They're often off the books

24 Compadre of Castro
25 Mountaineering attempts
26 World leader with an eponymous "mobile"
27 Guesstimate words
28 Where to find the only stoplight in a small town, typically
29 Picnic utensil
30 It's best when it's airtight
31 Towers on farms
35 Hurt
36 Pull up dandelions and crab grass
41 Harry Belafonte genre
42 It carries a shell
45 Flooring option
46 One needing detox
47 It's a plus
48 Tornado Alley city

51 Mortarboard tosser
52 ___ cream
53 Jiffies
55 Castaway site
56 Siouan speaker
57 Txts, e.g.
59 Symbol of slipperiness
60 Net judge's call

by Ruth B. Margolin

ACROSS

1 Pretty hard to find
7 Front
13 Orville Wright or Neil Armstrong
14 ___ Avenue (Mets' community website)
15 Sign at a neighborhood bar, part 1
17 Spars
18 Server of Duff Beer to Homer Simpson
19 Dry Idea alternative
21 Big, clumsy guy
22 Indeed
23 Quite a bit
24 Part 2 of the sign
28 Crowd drawer, often
29 Severely consternate
30 Go up, up, up
32 Made the first move
33 Play a round
35 General Motors subsidiary
37 Artist known as either Jean or Hans
40 Gatsby-era hairstyles
42 Some Coleridge colleagues
46 Accommodate, as passengers
48 Part 3 of the sign
50 Folly
52 Alliance HQ'd near the White House
53 Key molecule for protein synthesis
54 Fire
55 Adams of "American Hustle"
56 Prone to beefing
58 End of the sign
61 Epicurean explorer
62 "Anything Goes" composer
63 U.S.O. Care Package recipients
64 Coldly determined

DOWN

1 Redundant-sounding refreshment
2 Formed, as schoolyard teams, say
3 "Hit 'em where they ___"
4 Turns bad
5 Subject of many a viral video
6 Hardest substance in the human body
7 Forgery
8 Org. offering group practice membership
9 Ring of rebels
10 Columbus stopping point of 1493
11 Active when the sun shines
12 Provide, as a right
16 Slacks off
17 Pre-Columbian civilization
20 Like some blonds
22 Blond
23 Staple of Chinese cuisine
25 Many a tune in "The Sting"
26 Challenging employer for a maid
27 Seek to espouse
31 Second version
34 Patriot Act enforcer
36 Fiction course, for short
37 Locale of three Summer Olympics
38 Second version
39 Purchased
41 Time-stretching effect
43 Contract
44 Suede source
45 Canine command
47 Overdone
49 Easy hoops shots
51 Belief
55 All those in favor
56 Used to be
57 "In time we ___ that which we often fear": Shak.
59 Cut in the direction of the grain
60 Christie's offering

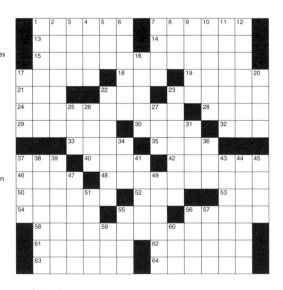

by Stanley Newman

ACROSS

1 Beret-sporting rebel, familiarly
4 Nutrition label units
9 Town with an eponymous derby
14 Bottom line?
15 Cuban salsa singer Cruz
16 Wide receiver's pattern
17 Assent on the Hill
18 -
20 More than a lot
22 eHarmony users' hopes
23 Graph marking
24 -
28 Act the sore loser, say
29 "Ciao, amigo!"
30 Move like the Blob
31 Render unreadable, in a way
33 Prefix with mural
34 Many a noble element
37 -
40 Bummed out
41 Money spent
43 Avoid, as a tag
45 Siouan tribesman
46 Flying machines, quaintly
48 Letter starter
52 -
54 Terra ___
55 Like "Goosebumps" tales
56 High-flying socialites
57 Phrase that defines (and describes) 18-, 24-, 37- and 52-Across
61 Create some drama
62 Reference work next to Bartlett's, maybe
63 Flip
64 Not just "a"
65 Nancy Drew creator Carolyn
66 Aquaria
67 Last letter in "Boz"

DOWN

1 Trophy winners
2 "Psst!"
3 "Kick it up a notch" TV chef
4 Popular instant-messaging app
5 One of two in an English horn
6 What a gimel means on a dreidel
7 "Cool" amount
8 Dictated, as a parent might
9 Aria title that means "It was you"
10 Late 1990s fad
11 They have umbras and penumbras
12 Ear-related prefix
13 Sound from an Abyssinian
19 Domino often played?
21 Tattoo parlor supply
24 It may be bounced off someone
25 Like half of all congressional elections
26 Cornell of Cornell University
27 Out of juice
29 Word often abbreviated to its middle letter, in texts
32 "Game of Thrones" network
33 Roadside bomb, briefly
34 Tasty
35 Prefix with pilot
36 Fred and Barney's time
38 Plum relative
39 Conservatory student's maj.
42 Exact revenge
44 Mark one's words?
46 Words clarifying a spelling
47 Barely make
49 Like Splenda vis-à-vis sugar
50 Don of "Trading Places"
51 Squealed on, with "out"
53 Glacial ridge
54 Satellite broadcasts
56 Kind of mail or bond
57 Rub the wrong way
58 Furrow maker
59 Pro that may be replaced by TurboTax
60 "Total Recall" director Wiseman

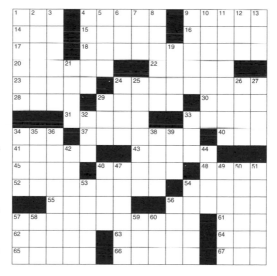

by Evan Birnholz

106 ★ ★

ACROSS
1 Side pieces
6 Tenor in a barbershop quartet, e.g.
10 Lot
14 Quick
15 Singer India.___
16 Modern yogurt flavor
17 Strictness
18 Pepsi-owned beverage brand
19 Cajun French, e.g.
20 Ones little-known in their fields
22 TLC, e.g.
23 Doesn't waste an opportunity
26 Agrees
27 Quickly
28 Qatari leader
30 Ingredient in many Asian desserts
31 Dallas-to-Amarillo dir.
33 Common situation near the start of an inning
36 Many a shot in the arm, for short?
37 Platform . . . or something that appears four times in this puzzle?
39 Decks, in brief
41 Management's counterpart
43 Royal son of the comics
44 First word, maybe
45 Seoul soldiers
47 Assumed
49 24-___
52 Device that converts pressure into a rotating motion
54 "Some Kind of ___" (Dick Van Dyke comedy)
55 Double-___
56 Actress Andersson
57 "Come here often?," e.g.

58 Japanese watch
62 Redding of R&B
63 Blue hue
64 British poet laureate ___ Day-Lewis
65 Honey-soaked dessert
66 Some fund-raising grps.
67 Upright

DOWN
1 Rattle
2 Athlete with the autobiography "The Soul of a Butterfly"
3 Computer storage unit, informally
4 Military decoration
5 German beer now owned by the Pabst Brewing Company

6 Annual parade locale
7 Wine feature
8 Kind of steak
9 Casual wear
10 Traction provider
11 Sharp
12 Prima ___
13 Fuentes and Puente
21 Socialize professionally
23 Land name before 1939
24 Heavenly figure, in Hesse
25 "___ lovely time"
26 Curse
29 Opalescent gems
32 New Deal inits.
34 Relative of a giraffe
35 "Tullius" in Marcus Tullius Cicero
37 Pipe buildup

38 European city whose airport is the world's largest chocolate-selling point
40 Singer with the 1986 #1 album "Promise"
42 Capital on the Danube
44 Character in Clue
46 Nascar's ___ Cup Series
48 Paris-based grp. since 1945
49 Item purchased at many a food cart
50 "West Side Story" woman
51 Cube creator
53 Aegean region
55 Pat-a-cake element
59 Cube makeup
60 It's all relatives
61 Familiar

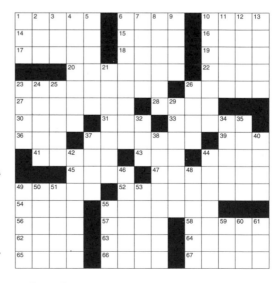

by Daniel Raymon

ACROSS

1 White breakfast beverage
5 Orange breakfast beverage
10 Tan breakfast beverage
13 Blunted blade
14 What a "V" signals to a violinist
15 Sock
17 Middle of a simile
18 Work like a dog
19 Body lotion brand
20 Admonition to the overly curious
22 Nut often found on a sticky bun
23 Agitated state
24 Ungentlemanly sort
25 R. E. Lee's org.
28 Like some shopping
31 Best-liked, in chat rooms
34 Kid's retort
36 Words said while tapping on a watch
38 "I'm buying!," at a bar . . . or a hint to this puzzle's theme
41 Good-looking person?
42 "10" star
43 Density symbol
44 Alternative to pasta
47 Agcy. for retirees
48 "___ Misérables"
49 They build up in pores
51 Rainbow-shaped
54 Story threads
59 Bet
60 Fire-starting aid
61 ___ bene
62 One of Isaac's twins
63 Start of an elimination rhyme
64 Endor denizen
65 Fizzy dinner quaff
66 Plain dinner quaff
67 Genteel dinner quaff

DOWN

1 Product of fermenting honey
2 ___ facto
3 Not marbled, say
4 Jonathan and Martha of Smallville
5 Newly arrived
6 Pulling an all-nighter, o.g.
7 Letter-shaped construction component
8 Pirate hide-out, often
9 Meadow mother
10 Clucked
11 G.E. component: Abbr.
12 Halo, e.g.
16 Clear libation popular in England
21 Hornswoggled
22 Cutout toy
24 Knocked-out state
25 Product of fermenting apples
26 England's Fergie, formally
27 Bud in the Southwest
29 Fifth-century pope called "the Great"
30 Before, briefly
31 Trey beaters
32 Moorehead of "Citizen Kane"
33 Clear libation popular in Russia
35 Presenter of many a spoof, for short
37 Stocking stuffer?
39 Six, in Seville
40 Old-timey agreements
45 Nickname for the $2 Canadian coin
46 Nervous giggle
48 Was a prelude (to)
50 Muscle connector
51 Product of fermenting barley
52 Speak like a tough guy, say
53 "Ta-ta!"
54 "Nolo contendere," e.g.
55 Dryer fuzz
56 "___ get it!"
57 School for James Bond
58 Clear libation popular in Japan
60 Not a lot

by Jeff Chen

ACROSS

1 Swine
6 "Giant" novelist, 1952
12 Country that calls itself the "Abode of Peace"
13 Shakespeare character who says "Unhappy that I am, I cannot heave / My heart into my mouth"
15 Like only one Best Picture in Academy Award history (1969)
16 Essay locale
17 Stylish 1960s luxury coupe
18 Louis Malle's "___ Amants"
19 Scottish exclamation
20 Fruit juice
21 Like much music, starting in the late 1980s
23 Gold units: Abbr.
25 2000 Richard Gere title role
26 D
28 Mycobacterium, e.g.
30 One of the vertices of the Summer Triangle
31 Start to break up a fight, say
32 Boston legend Phil, to fans
35 Rembrandt van ___
37 Foundation stone abbr.
38 Dirty dog
41 Conrad of the silents
44 Noted part of a book?
45 Eye part
46 Diamond stats
49 Operative: Abbr.
50 Subj. of 1991's Start treaty
52 Women's shoe style

54 Line score inits.
56 Highball?
57 Approval of an order
58 Play to the balcony?
60 Lassitude
61 Faint
62 11th-century founder of Scholasticism
63 Not hypothetical
64 "___ lift?"

DOWN

1 Like the Cowardly Lion at the end of "The Wizard of Oz"
2 Best on stage, say
3 Re
4 Bureaucracy
5 Mashie niblick
6 Some diet drinks
7 Teacher's advanced deg.
8 "___ Man"

9 2010 installment in the Call of Duty series
10 Like some primitive game graphics
11 "The Facts of Life" actress
12 Leave a lasting mark on
13 Kid's art activity . . . or something seen four times in this puzzle's solution?
14 Public
22 SFO opponent in the 2012 World Series
24 Elate
27 Key preposition?
29 Line holder
30 Vietnamese currency
32 Title character from the village of Highbury, 1815

33 Teal relative
34 Not too hard a golf hole
36 Part of U.S.N.A.: Abbr.
39 Certain grandson
40 Vatican City vis-à-vis Rome
42 Sunbathe
43 "Piece of cake!"
46 Hung
47 Radio activity?
48 ___ whale
51 Foreshadow
53 Breviloquent
55 Reef dwellers
58 Kind of trail
59 Rejections

by Alex Vratsanos

ACROSS

1 Easy, in adspeak
9 Like the stars
15 Tooth next to a canine
16 The "cave" of "cave canem"
17 Go away as a marathoner might?
18 Go away as a Michael Jackson impersonator might?
19 Z abroad
20 Yank rival
21 Pothook shape
22 Go away as an outdoorsman might?
26 Augment
28 Olympics chant
29 Some Marine NCOs
31 Neural conductor
32 Wrinkle-reducing shot
35 Step up or down
37 Go away as a bumblebee might?
40 Go away as a speaker of pig Latin might?
44 Particle theorized in 1977
46 Carnivore that both hunts and scavenges
47 Overwhelm with flattery
50 "Wonderful!"
53 Word with living or dead
54 Caffeine-laden nuts
56 With 63- and 65 Across, go away as a soda jerk might?
59 "___ be a pleasure!"
60 They're checked at the door
62 ___ instant
63 & 65 See 56-Across
69 A solar system "ice giant"
70 Sculptor's works
71 "For heaven's sake!"
72 F. A. O. Schwarz, for one

DOWN

1 "Science Friday" airer
2 Tulsa sch. with a Prayer Tower
3 Mud, when wet bird, idiomatically
4 Knock the socks off
5 Form of flamenco
6 Poky sorts
7 Hawaiian verandas
8 Joule fraction
9 Group featured in "Mamma Mia!"
10 "Later!"
11 Carrier in "The Aviator"
12 Hard-core
13 British upper-cruster, for short
14 Reveals one's feelings
20 Volkswagen model since 1979
22 Ernest of country music
23 Not worth ___
24 Willy who lent his name to a historic Manhattan deli
25 British scale divs.
27 "Pride and Prejudice" protagonist
30 College football star Michael in 2014 news
33 Conductor Seiji
34 Worthless tic-tac-toe row
36 "Sorta" suffix
38 Garden of Eden tree
39 Much paperwork
41 Need a bath badly
42 Hathaway of "Becoming Jane"
43 When tripled, a Seinfeld catchphrase
45 Museum-funding org.
47 One often in need of a lift?
48 Official with a seal
49 Racetrack has-been
51 Closely resembling
52 Like some short-term N.B.A. contracts
55 Hole in one's head?
57 Stands the test of time
58 Raw data, often
61 Usain Bolt event
64 "It's ___-brainer"
65 Prince Edward Island hrs.
66 Mekong Valley native
67 Sale rack abbr.
68 Rope on a ship

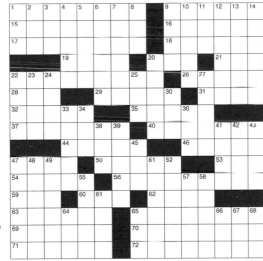

by Samuel A. Donaldson

110

ACROSS

1 "Paul Bunyan and Babe the Blue Ox," e.g.
5 Alternative to a game hen
10 Young brothers' band
14 "A Clockwork Orange" protagonist
15 1/16 of a 17-Across
16 Explorer with a friend named Boots
17 See 15-Across
18 Gripping read ["Get back!"]
20 New York City's ___ Place
22 Two in Toledo
23 Fit for a king
24 Oil containers ["Get down!"]
26 Slight
27 The opposing side
29 Super bargain
30 6 Series cars
33 -
35 Hiss cause
38 Make public
39 First word of "Huckleberry Finn"
40 One passing a gate
41 Pole connector
43 -
45 Actress Stapleton
46 Mall cop weapon
48 Vegetable rich in calcium and vitamin K
50 Amherst and Orono, for two ["Get up!"]
52 Where Maria and the Captain have their first kiss in "The Sound of Music"
56 Speak to the people?
57 Economy-size container
60 Lop off
61 1977 W.W. II film ["Get lost!]

64 Nickname for Anaheim's Angel Stadium
65 Buster Brown's dog
66 In front of, old-style
67 Name series condenser
68 Suffix with mob
69 Stuck together
70 Perspective provider

DOWN

1 Spanish starters
2 Those with no problem getting in
3 Slowly
4 Makes pay, in a bad way
5 Concession
6 Campus area
7 Golden rule word
8 Superb, in slang
9 Ask for a biscuit, say
10 ___ gland
11 Brazzaville inhabitants
12 Gloomy, in poetry
13 Eric who wrote "The Very Hungry Caterpillar"
19 Press
21 Cousin of "¡Olé!"
25 -
26 "___ over"
28 Cleveland was one in Buffalo
29 Leave scoreless
30 When repeated, a nursery rhyme call
31 Mingle
32 Presented prominently
34 First word of "Richard III"
36 Alias
37 Blood
42 More like sailors' talk, stereotypically

43 -
44 Have a dip
45 Prominent feminist blog
47 Assigned position
49 Velázquez's "___ Meninas"
50 Covers
51 What an astronaut may be in
53 What you might get for a party nowadays
54 Founded
55 Stage in a Ph.D. program
57 Tasteless stuff
58 Subjects of some 911 calls
59 Uncovered
62 Clodhopper
63 Like cherry-flavored things

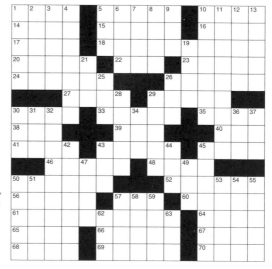

by Victor Barocas

111

ACROSS

1 "Foucault's Pendulum" author
4 Legendary predator of elephants
7 Entertainers at many 49-Downs, for short
10 Super Mario Bros. console, for short
13 Jobs offering
14 Stop ___ dime
15 Radio station listener's call-in, perhaps
17 Asthmatic's device
19 "Checkmate!"
20 Experiment site
21 Alternative to dice
22 1952 Winter Olympics host
23 ___ Sea, waters depleted by irrigation projects
24 "Spider-Man" director Sam
27 Abalone shell lining
30 "___ all good"
33 Politico Hatch of 54 Down
34 Clumsy sorts
35 Pick up
36 Holey plastic shoe
37 Off one's rocker
38 Drag racers' org.
39 "The Wizard of Oz" locale: Abbr.
40 Absorb, as gravy
41 ___-Grain
42 "Dee-lish!"
43 Bonnie's partner
44 :-(
45 ". . . ___ in Kalamazoo"
47 Eldest Stark child on "Game of Thrones"
49 Australia's Port ___ Bay
52 In hiding
56 Team leader of song
57 Retired academics
58 Tee-shot club

59 Well-put
60 Vintner's vessel
61 I.S.P. with a butterfly logo
62 After-afterthought on a letter: Abbr.
63 Many aging A.L. sluggers
64 ___ moment

DOWN

1 Send out
2 One of man's three legs, in the riddle of the Sphinx
3 Protest singer Phil
4 Arrives, as fog
5 N.B.A. great in Icy Hot commercials
6 *Typist's duplicate of old
7 Prohibitionists
8 Game show with the theme music "Think!"
9 Knights' attendants
10 *They're big on Broadway
11 "To be," to Brutus
12 Suffix with slick
16 Radius neighbor
18 With 38-Down, property of the first part of the answer to each starred clue (appropriately positioned in the grid)
24 First sports movie to win Best Picture
25 Pianist Claudio
26 *Medieval device with spikes
28 One way to read
29 *Anti-Civil War Northerner
31 ___ firma
32 Unflashy

37 Kid's post-haircut treat, maybe
38 See 18-Down
40 Bit of surf in surf and turf
41 Green Giant canned corn
46 Radiant look
48 Zip
49 Gym ball?
50 Barbaric sorts
51 Nth degrees?
53 Demanding sort
54 See 33-Across
55 Gyro bread

by Alex Vratsanos

112 ★ ★

ACROSS

1 Clay pounder?
7 Sounds at spas
10 With 66-Across, back to the beginning . . . or a description of 21- and 48-Down?
14 Gobble quickly
15 Persians, to the 300, e.g.
16 Required to serve, maybe
17 Healthy spirit?
18 Diverts
20 Best seller about shipwreck survivors
22 Honey pie
23 Airing, in a way
24 September through April, in a culinary guideline
26 "Shall ___ . . . ?"
28 Settled up
29 Sleepytime ___
32 Designate
34 Hindmost
35 Ring
36 Temple of ___, one of the Seven Wonders of the Ancient World
40 Finalized
42 Big laugh
43 Tap site
45 Constitution Hall grp.
46 Patient helpers, for short
47 Where to find "Yesterday" on the album "Help!"
49 High note?
53 Tom Selleck title role
55 Celebrity cosmetician Laszlo
56 What gives?
58 "The Godfather" parts I, II and III, e.g.

61 It might be held on a flight
63 Spheres
64 Nike competitor
65 Spanish valuable
66 See 10-Across
67 Tandoori flatbread
68 2012 YouTube sensation
69 Shows subservience, say

DOWN

1 Stay out of sight
2 Queued
3 Goes from first to second, say
4 Shirker of one's duties?
5 Smorgasbord
6 Hasbro brand
7 Great Rift Valley locale: Abbr.
8 Do-si-do whoop-de-dos
9 Courted with love notes?
10 County fair organizer
11 Green
12 Some jeans
13 Hindmost
19 Like some cereals
21 See 10-Across
25 Daisy ___
27 "Tasty!"
30 Loire contents
31 One above the Lötschberg Tunnel
33 It wraps around a chest at the beach
35 Hang in there
36 Gun, e.g.
37 Gun, in slang
38 Southernmost state
39 Sirens

41 W.W. II service member
44 Definite keeper
47 Friday and others: Abbr.
48 See 10-Across
50 Frog's alter ego, in a fairy tale
51 Low tie
52 Flings
54 ___-American
56 Abba not known for singing
57 Soap with pumice
59 Connie ___, Philadelphia Athletics manager for 50 years
60 ". . . now ___ the future"
62 Dale's partner

by Jean O'Conor

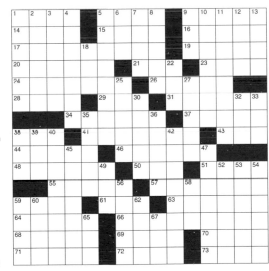

ACROSS

1 Miami's county, familiarly
5 Stalled driver's request
9 Inexperienced with
14 Words after pour or pass
15 Beast in the documentary "Blackfish"
16 Amtrak bullet train
17 Weapon part that's out of this world?
19 Chaim who created Asher Lev
20 Kurt of Nirvana
21 Spanish diminutive suffix
23 Pronoun in a wedding statement
24 Paper tiger, maybe
26 One-room home
28 ___-Ball
29 Sturm ___ Drang
31 Skedaddled
34 Wintertime airport supply
37 Victoria's Secret garment
38 Swell place?
41 Attack on a Mideast land that's out of thin air?
43 ___ Lanka
44 Boxer's prize
46 Protracted battles
48 Lady Schick target
50 "A revolution is not a dinner party" writer
51 Jewelry designer Peretti
55 Cries of pain
57 Some lines on a GPS screen
59 "And ___ word from our sponsor"
61 Anxious condition, for short
63 Bites playfully
64 Plumber's unclogger

66 Fisherman's feat that's out of character?
68 Happy gatherings
69 Cameo stone
70 Give the appearance of
71 "Whoopee!"
72 Insect repellent ingredient
73 "___ Little Tenderness"

DOWN

1 Places where people hustle?
2 On the job
3 Rock's ___ Brothers
4 Steamed
5 Sierra Club founder
6 Mentalist Geller
7 Mid 12th-century year
8 Singer Smith of punk music
9 Day care break
10 Environmental transition area
11 Drenched gangsters who are out of the woods?
12 The so-called "potted physician"
13 Box-office receipts
18 24 horas
22 Cabinet-level dept. since 1889
25 Pachacuti's people
27 Drink that may feature "foam art"
30 Blue wear
32 Yalta Conference monogram
33 Memo-heading initials
35 Letters in a children's refrain
36 Ostrich cousins
38 Aromatherapy spot
39 Liechtenstein's locale: Abbr.

40 Military laundry that's out of harm's way?
42 Challenger's announcement at a pickup game
45 Have a talk with
47 Purposely overlook, as a fault
49 Wee hour
52 NBC anchor Holt
53 Actress Dash of "Clueless"
54 Inhaler user's malady
56 Atlantic fish
58 Documentarian Burns who's the brother of Ken
59 Office-inappropriate, in web shorthand
60 Suitable for induction
62 Hamlet, e.g.
65 "___ Beso"
67 Manhattan ingredient

by David Levinson Wilk

114

ACROSS

1 Some interruptions
6 "That's that!"
14 Contacts ship-to-ship, maybe
16 Outbreak caused by the H2N2 virus
17 December display
19 Three-stringed Eastern instrument
20 Lifts
21 Common noninvasive med. test
23 Sin relative?
24 Mathematical field that includes the so-called "butterfly effect"
30 "___ culpa"
33 Circulation line
34 Co. in a 2001 merger with American
35 Hamilton ___, two-term secretary of state under Grant
36 One of literature's "three sisters"
40 It's big and brassy
41 City in Kyrgyzstan
42 Off land
43 Relatives of texts, for short
44 Went from butt to butt?
47 Flattens, in brief
48 Didn't move, as a product
49 Easy-peasy
52 Part of a chest
58 Chorus starter in a 1972 David Bowie song . . . or the theme of this puzzle, phonetically
62 Boxer who competed on "Dancing With the Stars"
63 Maze solver
64 Like socks right out of the dryer
65 Marks for life

DOWN

1 Things that are tossed usually go in them
2 "Joke's on you!"
3 Gouda alternative
4 Fun-size, say
5 ___-chef
6 Slangy negative
7 Mil. branch
8 Interjection of disgust
9 Many a sci-fi devotee
10 Prominent part of an aardvark
11 '60s do also called a "natural"
12 "Now ___ me down to sleep"
13 "Obviously!" remarks
15 Kind of shooting
18 Key of the Nile
22 "Would you believe . . ."
23 Zodiac symbol
24 Arizona sights
25 "You're boring me"
26 One side in a 1967 war
27 ___ vez (again: Sp.)
28 1942 title role for Rita Hayworth
29 Not be squared up, say
30 Eastern European capital
31 Makeup magnate Lauder
32 Up
35 Picture, informally
37 Some reactions to fireworks
38 Airport inits.
39 Zodiac symbol
44 54, e.g., in old TV
45 Snitch (on), in slang
46 Big name in power tools
47 Artist Frida with many self-portraits
49 Org. concerned with due process
50 Young-adult fiction author Darren
51 CBS military procedural
53 Farm cries
54 Lawrence Kudlow's network
55 City SSE of New Delhi
56 Duds
57 Guesses: Abbr.
59 It may collect tips . . . or be tipped
60 Indians' home: Abbr.
61 Veiled

by David Benkof and Jeff Chen

ACROSS

1 Furtive attention-getter
5 Handles roughly
9 Like some scents for men
14 Arabian Peninsula land
15 James who won a posthumous Pulitzer
16 State one's case
17 Knight's contest
18 Cut back
19 ___ wrench
20 Will Smith biopic
21 Cottonmouth, e.g.
23 Capable of being stretched
25 Trivia whiz Jennings
26 Cineplex ___ Corporation
27 Was on both sides of
33 Pixel density meas.
35 Muesli morsel
36 A low one is best, for short
37 Question asked by a customs officer or a kid on Christmas . . . with a hint to this puzzle's circled squares
43 "The Mikado" accessory
44 "Didn't know that!"
45 Prepare for a spike, in volleyball
46 Verbiage
50 Abs worker
54 Tangent of 45 degrees
55 Rock, so to speak
57 Dawn
61 Grass from a farm
62 Seminomadic Kenyan
63 New York's ___ Stadium
64 Title derived from the name "Caesar"

65 Ingredients in old-fashioneds
66 "Little piggies"
67 Mezzo's choirmate
68 Stuck-up sort
69 Some linemen
70 First lady before Mamie

DOWN

1 Latke component
2 Heeded the photographer, say
3 IV solution
4 Blasting stuff
5 ___ States
6 Banded gemstones
7 "#1" may follow it
8 Futures dealer?
9 Bellyached
10 Higher ground
11 Product of a domesticated insect

12 Proposer's prop?
13 Its banknotes have denominations from 1,000 to 10,000
21 Cellar stock
22 Roller derby need
24 Microsoft Excel command
28 Schleps
29 When repeated, super-enthusiastic
30 N.Y.C. ave. parallel to Park and Madison
31 Bard's preposition
32 Prosecutors, for short
34 Seal engraved on a ring
37 "Holy cow!"
38 "Game of Thrones" network
39 Bring up, as a grievance

40 Word in many a woman's bio
41 Attack from all sides
42 Ear-related
47 El ___ (fabled city)
48 Refuse to yield
49 Said "alas," say
51 Shoving match
52 W.W. II threats
53 Three-time Cy Young winner Martinez and others
56 Magnus Carlsen's game
57 "April Love" composer Sammy
58 "There ___ 'I' in 'team'"
59 After the whistle
60 "The heat ___!"
62 ___ Paul's (seafood brand)
64 Bill

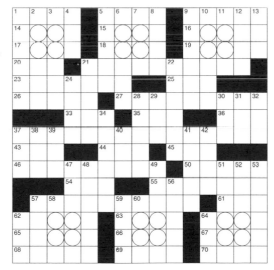

by John E. Bennett

ACROSS

1 Ute relative
4 Hardly 100%
7 Where Whole Foods is headquartered
13 *Kind of affair
15 Fast-food chain founded by Italian immigrants
16 Distress
17 Alma mater for Toni Morrison and Zora Neale Hurston
18 Swamp
19 *1971 song with the lyric "Helter skelter in a summer swelter"
21 Gray ___
23 One way to stand
24 ___ meeting
25 *Creator of Sheriff Deadeye and Cauliflower McPugg
30 Bench warmer?
31 Sabin's study
32 Not the most sophisticated humor
33 *Sketchy history
37 No-luck connector
38 Cosmetic problem
39 It might come with a bill
40 *January events
45 Exclamation often followed by multiple exclamation points
46 First song on "More of the Monkees"
47 Table poker?
48 *Some illegal transmissions
54 Training ___
55 Buddy
56 Feature of some stationery
58 Emergency room agent
59 Popular day trip destination . . . or a hint to the starts of the answers to the starred clues
60 Vehement venting
61 Switch halves
62 Sweet ending?

DOWN

1 Nobelist who won an Emmy
2 Made it?
3 Zapper target
4 Couple of stars, say
5 ___-blog
6 Not just a side glance
7 8-Down sinker
8 See 7-Down
9 Like logs, quaintly
10 Hide seekers
11 Pebble in one's shoe, e.g.
12 Honey-do list rejection
13 "Le petit éléphant"
14 Rio maker
20 2004 Google event, briefly
22 Facet
26 ___ Industries (oil giant)
27 Alberta's ___ Island National Park
28 Fictionalize?
29 Sculpture subjects
30 Find hilarious
32 They face liabilities in their work, in brief
33 CBS spinoff that was filmed mostly in California
34 More ambitious
35 Defib administrator
36 Mark in the '60s
39 Tot, affectionately
40 Word often redundantly preceded by "from"
41 2013 Best Picture nominee
42 Some September babies
43 Cause to boil
44 Fashion lines?
46 Restrained
49 Film dog
50 Playground rejoinder
51 Whack
52 "Suicide Blonde" band
53 Cartoon sound effect
57 Day-___

by David Steinberg

ACROSS

1 Bound
5 Cuddly sci-fi creature
9 Actors Sharif and Epps
14 ___ cry
15 Kind of curriculum
16 Tackles
17 Nirvana seeker
18 Brain part
19 Pickling liquid
20 Post-christening event
23 Pitch tents, say
26 Feedbag morsel
27 Hair goop
28 What scientists use to predict the rates of chemical reactions
32 "Winnie-the-Pooh" young 'un
33 Golf's Ernie
34 TV
35 Felix of "The Odd Couple"
38 "Krazy ___"
40 Hindu honcho
44 Contra-contraband org.
46 Bloviation
48 Author Umberto
49 Small part that's visible
55 Lead-in to meter
56 ___-de-France
57 Eschews nuptial formalities, say
58 Headline of April 16, 1912
62 Saw
63 Clump of hair
64 Clump of hair
68 Soda bottle measure
69 When repeated, kind of show
70 Dust Bowl migrant
71 Floor
72 "Goodness gracious!"
73 Cry at a deli

DOWN

1 Noisy bird
2 One side in a close encounter
3 ___ wheels
4 Kind of instinct
5 Sun block?
6 Lumber
7 "Eat ___ eaten"
8 Liking a lot
9 Winnie-the-Pooh catchphrase
10 Crèche figure
11 Italian cheese
12 Texas lawman
13 Unyielding
21 Godard, to Truffaut, e.g.
22 Vintners' vessels
23 Relative of beige
24 Eleven plus one
25 Plumbing problem
29 Sort
30 Oklahoma Indian
31 Amtrak listing, for short
36 Tokyo's former name
37 Facility often found near a port
39 Mai ___
41 Grand Cherokee, e.g.
42 Parcel of land
43 Arkansas footballers, informally
45 Mythical king of the Huns
47 Fragrant
49 Wrecks
50 Cry of success
51 Stew ingredient
52 Give a hard time, in a way
53 Yellowstone bugler
54 Globe's place
59 New ___
60 Catch
61 Smidgen
65 Maui music-maker
66 Pickle
67 Vietnamese New Year

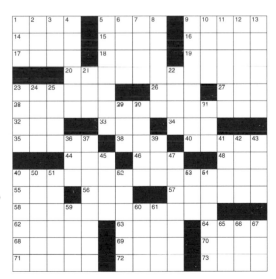

by Michael Dewey

ACROSS

1 Mob muscle
5 Little bit
8 A pop
12 "You know nothing about me"
14 Open-mouthed state
15 Astronomer ___ Brahe
16 "America's Most Wanted" host John
17 "Toy Story" character
18 Subway fare?
19 Superior skill
21 Pioneer in New Criticism
23 With 13-Down, blew one's stack
24 With 15-Down, spent way too much money for something
25 Song that may be performed with supertitles
27 Turn on
28 Soft and light
31 "That put me over the edge!"
35 "What?!"
36 "Fine and dandy," in old slang
37 Symbols for statistical means
38 What pitchforks pitch
39 Summer in Québec
40 Slick trick
42 H.R.E. part: Abbr.
43 With 30-Down, hit dead-on
45 With 61-Across, carefully consider . . . or a clue to this puzzle's theme
46 With 32-Down, followed a career ladder
47 Not ___ (meh)
49 Big club?
50 Hardy hog breed
51 Opposite of paix

53 World powerhouse in curling
54 Botanist Gray
55 Seasoned veterans
59 Wii forerunner, for short
60 Debussy's "La ___"
61 See 45-Across
62 Kit ___ bar
63 Winter D.C. setting
64 Bullet points
65 '60s campus org.

DOWN

1 Stare with an open mouth
2 Palestinian nominee for Best Foreign Language Film of 2013
3 Simmering
4 "Easy peasy"
5 Throws off balance
6 "I ___ you"

7 Emoticon medium
8 They're usually heavier at night
9 Stinging
10 Toy train sound
11 Human in "Alien," e.g.
13 See 23-Across
15 See 24-Across
20 Can't do well
22 Go caving
26 Wife of Muhammad
27 French writer de Beauvoir
28 Metaphor for diplomacy
29 Heads for the woods?
30 See 43-Across
32 See 46-Across
33 "My parents are going to kill me!"
34 Pigeonholes, in a way

41 Little jerk
44 A.L. East squad
46 Go quickly
48 Go quickly
50 Go quickly
52 Pre-coll. years
53 Teeth
56 "The 5,000 Fingers of ___" (1953 Seuss film)
57 "The Purloined Letter" writer
58 Main ingredient in pirates' grog

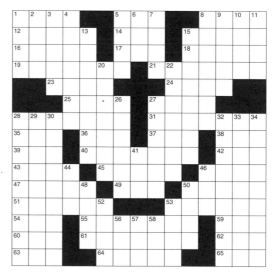

by Mary Lou Guizzo and Jeff Chen

ACROSS

1 WALLY
8 GUS
15 Whittling away
16 Like some email addresses
17 Blow the joint
18 Volatile solvents
19 50–50
20 Regina's locale: Abbr.
22 Burmese, for one
23 Sites for kites
25 What is cast, in a saying
28 River of Hesse
31 Not just hot
34 Bub
37 Improper
39 Animal with stripes
40 In the style of
41 ALAN
43 Place for a baseball insignia
44 Many a classical sculpture
46 Sandbank
47 Copy desk workers, e.g.: Abbr.
48 Very high trumpet note
50 "Splendor in the Grass" screenwriter
51 Gloomy donkey of fiction
53 Mark up or down, say
58 Caller on a cell phone?
60 Library refs.
62 Keyboardist Saunders
63 Stab
66 International agreement
69 "Luck Be a Lady" composer/lyricist
70 "I envy Seas, ___ He rides": Emily Dickinson

71 With 1-Down, first American astronauts
72 DEKE

DOWN

1 See 71-Across
2 Ardently want
3 They're mobile in a trailer park
4 "___ believe it!"
5 2016 Olympics city
6 E.R. personnel
7 A really long time
8 Grind
9 NASA vehicle
10 Fury
11 Firmed up
12 Old U.S./Soviet rivalry
13 It's a crock
14 Best-selling PC game of the 1990s

21 Weakened due to inactivity
24 Kind of perception
26 School desk drawer?
27 Nettle
29 Play-___
30 Verb with "vous"
32 ___ Mini
33 Some market fluctuations
34 Gym surfaces
35 Baseball family name
36 SCOTT
38 Unstable subatomic particle
42 Tease
45 Envision
49 GORDON
52 Hear again in court
54 File material
55 Guiding belief
56 "Star Wars" droid
57 JOHN

58 Unruffled
59 Plains tribe
61 Ends, with "up"
64 PC key
65 Where Magic Johnson played college ball, for short
67 Org. with Sharks and Predators
68 It may be herbal

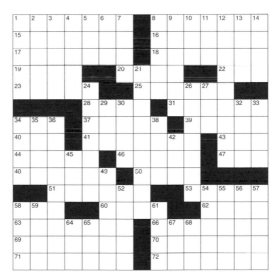

by David J. Kahn

ACROSS

1 Weapon with knots
5 Soprano Gluck
9 Grass shack dances
14 It means "skyward"
15 Wassailer's tune
16 City near Rome
17 Religious act
18 Distinctive dress
19 What walls might hide
20 The theme, part 1
23 It may be felt
24 Gibson or Brooks
25 Four-yr. degrees
28 Ends up even
30 Not too awful
32 French department
36 Overclever
38 Chekhov "Sister"
39 The theme, part 2
42 Negative points
43 "Argo" setting
44 Tablet smasher
45 G.M. option
47 Mrs. James Joyce
49 House call, often
50 Business honcho
52 Bach choral work
57 The theme, part 3
60 Dish inventor
62 "That's fine with me!"
63 It's a long time
64 Bothered a lot
65 Bureau, for short
66 Track assignment
67 Singer Simon
68 No gentleman
69 A reduced state

DOWN

1 Hat worn by Che
2 Shade like khaki
3 Scratch-card layer
4 On the lookout
5 Luanda's land
6 Wheels for a while
7 Pure and simple
8 Best-selling Mitch
9 Disco line dance
10 45th state
11 Flotation gear
12 Virtuoso
13 Finnair rival
21 "Oh my goodness!"
22 Golf cup sponsor
26 Hidden motive
27 Hotel visits
29 "Lazy" lady
31 Conan nickname
32 Colleague of Kirk
33 Using no help
34 Attempts to catch
35 Hive, in effect
37 Break time, perhaps
40 LinkedIn client
41 "Spillsaver" brand
46 Mental sharpness
48 Public-road race
51 Trash can dweller
53 What takes a stand?
54 Food for tadpoles
55 Some freezing temps
56 Surefooted beasts
58 Demanding test
59 Class at a Y
60 "12" preceder
61 Docking info

ACROSS

1 Hall-of-Fame rock band or its lead musician
8 It sends out lots of streams
15 Very long European link
16 Rust or combust
17 It flies on demand
18 Skunk, at times
19 Some P.D. personnel
20 One who may be on your case
22 The Spanish I love?
23 What a couple of people can play
25 Stand-out performances
26 Chocolate bar with a long biscuit and caramel
27 Subject of the 2003 book "Power Failure"
29 Without hesitation
30 Subsist on field rations?
31 Its flowers are very short-lived
33 Like a sawhorse's legs
35 Critical
36 Party staple
37 Catered to Windows shoppers?
41 Noodle taxers?
45 Observes
46 Abbr. after 8-Across
48 Last band in the Rock and Roll Hall of Fame, alphabetically
49 "The Hudsucker Proxy" director, 1994
50 Columbia and the like
52 French river or department
53 "___ mentioned . . ."

54 Images on some lab slides
56 Lima-to-Bogotá dir.
57 Frankenstein, e.g.
59 Its passengers were revolting
61 Theodore Roosevelt Island setting
62 Destroyer destroyer
63 Colorful cooler
64 Makeover options

DOWN

1 Like some milk
2 Sashimi staple
3 Changing place
4 Blockbuster?
5 Mediums for dummies, say: Abbr.
6 Where it all comes together?
7 Ex amount?
8 Appointment disappointments

9 Nationals, at one time
10 Flag
11 Tablet banner, say, briefly
12 Reserve
13 Inventory
14 Duped
21 Gradual, in some product names
24 Giant in fantasy
26 Bar that's set very high
28 Physicist Bohr
30 Display on a red carpet
32 Basic solution
34 Without hesitation, in brief
37 Does some outdoor pitching?
38 "Don't joke about that yet"
39 Took away bit by bit

40 Event occasioning 7-Down
41 Cryotherapy choice
42 Artificially small
43 What might take up residence?
44 Truncated trunks?
47 Zero times, in Zwickau
50 Back-pedaler's words
51 About 7% of it is American
54 Vapor: Prefix
55 Apple assistant
58 Lib. arts major
60 Coral ___ (city near Oakland Pk., Fla.)

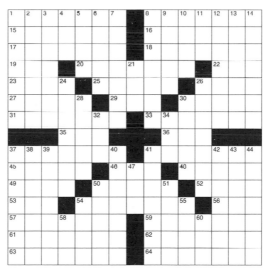

by Bruce R. Sutphin

ACROSS

1 It may provide closure in a tragedy
8 Discarded
15 City named for Theodore Roosevelt's vice president
17 Word search technique?
18 Webby Award winner who accepted saying "Please don't recount this vote"
19 With 11-Down, animal called "stubbin" by locals
20 Nascar stat that rises under caution flags
21 Diddly
22 Opening in the computer business?
23 Bad thing to lose
24 Flights
25 Taste makers?
26 Has it bad for, so to speak
27 -i relative
28 Largest city in Moravia
29 Mob member, informally
30 Morale
35 Second in command?
36 Cloverleaf section
37 Flat top
39 Blended dressing?
42 Shutter shutter
43 Literally, "I do not wish to"
44 Sauna exhalations
45 Solomonic
46 Chewed the fat
47 Watson's creator
48 Lowest of the low?
49 Prankery
50 1965 Beach Boys hit
53 Mission

54 Jason Mraz song that spent a record 76 weeks on Billboard's Hot 100
55 Outcries

DOWN

1 Outgoing
2 Lot arrangement
3 Draws
4 Some refrigerants
5 Reinforcement pieces
6 Mantel piece
7 Nissan bumpers?
8 Annual event since 1929, with "the"
9 Hard to pick up
10 Cigarette paper source
11 See 19-Across
12 Author of 1980's "The Annotated Gulliver's Travels"
13 Macedonia's capital

14 "El día que me quieras" and others
16 Large monitors
22 Abandon one's efforts, informally
23 "The Hound of the Baskervilles" backdrop
25 It's around a cup
26 1 Infinite ___ (address of Apple's headquarters)
28 Dover soul
29 Force in red uniforms: Abbr.
31 Course data
32 Palliate
33 Hit hard, as in an accident
34 Tip used for icing
38 They will be missed
39 Lightly hailed?
40 Major report
41 "Yowza!"

42 Hound
43 Dresden decimator of 1945
45 Something beyond the grate divide?
46 Herod's realm
48 1879's Anglo-___ War
49 "Fantastic Mr. Fox" author
51 War on Poverty agcy.
52 Advisory grp. that includes the drug czar

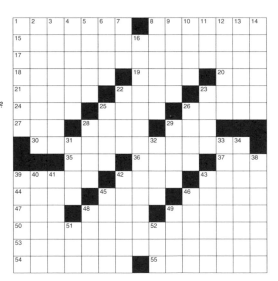

by Byron Walden

ACROSS

1 Forest newcomer
5 Group whose last Top 40 hit was "When All Is Said and Done"
9 To-do list
14 Sound after call waiting?
15 Sense, as a 14-Across
16 Nobel winner Joliot-Curie
17 Turkey sticker
20 "Everybody Is ___" (1970 hit)
21 Response to a threat
22 Old co. with overlapping globes in its logo
23 1960s civil rights leader ___ Brown
25 Katey who portrayed TV's Peg Bundy
27 Benchwarmer's plea
33 Drain
34 Bobby's follower?
35 Fibonacci, notably
36 Hockey Hall of Fame nickname
38 Alternative to ZzzQuil
40 Stat. for Re, La or Ti
41 "___ needed"
43 Papa ___ (Northeast pizza chain)
45 Now in
46 "That subject's off the table!"
49 Luster
50 They have edible shells
51 Whse. sight
53 "Philosophy will clip an angel's wings" writer
56 French class setting
59 Universal query?
62 Uncle Sam, say
63 One featuring a Maltese cross

64 Turkic word for "island"
65 Browser history list
66 Couldn't discard in crazy eights, say
67 Court suspensions

DOWN

1 Relief provider, for short
2 Blasts through
3 "And now?"
4 Sealing worker
5 "Per-r-rfect!"
6 ___-red
7 Alfred H. ___ Jr., founding director of MoMA
8 Like G.I.'s, per recruiting ads
9 Interval
10 Were present?
11 Gets payback
12 Sensed

13 They may be used in veins
18 They may be used around veins
19 All-Star Infante
24 Drone
26 1998 hit from the album "Surfacing"
27 False start?
28 Stockholder?
29 Like some hemoglobin
30 ___-A
31 Plantation habitation
32 Cybermemo
37 Something taken on the stand
39 Ring
42 They're on hunts
44 Revolving feature
47 Revolving features?
48 "Psst . . . buddy"
51 1/20 tons: Abbr.

52 Whence the word "bong"
54 Day of the week of Jul. 4, 1776
55 Wizened up
57 Indiana, e.g., to Lafayette
58 Some use electric organs
60 River Shannon's Lough ___
61 Sudoku segment

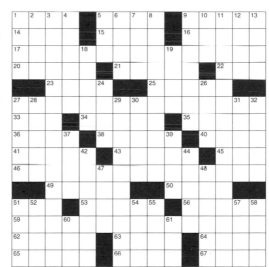

by Peter A. Collins

124 ★ ★ ★

ACROSS
1 Angry missive
10 Body parts often targeted by masseurs
15 Trailing
16 Hatch in the upper house
17 Chutes behind boats
18 Treaty of Sycamore Shoals negotiator, 1775
19 Taking forever
20 Antimissile plan, for short
21 Part of Duchamp's parody of the "Mona Lisa"
22 Octane booster brand
24 San ___, Calif. (border town opposite Tijuana)
26 Discount ticket letters
29 In the main
31 Stuffed bear voiced by Seth MacFarlane
34 Not likely to be a "cheese" lover?
36 Pens for tablets
38 Learn to live with
39 Like the sound holes of a cello
41 1986 Indy 500 champion
42 Champion
44 Venetian mapmaker ___ Mauro
45 Driver's license requirement
47 Portugal's Palácio de ___ Bento
48 What a movie villain often comes to
50 Faced
52 Enter as a mediator
54 Tribe whose sun symbol is on the New Mexico flag
56 Grandson of Abraham
60 Roadster from Japan

61 Sites for shark sightings
63 Gut trouble
64 Group in a star's orbit
65 Disney Hall architect
66 Sci-fi battle site

DOWN
1 Beats at the buzzer, say
2 Like a control freak
3 Houston ballplayer, in sports shorthand
4 Spring events
5 Word spoken 90 times in Molly Bloom's soliloquy
6 Desperately tries to get
7 "Criminal Minds" agent with an I.Q. of 187

8 Singer of the #1 single "Try Again," 2000
9 Half a couple
10 Vacancy clause?
11 Like the crowd at a campaign rally
12 Some mock-ups
13 One in a Kindergarten?
14 Three-time All-Pro guard Chris
21 Owen Wilson's "Midnight in Paris" role
23 Glenda Jackson/ Ben Kingsley film scripted by Harold Pinter
25 Cunning one
26 Wolf (down)
27 ___ gun
28 Battle site of June 6, 1944

30 Grand Slam event
32 John Paul's successor
33 Inflicted on
35 Green org.
37 Shade that fades
40 Musical with a cow that's catapulted over a castle
43 Area inside the 20, in football
46 Appetite
49 More likely
51 Sadness symbolized
52 Complacent
53 Plaza square, maybe
55 Least bit
57 Blind strip
58 Morsel for a guppy
59 One with a password, say
61 Street crosser, briefly
62 "You wanna run that by me again?"

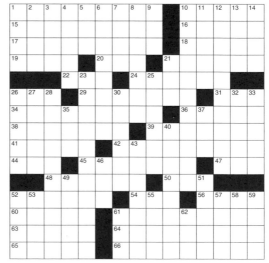

by John Farmer

ACROSS

1 1999 rap hit featuring Snoop Dogg
9 "Sin City" actress
13 Classic TV family
15 Represent
16 45°, for 1
18 Wild things?
19 Puts on eBay again
20 Cuban province where Castro was born
22 Zoological groups
23 Diamond deal
24 Software plug-in
25 Mode of transportation in a 1969 #1 hit
26 Filmdom family name
27 Israel's Sea of ___
28 Silence fillers
29 Informal name of the 45th state
30 Softball question
33 Clean, now
34 Songbird Mitchell
35 Turkey ___, baseball Hall-of-Famer from the Negro leagues
37 Breaks
38 They get tested
39 ___ system, part of the brain that regulates emotion, behavior and long-term memory
40 2000s CBS sitcom
41 Sextet at Woodstock
42 "El Condor ___" (1970 Simon & Garfunkel hit)
43 Golda Meir and Yitzhak Rabin led it
45 Division d'une carte
46 Place of outdoor meditation
47 Mock words of understanding
48 Price of an opera?

DOWN

1 Gangster nickname
2 "Carmen" figure
3 Covers
4 Share a secret with
5 From the Forbidden City
6 Bad impressions?
7 Poverty, metaphorically
8 Dutch city ESE of Amsterdam
9 Shape shifters?
10 Try to hear better, maybe
11 Knock-down-drag-out
12 First name in shooting
14 Winter set
17 Didn't make it home, say
21 Arm
23 Email ancestors
25 "Wordplay" vocalist, 2005
27 "In your dreams!"
29 Mary ___ (doomed ship)
30 Italian region that's home to Milan
31 Chances that a year ends with any particular digit
32 Florida's Key ___
33 Musician who arranged the theme from "2001"
34 Fruit-filled pastry
35 Where to bury the hatchet?
36 Olympic ice dancing gold medalist Virtue and others
37 ___ Alley
38 Hypercompetitive
39 About 40–60 beats per minute
41 Volume measure
44 Volume measure

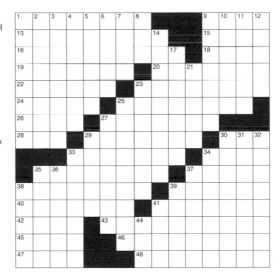

by David Steinberg

ACROSS

1 1980 new wave classic
7 1996 hybrid animation/live-action film
15 Cole ___, 2008 World Series M.V.P.
16 "Ahh" sloganeer
17 Juices
18 Hot numbers
19 "Bait Car" channel
20 Some hotels and old cars
21 Lays flat
22 It can precede masochism
23 Kind of mile: Abbr.
24 Location from which the phoenix rose
25 Ulan-___ (city in Siberia)
26 Biographer biographized in "Poison Pen"
29 Wear for Teddy Roosevelt
31 Amt. of copper, say
32 Surmounted
33 Dirty Harry fired them
37 Upstate N.Y. sch.
38 1985 #1 whose video won six MTV Video Music Awards
39 Rhode Island cuisine specialty
43 Rapper with the 2000 single "Party Up (Up in Here)"
44 "___ Story" (2007 Jenna Bush book)
45 Symbols of strength
46 Zales inventory
47 Give some juice
48 Benefits
50 Have thirds, say
51 Jockey competitor
53 Jin dynasty conqueror

54 Female novelist whose given name was Howard
55 Rhyme for "drool" in a Dean Martin classic
56 Something between 49-Downs
57 Out of alignment

DOWN

1 "How's it goin', dawg?"
2 Hobby with Q codes
3 Fresh
4 Gnocchi topper
5 "___ It" (2006 Young Jeezy single)
6 100 metric drops: Abbr.
7 Dirt, in slang
8 Like the Simpson kids' hair
9 Dramatic opening
10 Lewis ___, loser to Zachary Taylor in 1848
11 Prefix with tourism
12 1995–2013 senator from Arizona
13 1985–93 senator from Tennessee
14 Raymond who played Abraham Lincoln
20 Cowboy feature
23 What a leadfoot may do
24 City that's headquarters for Pizza Hut and J. C. Penney
26 Former Australian prime minister Rudd
27 Supposed sighting off the coast of Norway

28 Where faces meet
30 Tight shoe wearer's woe
33 Mercury and Saturn, once
34 Follower of one nation?
35 Soup line
36 Marketing mantra
38 Return service
39 Sci-fi's ___ Binks
40 Many an early tie
41 Safe spots
42 First marketer of Cabbage Patch Kids
46 Outrageously freewheeling
48 ___ concours (unrivaled: Fr.)
49 Way off
50 Bearded mountain dweller
52 Bit of action
53 Deg. from 37-Across

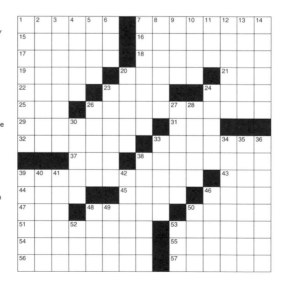

by Peter Wentz

ACROSS

1 Wiped the floor with
16 Use of blockades, say
17 Western daily
18 Lobby
19 Watch things
20 Limited edition?
21 Suffix with electr-
22 Blasting, musically
24 Bay, say . . . or bring to bay
28 Tempest, to Theodor
31 Bellyaches
33 ___ Rose
34 One may be tapped out
37 Brunch orders, briefly
38 McKinley's Ohio birthplace
39 Title priestess of opera
40 Aim
42 Setting of 10, maybe
43 Sony output
44 Bulldogs' sch.
46 Painter ___ della Francesca
48 Certain advertising medium
55 It's not word-for-word
56 Old French epics
57 Idolizes

DOWN

1 1970s–'80s sitcom setting
2 "I'm ___" (Friday declaration)
3 Doctor's orders
4 Passing people
5 What Hamilton called the wealthy
6 "Sure, let's try"
7 ___ Arden Oplev, director of "The Girl With the Dragon Tattoo"
8 Mid third-century year

9 Gershwin biographer David
10 Guarders with droopy ears and pendulous lips
11 Some collectible lithographs
12 It hasn't happened before
13 Sans spice
14 Sought-after rock group?
15 Fun or laugh follower
22 Send quickly, in a way
23 Finders' keepers?
25 What stars may indicate
26 Cause of a class struggle?
27 Allure alternative
28 Sun blocker
29 Pearl Harbor attack initiator

30 Polaris bear
31 Limb-entangling weapon
32 Second-greatest period in the history of something
35 1931 Best Picture
36 Utility bill details
41 Light measures
43 Like much arable land
45 "I ___ Lonely" (1954 hit for the Four Knights)
46 Lead in to deux or trois
47 Particular paean penner
48 Ozone destroyers, for short
49 "What's Hecuba to him, ___ to Hecuba": Hamlet

50 Sinatra's "Meet ___ the Copa"
51 Biblical miracle setting
52 Police dept. personage
53 Touch
54 Law school newbie

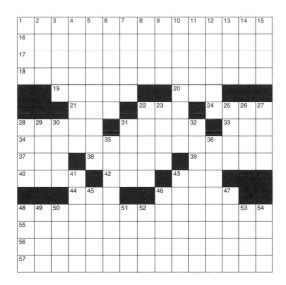

by Martin Ashwood-Smith

128

ACROSS

1 Domino's bottom?
11 Sing
15 Olympic Tower financier
16 Roman marketplaces
17 Lines to be cracked
18 Something to hold down
19 Asian silk center
20 Giving no performances
22 Aid in getting it together?
23 Off-limits
26 Al Bundy's garage, e.g.
28 Spot with a talking bear, maybe: Abbr.
31 XII, perhaps
33 Hailstorm, e.g.
34 Sarah Palin called herself an average one
37 How fresh paint glistens
38 "The Tourist" novelist Steinhauer
39 Best final result
41 Literary character who says "I'll chase him round Good Hope"
42 Kind of horoscope
44 Kids' party game
46 Bell heather and tree heath
48 Topic in a world religions course
49 Follower of Gore?
50 Like some laptop keyboards
52 Minable material
54 Part of un giorno
55 "I'll send for you ___": Othello
57 Record held for decades?
61 Swimmer featured in the 2013 film "Blackfish"

63 Important stud farm visitors
66 Ape's lack
67 Pre-Raphaelite ideal
68 Bad side of literature?
69 Sings

DOWN

1 Spotted South American mammal
2 The white surrounds it
3 99+ things in Alaska?
4 2008 title role for Adam Sandler
5 Buttercup family member
6 See 8-Down
7 Letter string
8 With 6-Down, old wheels
9 When hands are extended straight up and down

10 It may be over a foot
11 Closest bud, briefly
12 Head-turning cry
13 Make a fashionable entrance?
14 Its contents provide juice
21 Apprehended
24 Big name in Hispanic food
25 Juice
27 Sports stud
28 DC transformation location
29 Collection of green panels
30 CH_3COOH
32 Some pleas, briefly
35 Flair
36 Like some colors and cornets
40 Grp. concerned with feeding the kitty

43 Karaoke stand-in?
45 Raiser of dogs?
47 Penalty box, to sports fans
51 Trattoria dessert
53 "32 Flavors" singer Davis, 1998
56 "Barney Miller" Emmy winner Pitlik
58 Armenia's basic monetary unit
59 French suffix with jardin
60 Proposal figs.
62 Draught
64 Jubilant cry
65 Trash

by Barry C. Silk

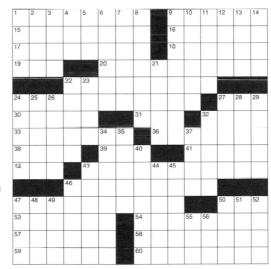

ACROSS

1 Common catch off the coast of Maryland
9 Light, in a way
15 Crude alternative
16 Jewelry box item
17 Like a bout on an undercard
18 Dickens's Miss Havisham, famously
19 ID clincher
20 Challenge to ambulance chasers
22 Arcade game prize grabber
24 Fiacre, to taxi drivers
27 "___ reminder . . ."
30 Nook occupier
31 Toshiba competitor
32 Some camcorders
33 Besmirch
36 Isaac Bashevis Singer settings
38 Culmination
39 Only proper noun in the Beatles' "Revolution"
41 "Something to Talk About" singer, 1991
42 Golf commentator's subject
43 Classic kitschy wall hanging
46 Slip for a skirt?
47 "Billy Bathgate" novelist
50 Ex-G.I.'s org.
53 Washington State mascot
54 Pre-W.W. I in automotive history
57 "If music be the food of love . . ." speaker in "Twelfth Night"
58 Cry of despair
59 Nothing: It.
60 Periods of warming . . . or cooling off

DOWN

1 M asset
2 Royal Arms of England symbol
3 Bone under a watchband
4 The Orange Bowl is played on it: Abbr.
5 Acupuncturist's concern
6 Croupier's stick material
7 Acknowledges
8 Tab carrier in a bar?
9 Tourist attraction on Texas' Pedernales River
10 Face in a particular direction
11 "Champagne for One" sleuth
12 Shot, informally
13 Serena Williams, often
14 Novel in Joyce Carol Oates's Wonderland Quartet
21 Exasperates
22 Cauldron stirrer
23 "The Avengers" villain, 2012
24 Bit of sachet stuffing
25 Classroom clickers of old
26 Singer who once sang a song to Kramer on "Seinfeld"
27 When "Ave Maria" is sung in "Otello"
28 1970s pact partly negotiated in Helsinki
29 Right hands: Abbr.
32 Arena
34 Orange garnish for a sushi roll
35 Fox hunt cry
37 Bay, for one
40 Prompt a buzzer on "The Price Is Right"
43 Unoccupied
44 Massive, in Metz
45 Block
46 Keep from taking off, as a plane with low visibility
47 Nobel category: Abbr.
48 Loughlin or Petty of Hollywood
49 Italian actress Eleonora
50 Let it all out
51 Unoccupied
52 Rolls of dough
55 One of the Ms. Pac-Man ghosts
56 "There is no ___ except stupidity": Wilde

by Brad Wilber

ACROSS

1 Insignificant row
9 Traffic reporter's aid
15 Big rush, maybe
16 Twin's rival
17 Offerer of stock advice
18 Grown-up who's not quite grown up
19 No big shot?
20 Nasty intentions
22 Threatening word
23 Overseas rebellion cry
25 One may be played by a geisha
26 Wasn't given a choice
27 "You Be ___" (1986 hip-hop hit)
29 Super German?
31 Pressure
33 Launch site
34 Where many airways are cleared, briefly
35 Antithesis of 32-Down
37 Common sound in Amish country
39 Large amount
42 Classics with 389 engines
44 Scrammed
48 Like Fabergé eggs
51 Schoolyard retort
52 Carry ___
53 So great
55 Paving block
56 Golf lesson topic
57 Goes downhill
59 Troubling post-engagement status, briefly
60 Doctor
62 They were labeled "Breakfast," "Dinner" and "Supper"
64 2002 César winner for Best Film
65 Real rubbish
66 Least significant
67 It really gets under your skin

DOWN

1 Determine the value of freedom?
2 Carp
3 Scandinavia's oldest university
4 Sneeze lead-ins
5 Austrian conductor Karl
6 Recess
7 Be quiet, say
8 Savor the flattery
9 It's bad when nobody gets it
10 "The Guilt Trip" actress Graynor
11 Like some cartilage piercings
12 "Possibly"
13 Dream team member
14 Planet threateners
21 Like a top
24 Stain producers
26 Gallant
28 Result of knuckling down?
30 Hollow
32 Antithesis of 35-Across
36 Pageant judging criterion
38 Ed supporters
39 Park Avenue's ___ Building
40 Radical
41 Shaking
43 Sniffing a lot
45 What a slightly shy person may request
46 1967 Emmy winner for playing Socrates
47 "As you like it" phrase
49 What a bunch of footballers might do
50 Game in which the lowest card is 7
54 Marriott rival
57 Preventer of many bites
58 Bit of action
61 Household name?
63 Soreness

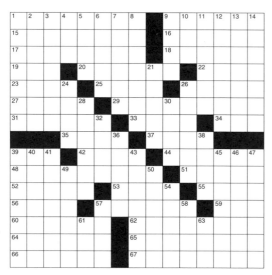

by Tom Heilman

ACROSS

1 African city of 4+ million whose name means, literally, "haven of peace"
12 Seeing things
14 "Why such a fuss?"
16 Start of a Jewish holiday?
17 Put one's two cents in?
18 Arizona's Agua ___ River
19 Not natural for
21 Like Beethoven's Piano Sonata No. 6 or 22
24 Tilting figure: Abbr.
25 ___ Ximénez (dessert sherry)
26 Manipulative health care worker
29 Smash letters
30 Destroy, informally
32 Range ridges
33 Classified
35 Eatery where the Tony Award was born
38 Pitch
39 Juan's "Hey!"
42 Perseveres
44 Some Deco pieces
46 Lead film festival characters?
47 Rhineland Campaign's arena: Abbr.
48 Frito-Lay snack
50 Silver of fivethirtyeight.com
52 California city near Fullerton
54 Author Janowitz
55 Opening line of a 1966 #1 Beatles hit
59 One-hit wonder
60 Events for some antiquers

DOWN

1 Demonstration exhortation
2 A bee might light on it
3 Some N.F.L.'ers
4 Irritate
5 Dopes
6 Restoration notation
7 Even though
8 Polynesian island chain?
9 Lee with an Oscar
10 Home row sequence
11 Kalahari Desert dweller
12 Irritability
13 Femme canonisée
14 Deli menu subheading
15 Foundation for some roofing
20 Silence
22 Verges on
23 Anticipate
27 Mind
28 Irritable state
31 Election surprise
33 What some bombs result in, in brief
34 Fanciful notions
35 Dead
36 Pair of boxers?
37 Give a makeover
39 Pontiac and others
40 "Star Trek" extra
41 It's definitely not the short answer
43 "That's that"
45 Fix a key problem?
49 Kind of yoga
51 Important info for people with connections
53 Clément with two Oscar-winning films
56 Düsseldorf direction
57 La la lead-in
58 Allen of play-by-play

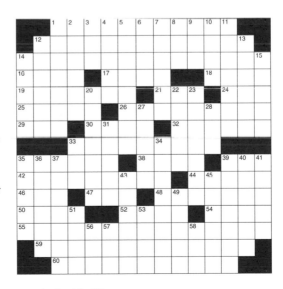

by Alan Arbesfeld

132

ACROSS

1. Made a seat-of-the-pants error?
11. "Your mama wears army boots," e.g.
15. Rioting
16. Popular pizza place, informally
17. Washington, D.C., has a famous one
18. Greets enthusiastically, in a way
19. One working in a corner in an office?
20. Eastern Woodlands native
22. Noted eavesdropper, for short
23. Covenants
25. Splendiferous
27. Bar supply
30. ___ Valley
31. Sulky
32. Tandoori-baked fare
34. "Yes" to an invitation
36. One way to stand
37. They may result when you run into people
40. Hognose snake
41. Of two minds
42. ___ work
43. Lender, legally speaking
45. Lo ___
47. 50% nonunion?
48. "Gunsmoke" setting
49. Marina sight
51. Classic Northwest brewski
52. Charlie's land
54. Like a tennis match without a break?
58. Like many a gen.
60. Mother of Andromeda
62. "Iliad" locale
63. Settles in, say
64. Job application info, for short
65. Nootropics, more familiarly

DOWN

1. Internet prowlers
2. Hand or foot
3. Cry frequently made with jazz hands
4. Georg von ___
5. Vice president after whom a U.S. city is thought to have been named
6. Ninny
7. Best Picture of 1960, with "The"
8. ___ Palmas
9. Breastplate of Athena
10. "The High One"
11. Where a canine sits?
12. Whole
13. Winter Olympics sight
14. They use blue books
21. TV show headed by a former writer for "S.N.L."
24. "Mom" and "Mama's Family"
26. Poetic expanses
27. Grumpy
28. They use Blue Books
29. "The Wishing-Chair" series creator
33. Manage
35. Whiner, of a sort
38. Kind of compressor
39. Yankee, once
44. Passes
46. "Uh-uh!"
50. #2 pop
53. Title with an apostrophe
55. Appear stunned
56. Apothecary item
57. Din-din
59. Prefix with peptic
61. 2 Tone influence

by Michael Ashley

ACROSS

1 Their drinks are not on the house
9 Rough limestone regions with sinkholes and caverns
15 Novel title character with a "brief, wondrous life"
16 Hawaii's Forbidden Isle
17 ". . . period!"
19 One buzzing off?
20 Three Stooges display
21 Some lab leaders, for short
22 Like most hall-of-fame inductees: Abbr.
23 Gave belts or socks
24 Swamp
25 Female friends, to Francisco
27 Early-millennium year
28 Jet black
29 Some are soft-shell
30 Spread out
32 He cast the Killing Curse on Dumbledore
33 What the Flying Wallendas refuse to use
34 Powerful Hindu deities
38 That same number of
40 Diner's words of thanks
41 Unlucky accidents, old-style
44 Co. led by Baryshnikov in the 1980s
45 It broke up in the age of dinosaurs
46 Not procrastinating
47 Midday assignation, in slang
49 Stink
50 Olive ___

51 More pointed
52 Give an underhanded hand?
53 Assertion more likely to be correct if 8-Down is given
56 Decision makers
57 Axis, e.g.
58 "Fingers crossed"
59 Whose eyes Puck squeezes magical juice on

DOWN

1 "Well done!"
2 With no dissenters
3 Common result of a slipped disk
4 Foil feature
5 Realty ad abbr.
6 Lies ahead
7 What a vacay provides

8 What an interrogator might administer
9 Bring home, as a run
10 Light as a feather
11 One in a cage
12 Confined
13 Vast historical region controlled by the Mongols
14 Kingdom next to Kent
18 See 24-Down
23 They aid responses, in brief
24 With 18-Down, life today
26 Transcend
30 Speaking of repeatedly, to a Brit
31 1984 award for Elmore Leonard
35 Drifting type

36 Good hand holding in Omaha Hi-Lo
37 It has the densest fur of any animal
39 Alpine skier Julia who won Olympic gold in 2006
41 Still-produced stuff
42 Slangy segue
43 Awful accident
45 Hazards
48 Afresh
51 Film and theater
52 Actor Rickman who played 32-Across
54 Low numero
55 ___ Fáil (Irish coronation stone)

by David Woolf

ACROSS

1 Air protection program?
10 Italian alternative
15 Tight squeeze for a couple?
16 Where Union Pacific is headquartered
17 1992 chart-topper that mentions "my little turn on the catwalk"
18 Tar
19 65-Across's title: Abbr.
20 Evian competitor
21 Gun shows?
22 A or O, but not B
24 First name in fashion
26 One going for the big bucks
27 ___ Fund Management (investment company)
29 Strike-monitoring org.
30 Contact on Facebook
31 Time reversal?
33 Tore to shreds
35 Diehard sort
38 Dangerous things to go on
39 Long, slender glass for drinking beer
41 River to the North Sea
42 Lowly one
43 Quarterly magazine published by Boeing
45 Norwegian Romanticist
49 Anti
50 Sch. in Madison, N.J.
52 ___ Gunn, "Breaking Bad" co-star
53 Killing it
56 Make a touchdown
58 Star opening?
59 Turning blue, maybe
60 Prevent a crash, say
62 Triumphant cry
63 "Buy high and sell low," e.g.
64 Baselines?
65 Case worker

DOWN

1 Springblade producer
2 Marmalade fruit
3 Green piece
4 Wall Street inits.
5 ___ Musk, co-founder of Tesla Motors and PayPal
6 Millan who's known as "the Dog Whisperer"
7 Temporarily inactive
8 ___ Place (Edmonton Oilers' arena)
9 Frozen food aisle eponym
10 See 11-Down
11 She loves, in 10-Down
12 "G-Funk Classics" rapper
13 Iroquoian tongue
14 Provincials
21 "Holy smokes!"
23 Long Island Rail Road station
25 Old phone trio
28 Spartan gathering place
30 Bakery/café chain
32 Schwab rival
34 Rhames of "Mission: Impossible"
35 Pioneering underground publication of the 1960s
36 Early tragedienne Duse
37 1990s sci-fi series
40 Alternative to die
41 In the direction of
44 Make further advances?
46 Sense
47 Former Italian P.M. Letta
48 Boot covering
51 Open, in a way
54 Kind of threat
55 Certain spirits
57 Frankie Avalon's "___ Dinah"
60 Org. with a top 10 list
61 Shopper's choice

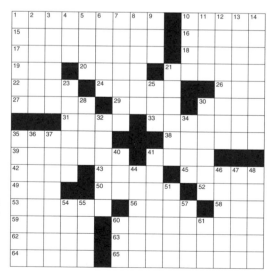

by David Steinberg

ACROSS

1 Milk additive
6 TV actor who lived, appropriately, in Hawaii
14 Hoyt who wrote "Joy to the World"
15 Go-getter on the hunt?
16 Catch
17 Reverse order?
18 "Wrong" way to spell a world leader's name in a New York Times crossword, according to a 1999 episode of "The West Wing"
20 Gets ensconced
21 Altdorf's canton
22 19th-century abbot and scientist
24 Word that begins with an apostrophe
25 Cheese made from the milk of Friesian cows
27 Reposes
28 Relative of a leek
30 Otherworldly
32 Showing irritation
33 On-deck circle?
36 First name in pop
37 Arm bones
38 Charles who was born Angelo Siciliano
39 Reproductive cell
40 Bar in a shower stall
44 Moniker
45 Johns Hopkins program
47 Beat oneself up about
48 Authorized, as to read secrets
51 Paternity prover
53 Dicey issue
55 Light-reflecting shade
56 Deep-fried treat
57 Third-place finisher in 2004 and 2008

58 Unwelcome benchmark?
59 Cygnet's parents

DOWN

1 Language of Navarre
2 City that hosts the California Strawberry Festival
3 Places for races
4 Drapery attachment
5 Wee hour
6 One of the Bushes
7 Makes up (for)
8 Monstrous
9 Modelists' purchases
10 Took a powder
11 Milk additive
12 Stereo system component
13 Showing some wear?

15 Only so-called "Decade Volcano" in the continental U.S.
19 ___ González, longest-serving democratically elected Spanish P.M.
23 Star of Buñuel's "Belle de Jour"
26 Group that offers "protection"
28 Beloved, in Bologna
29 Possible skin test reaction
31 Cinematography choice
32 Scribes
33 Never mind
34 Phone line?
35 Title sort of person in 2008's Best Picture
36 Purina product

39 Officially make
41 Brand in the frozen food aisle
42 "Northanger Abbey" novelist
43 Dwindles to nothing, with "out"
45 ___ dish
46 Begins to develop
49 Each
50 Author Jaffe
52 Détente
54 Shell filler

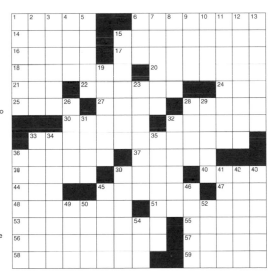

136

ACROSS

1 It includes pinning and throwing
8 "Chicago" setting
15 Rapture
16 Skyrocket
17 Prepare to pull the trigger
18 Couple seen at a baby shower
19 Hard knocks
20 It might hold up a holdup
22 Reason for a semiannual shift: Abbr.
23 Skunk and such
24 Star in Virgo
25 Aid in getting a grip
26 Check spec.
27 Abyss
28 Modern Persian
29 "That's clever!"
31 California's ___ Sea (rift lake)
32 Got a 41-Across on
33 Billy who played the Phantom in "The Phantom"
34 Person with small inventions
37 Slam dunk stat
41 Benchmark mark
42 They have seats
43 Crew's director
44 "Que ___-je?" ("What do I know?": Fr.)
45 "The Great Caruso" title role player
46 Perpetual 10-year-old of TV
47 Wile E. Coyote buy
48 Too, to Thérèse
49 Board game with black and white stones
50 Pupil of Pissarro
52 Like many laptop cameras

54 First name among Italian explorers
55 With ramifications
56 Galls
57 Does some farrier's work on

DOWN

1 One feeling 15-Across after Super Bowl III
2 Title name written "on the door of this legended tomb," in poetry
3 Home of Southeast Asia's largest mosque
4 News briefs
5 Colombian kinfolk
6 "___ see"
7 Like the human genome, before the 1990s
8 "St. John Passion" composer
9 Now, to Nicolás
10 Choice for a long shot
11 Sound in the comic "B.C."
12 Groveled
13 Tepid consent
14 Sitcom pal of Barbarino and Horshack
21 Grammy-nominated Ford
24 No-yeast feast
25 Parking meeter?
27 Cuts up
28 Adder's defense
30 They're off-limits: Var.
31 Pole star?
33 Its main island is Unguja
34 Asset in a drag contest

35 Whence a girl who's "like a samba," in song
36 Member of 31-Down's team
37 Geiger of Geiger counter fame
38 "You're not the only one!"
39 Recess for a joint
40 Reaches
42 Leisurely strolls
45 It's often parried
46 Impolite interruption
48 Indigo source
49 Spinal cord surrounders
51 Rescue vessel?
53 Relative of Aztec

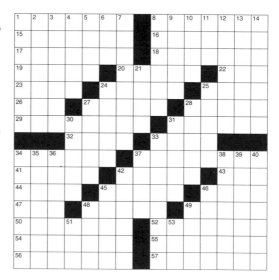

by Frederick J. Healy

ACROSS

1 Cartoon canary's bune
9 Lymph liquid
14 Launch
15 Many a predictable plot
16 Rests
17 One with a game collection, maybe
18 Gate announcement, briefly
19 Longtime model Parkinson of "The Price Is Right"
20 One with a game collection
21 Home to Bar-Ilan Univ.
22 Grp. supported by 17-Acrosses
23 Something groundbreaking
27 Post rival
32 "That is so obvious!"
33 What corned beef is often served on
34 Weights, to a weightlifter
35 Heart-felt thing?
36 Where to take stock?
37 Lamb accompaniment
39 Shade similar to bay
40 One getting into briefs?
41 Least brazen
42 "Eldorado" inits.
43 Forbid
44 Urban phenomenon
48 Coastal diver
49 Sun Devil Stadium's sch.
52 Chill
53 Labor leader?
55 Ray Charles's Georgia birthplace
56 A sprinkling
57 Inc. magazine topic
58 Voice of 1-Across

DOWN

1 Ton
2 Ton, e.g.
3 Quit running
4 Detoxing woe
5 Bagel source?
6 Many a Taiwanese
7 More than bickering
8 It has eight neighbors: Abbr.
9 Stars and stripes, say
10 Tod's sidekick on "Route 66"
11 Court records
12 Hammer and sickle holder, maybe
13 Trivial
15 Delta lead-in
22 Like many holiday letters
23 Jungian principle
24 In favor of the idea

25 Words before know and care
26 Tutu
27 See 29-Down
28 Sarcastic "I can't wait"
29 With 27-Down, her last film was "High Society"
30 Some food festival fare
31 French body of law?
33 Derby favorite
35 10 or 15 yards, say
38 One shot in a cliffhanger
39 Inner ear?
41 Stall near the stacks
43 Designer Geoffrey
44 Evidence of damage
45 John Paul II, e.g.
46 ___-call
47 Creator of bad apples?

48 Hartmann of talk radio
49 Mont. neighbor
50 Wrapped (up)
51 Grp. with national antidoping rules
54 It might end in "mil"

by Ned White

ACROSS

1 1960s sitcom character with the catchphrase "I see nothing!"
11 Kvetch
15 Pitchblende, e.g.
16 Disney title character surnamed Pelekai
17 Singles collection?
18 Hostile
19 Malignant acts
20 "Not serious!"
21 Lose one's place?
22 Itches
23 Places gowns are worn, for short
24 Setting for many reprises
26 Elated outpouring
28 Hercules type
29 Result of some fermentation
33 Ingredient in Worcestershire sauce
35 Still in the 17-Across
37 Still
38 Second baseman in both of the Dodgers' 1980s World Series
40 Like South Carolina vis-à-vis North Carolina, politically
41 Storied abductee
42 Sports mascot who's a popular bobblehead figure
44 Ring
46 Comfort's partner
47 "The X-Files" project, for short
51 Verb in the world's first telegraph message
52 Watergate units: Abbr.
54 Embroidery loop
55 Brand once pitched by Garfield
56 Where filing work is done
58 Relative of aloha or shalom
59 Home of the W.N.B.A.'s Silver Stars
60 Transcendental aesthetic developer
61 Accent for plus fours, often

DOWN

1 Like many drafts
2 Lollipop selection
3 Tarte ___ (French apple dessert)
4 Uncooperative moods
5 What César awards honor
6 Stick close to
7 One paid to make calls
8 Considers
9 "Star Trek: T.N.G." role
10 Literary wife in "Midnight in Paris"
11 Nearly set?
12 Judicious state
13 Minor payment
14 Early riser?
23 Locales that may be well-supplied?
25 Digs on a slope
26 Recognition not sought by Benjamin Franklin
27 Rapper with the 2012 album "Life Is Good"
29 Clear one's way, in a way
30 Latin condenser
31 Cookware that's often hinged
32 Cared
34 Overcome by mud
36 Weir
39 Blue label
43 Lose
45 Medieval merchants' guild
47 Grain elevator components
48 Discount, in combination
49 Vodka ___
50 "There, there"
53 "Up to ___" (1952 game show)
54 Fancy spread
57 Show on Sen. Franken's résumé

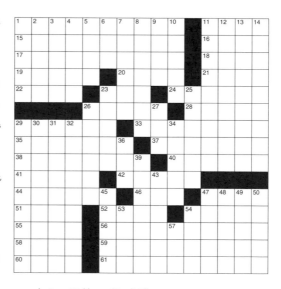

by Byron Walden and Brad Wilber

ACROSS

1 Innocent one
6 Short shrift?
10 Judgmental clucks
14 Influential style of the 1960s
15 Au courant about
16 Home of Sunset and Paradise
17 Pitching staff work areas
19 Plea opener
20 Coffee order
22 Theology inst.
23 "Praise the Lord!"
26 "Stanley & Iris" director Martin
29 A bit of cheer?
32 "Aw, sorry about that . . ."
33 Here, to Henri
34 B, to scientists
36 Untwisted silk fibers
37 Ganache ingredient
40 Brisbane buddies
41 Country that split in two in 2011
42 22-Across subj.
43 Puts on a pedestal
45 Door sign
46 Combines
47 Cold war defense system
49 Semi part
51 Dancers known for their Japanese street-style wardrobe
57 Water bearer
59 Singer whose first top 10 hit was "Where Does My Heart Beat Now"
60 In Australia her name is Karen
61 1980s Chrysler offering
62 Harper Lee's given name
63 Castaway's spot
64 Amtrak stops: Abbr.
65 "Skyfall" singer

DOWN

1 "The aristocrat of pears"
2 On ___ with
3 Like one end of an electric cord
4 Nursing locale
5 "Hello, ___"
6 Subatomic particle more massive than an electron
7 Many a museum audio guide
8 Chinese menu words
9 Relative of a raspberry
10 Sushi order
11 Plot device?
12 Early "Doctor Who" villain
13 "Nurse Jackie" channel, for short
18 Musket loader
21 Make jokes about
24 Like many turkeys
25 Collectible cars
26 Encircled
27 Producer of cold cuts?
28 Carnival ride since 1927
30 Ones going in circles?
31 [Zzzzz]
34 Get moving
35 Anatomical knot
38 Prevaricate
39 Popular spring break locale
44 They may be offered by way of concessions
46 Withstood
48 Deplane in moments
50 NASA's Gemini rocket
52 ___ Bator
53 Wine-and-cassis drinks
54 Make angry
55 Idle
56 "The Mikado" weapon
57 Penultimate Greek letter
58 Grafton's "___ for Alibi"

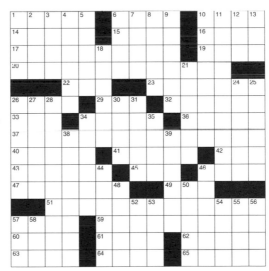

ACROSS

1 Big name in 25-Across treatment
9 Air piece?
14 Shrugs, maybe
16 Take it as a sign
17 "The Help" co-star, 2011
18 Decorative moldings
19 First of a succession of 13
20 Coot
22 Johnny-jump-up, e.g.
24 Nude medium, often
25 See 1-Across
27 90° from ouest
28 Really
31 Area map
32 ___ d'âme (moods: Fr.)
33 Alternative to 53-Down
34 Secures
37 She's no puritan
40 Farm sounds
41 Station, e.g.
42 Repulsive
43 Get out of practice?
45 Sportscaster Nahan with a star on the Hollywood Walk of Fame
48 Keel extension
49 Unrefined type
50 Key setting
52 Like eggheads
56 Stockholder's group?
57 Universal work
58 Hack, say
60 Nonstop
61 Evidence of having worn thongs
62 Little ones are calves
63 Player of many a tough guy

DOWN

1 Olympian on 2004 and 2012 Wheaties boxes
2 Bach contemporary
3 Onetime pop star who hosted "Pyramid"
4 First name in erotica
5 Fortune subjects: Abbr.
6 Stalin defier
7 Stargazer's focus?
8 Street fair lineup
9 Lodge org.
10 Fryer seen at a cookout?
11 Harvard has an all-male one
12 Creation for many an account
13 Super Mario Bros. runner
15 Backing
21 ___ rating (chess skill-level measure)
23 So-far-undiscovered one
26 Name-dropper's abbr.?
29 Aid in making one's move?
30 So-far-undiscovered ones, briefly
32 Like a type B
34 Geishas often draw them
35 Wimp's lack
36 Wrest the reins
37 Crane arm
38 Ace's stat
39 Open love?
41 To the degree that
43 What mops may be made into
44 Feet with rhythm
45 Dealt with
46 Abercrombie design
47 Brought to ruin
51 Kick back
53 Alternative to 33-Across
54 Ripped
55 Drumroll follower
57 Group with family units
59 Actor Penn of "Van Wilder"

by James Mulhern

ACROSS

1 Kid in shorts with a cowlick
8 Soft soap relative
15 Twisting
16 Industrial production unit
17 What black licorice or blue cheese is, for many
19 What a parade may necessitate
20 Goulash
21 Give the ax
22 Organ showpiece
24 Things that are put on . . . or don't go off
25 Sound of a belt
28 Agitates
29 "Stand and fight" grp.
30 Like agateware and graniteware
32 One might be made for the shower
35 Goosed
36 Consolation prize recipient
37 Novel followed up by "The Boyhood of Christ"
38 Out to lunch
39 Need for muscle contraction, briefly
40 Person who may work a lot
41 One having a ball?
42 Like a Madrilenian millionairess
44 Apex
46 Geology topic
47 Plot element?
48 Singular publication
52 Line near the end of an infomercial
55 Get limited access?
56 Finish line?
57 Rural parents
58 Sexual desire, euphemistically

DOWN

1 Not much
2 Singular
3 Rushing home?
4 Bit of chichi wear
5 Smashed
6 Like a common printing process
7 The Skywalker boy, for short
8 Processes, as ore
9 Tennis star Petrova
10 Not suckered by
11 Inquiry made while half awake, maybe
12 Mojave Desert sight
13 Like some celebrities blogged about by Perez Hilton
14 Inn inventory
18 Chemistry Nobelist Hoffmann
23 Hernando's hundred
24 Go gaga (over)
25 English channel's nickname, with "the"
26 Being with une auréole
27 King John sealed it
29 Direct, as a confrontation
31 Israel Philharmonic maestro
32 Technology standard named for a Danish king
33 "Calm down now . . ."
34 Massachusetts motto opener
36 Hitch horses
38 All-Star 18 consecutive times from 1967 to 1984
40 "Where we lay our scene," in Shakespeare
42 Take up one more time, say
43 ___ Sendler, heroine of W.W. II's Polish Underground
44 Blocker working with a receiver
45 Out of sight
47 "Like ___ Song" (John Denver hit)
49 With 51-Down, unscented
50 Wind, in Chinese
51 See 49-Down
53 Midwest attachment?
54 Bearded ___ (reedling)

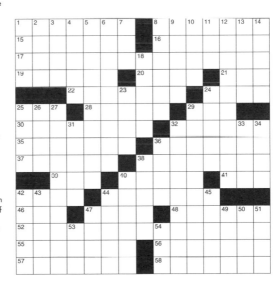

by Gary Cee

ACROSS

1 2015 Toronto event
11 Office staples
14 Slide
15 Protagonist in David Foster Wallace's "Infinite Jest"
16 "Corpus Christi" playwright
18 Ones united in France?
19 Manufacturer of boxy cars
20 Treasure
21 Loose end?
22 "Return to Never Land" role
23 Darkroom chemical solution
24 Pickle
25 Big gun
26 U.S. city that's almost as large in area as Delaware
35 Part of a French cabinet
36 Jumbo, e.g.
37 Shpilkes
38 Certain shell contents
39 Joan Sebastian's "___ y Más"
40 Pull out all the stops
43 Miracle site
45 Latin primer word
49 Hip to
50 Enterprise Klingon
51 Close call
52 Forrest Tucker's "F Troop" role
55 X-___ large
56 What solidifies things in the end?
57 Member of the E Street Band
58 Bit of forensic evidence

DOWN

1 Golfer Calvin
2 Quattro relatives
3 Quaint complaint
4 Husband of Otrera
5 TV ad unit: Abbr.
6 Not cover one's butt?
7 Formation from glaciation
8 Former first lady
9 List-ending abbrs.
10 When repeated, a breath freshener
11 Jacob's ladder, for one
12 Make a little lower?
13 More artful
14 Tank gun first produced by the Soviets in W.W. II
17 Ottoman ruler nicknamed "The Lion"
22 19th-/20th-century U.S. portraitist
23 ___ Brunelleschi, Italian Renaissance architect who developed linear perspective
24 Coupling
25 1958 41-Down by Samuel Barber
26 Mennen line
27 Scandinavian goddess of fate
28 Suffix with pluto-
29 "Ocean's Eleven" activity
30 Cagney classic of 1935
31 Big name in modeling agencies
32 "South Park" boy
33 The Garden of England
34 Song and dance
40 Flag wavers?
41 25-Down, for one
42 Common cleanser
43 Neighbor of Gabon
44 Holder of Leia's secret
45 Legend maker
46 Cuban revolutionary José
47 "Little Miss Sunshine" co-star
48 Souvenir buys
50 Keen
51 Flue problem
53 Literary inits.
54 Real-estate listing abbr.

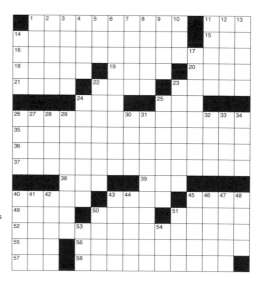

by Martin Ashwood-Smith

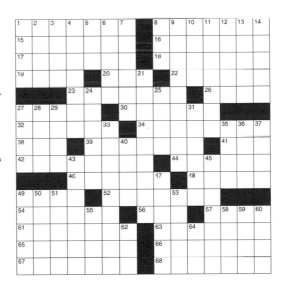

ACROSS

1 Locale that often includes a wet bar and large-screen TV
8 Picture with a number
15 Where it never gets above zero degrees?
16 One going around the bases?
17 Ends of some films
18 Warm-up?
19 Greasy spoon order
20 Where a bud hangs out
22 Successfully lure
23 Kind of figure
26 Highlighted, say
27 Toss
30 Mexican revolutionary of 1910
32 Moon of Mars
34 Draft pick?
38 Electric ___
39 Jacket option
41 "___ bad!"
42 Much of the Plains States
44 Palliate
46 Staple of the house in "The Real World"
48 Still
49 "___ con Dios"
52 Transport for Miss Gulch, in "The Wizard of Oz"
54 What a chair needs
56 Hawaiian for "white"
57 PC whiz
61 Controversial 1715 measure of Parliament
63 Touch-type?
65 Infomercial testimonial
66 Reply to a schoolmistress

67 It clears the air
68 "The Hangover" co-star

DOWN

1 Go well (with)
2 Soft shade
3 "The Sound of Music" chorus
4 TV game show on the Discovery Channel, 2005–12
5 Loved, with "up"
6 Person behind a curtain, maybe
7 Unreal
8 Joe
9 Handles online
10 Attend
11 Edward Murdstone, to David Copperfield
12 Sugar
13 Certain belly button

14 What polling may reveal
21 Chinese restaurant staple
24 ___ Belvedere (classic sculpture in the Vatican)
25 Great white shark prey
27 Particular, informally
28 "Clueless" protagonist
29 Hershey candy
31 Distilled pine product
33 Places to find in flight magazines
35 Advance on a table
36 Actor Jay of "Jerry Maguire"
37 Leave in
40 Lock opener?
43 Unreal
45 Former
47 "So long"

49 South American carrier founded in 1927
50 Heartburn
51 Cries of pain
53 Nursed, with "for"
55 ___ Torres, four-time Olympic swimming gold medalist
58 Company that follows Shin Bet security procedures
59 Tight-lipped sort
60 Border lines?
62 "Bad!"
64 Popular wood for wood chips

by Ian Livengood

144 ★★★

ACROSS

1. Girl's name in #1 1973 and 1974 song titles
6. With 20-Across, where the first-ever crossword puzzle appeared
13. Reserved parking spaces and others
14. Less light
15. Form of many a birthday cake
16. Jojoba oil is a natural one
17. Lead-in to now
18. Home of MacDill Air Force Base
19. Had ___ (flipped)
20. See 6-Across
24. Legal attachment?
25. Light unit
26. Acclaim for picadors
28. Certain sultan's subjects
30. They're not team players
34. Lab dept.
35. La ___ (California resort and spa)
36. Extended trial
38. Not for the general public
39. Morlocks' enemy
41. Saxony, e.g.
42. Shot
45. Creator of the first crossword
49. Kingdom vanquished by Hammurabi
51. Actor Tom of "The Seven Year Itch"
52. Ranch sobriquet
53. 1989 Peace Nobelist
55. Aviary sound
57. To a fault
58. Fruit whose name comes from Arawak
59. Year in which the first crossword appeared, on December 21
60. Firth, e.g.

DOWN

1. Where vaults can be seen
2. Jacket style
3. Noted geographical misnomer
4. "South Park" boy
5. Basic Latin verb
6. Hobbyist, e.g.
7. Jerry Orbach role in "The Fantasticks"
8. Early Chinese dynasty
9. Neighborhood org. since 1844
10. Chilling
11. Mulligans, e.g.
12. Mardi Gras group
14. Big sport overseas?
16. Babe in the woods
18. Sailors' chains
21. City on the Firth of Tay
22. "Star Wars" queen and senator
23. Canine vestigial structure
27. High-hatting
28. Cortés's quest
29. Graffiti, say
31. Like many nutrients
32. 1, for one: Abbr.
33. Poor, as an excuse
37. Rock singer?
38. Key never used by itself
40. Formal confession
41. Toni Morrison novel
42. Obscure
43. Like some vin
44. R. J. Reynolds brand
46. Borders
47. Brass
48. Hemingway, notably
50. T. J. ___
54. "Vous êtes ___"
55. Staple of sci-fi filmmaking
56. Ostrogoth enemy

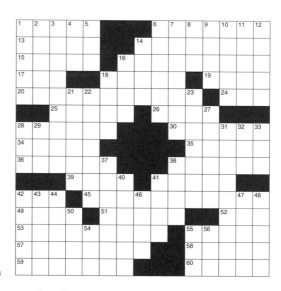

by Todd Gross and David Steinberg

ACROSS

1 Compliment after a dive
10 Word with cellar or door
15 2012 billion-dollar Facebook acquisition
16 Dermatologist's case
17 Things employed to show the passage of time à la "Citizen Kane"
18 Some saucers
19 Mixed ___
20 1950s–60s sitcom nickname
21 Cant
22 Identifies
24 Small jerk
26 Accord
27 Brown refreshers
30 Caustic soda, chemically
32 ___ kwon do
33 Gridiron datum: Abbr.
34 So-called "potted physician"
36 Oscar-nominated film featuring a dentist-turned-bounty hunter
40 Home of Sky Tower, the tallest free-standing structure in the Southern Hemisphere
41 "Uncle Tom's Cabin" girl
42 Morse bit
43 Contrarian's abbreviation
44 Island where Artemis was born
47 Phishing lures
49 Disperse
51 Double ___ Oreo
53 Lead-in to type
54 Two-master
57 Sushi fish
58 Leader of Uganda's independence movement
60 Subject of a landmark 2012 Supreme Court decision
62 Dice
63 Final say
64 Apply
65 Like Albert Einstein, ethnically

DOWN

1 Add zip to
2 "Hold on . . ."
3 Port on Lake Ontario
4 Result of drying out, maybe
5 Pasta, e.g., informally
6 "The African Queen" screenwriter
7 Attempt to cure
8 "Homicidal Psycho Jungle Cat" duo
9 Bounty letters
10 E, F and G in D.C.
11 Jennifer of "Bound"
12 Quite a long shot
13 Cause for some blacklisting
14 Who's who in publishing?
23 Move furtively
25 Class graded on a curve?
26 Gather at harvest
28 Whites, informally
29 Brown coat
31 Expressed some delight
35 Perfume holders
36 Some Lamaze assistants
37 Drink with a straw
38 Have no help
39 Some, in Salamanca
45 Parliamentary home
46 Newsman Ray
48 What stress may be good for
50 "Roasted in ___ and fire": Hamlet
52 Guy with a cooking show
55 Reassuring comment after a fall
56 Wide breach
59 What means the most at the end?
60 Beginnings of life
61 Bilk

by Ian Livengood and J.A.S.A. Crossword Class

ACROSS
1 Gut-busting side
11 Port. title
15 Alternative to 1-Across
16 Some GPS suggestions, informally
17 Shooting star?
18 College figs.
19 It means little in the Lowlands
20 Trimming gizmo
21 Like floppy disks, e.g.
22 Vino de ___ (Spanish wine designation)
23 Red shade
24 Santa Ana wind source
27 It may be up against the wall
29 Bring out
30 1975 hit song about "tramps like us"
33 Like Athena
34 Sharon's predecessor
35 Fig. for I, O or U, but not A or E
36 It may be said while wearing a toga
38 Manual series
39 Phoenix suburb larger than the Midwest city it's named for
40 Break through
41 Princess of ballet
43 Like red bell peppers
44 Orders
45 Key ring?
47 Scoutmaster, often
50 The moment that
51 It's not drawn due to gravity
53 Co-star in the U.S. premiere of "Waiting for Godot," 1956
54 Pride and joy

55 Abstainers
56 Question from a bully

DOWN
1 Slight pushes
2 One at the U.S. Mint?
3 Jonathan's wife in "Dracula"
4 A.L. East team, on sports tickers
5 Like many pregnant women
6 Where to get a cold comfort?
7 #1 spoken-word hit of 1964
8 "My Son Is a Splendid Driver" novelist, 1971
9 Castle of ___ (Hungarian tourist draw)

10 Old map abbr.
11 Like some pills and lies
12 Dilly
13 Bait
14 Listing on I.R.S. Form 8949
21 Summit success
22 Front runners
23 Engine buildup
24 Sound like a baby
25 Cartoon pooch
26 Hunky-dory
27 Rather informal?
28 Printer part
30 Port on the Adriatic
31 Like Bill Maher, notably
32 Supporter of shades
34 Unembellished
37 Stock to put stock in
38 Verbal alternative to a head slap

40 Go for a car-cramming record, say
41 Anciently
42 Tunisian money
43 ___ presto
45 Devotional period?
46 Insignificant
47 Twain's "celebrated jumping frog"
48 Talent show lineup
49 "___ Bones G'wine Rise Again" (spiritual)
51 Important card source: Abbr.
52 Deterrent to lateness or cancellation

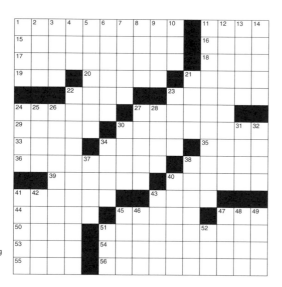

by Frederick J. Healy

ACROSS

1 Bite-size sweet
10 Complains loudly
15 Locomotive
16 1946 University of Pennsylvania invention
17 1950s–'60s sitcom headliner
18 Instagram filter
19 What many cats play
20 It's snowy in Florida
22 Left
23 Oxygen tent locale, briefly
24 Home of Harpers Ferry: Abbr.
25 Flock member
27 Literary adverb
28 Dundee denial
29 Nikkei unit
30 Salmagundi
32 Prefix with phobia
33 Basilica honoree
34 Former silkworms
36 Time indicator, of sorts
37 Media giant that owns the Detroit Free Press
39 4-Down inventory
40 Gedda or Ghiaurov of opera fame
41 "Cap'n ___" (Joseph C. Lincoln novel)
42 "Phooey!"
45 Singer who said "People make music to get a reaction"
46 "Tastes terrific!"
47 Actress Gardner
48 Oriole rival
49 Junior senator from Texas
51 Food whose name means "feathers"
53 Eatery
54 Nuclei
56 Profession for Laura Bush before the White House

58 Rushed
59 "Cinderella" stepsister
60 Perfect
61 Type-A types

DOWN

1 Linguistic 30-Across
2 Record glimpsed on Norman Bates's Victrola
3 1-Down, e.g.
4 Michelin Guide recommendations
5 Lun ___ (Tuptim's beloved in "The King and I")
6 Certain rate-hike circumvention
7 Pizzeria supply
8 One logging in
9 Cashes in
10 "___ on Prop . . ." (campaign sign)

11 Over
12 Many "Jackass" stunts
13 In a state of nirvana
14 Not stay together
21 Online realm since 2006
24 Common British Isles shader
26 "Where you book matters" sloganeer
31 Some Olympic coups
32 It's 8 for O
34 Artery
35 Not going astray
37 Trattoria dish
38 Delay
39 Midway missile
42 Cook, as Swiss steak
43 Erle Stanley Gardner pseudonym

44 Shenzi, Banzai and Ed, in "The Lion King"
50 Fraternity letter
52 Hombre, once
53 Techno- tack-on
55 Dict. demarcation
57 Sidebar requester: Abbr.

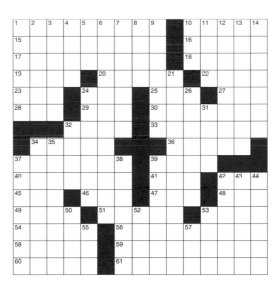

by Barry C. Silk and Brad Wilber

ACROSS

1. Like cork trees and flying lizards
6. "Jersey Shore" housemate's music-biz name
14. Jersey Shore vacation option
15. Big Dipper's setting
16. One offering help in passing?
17. Take up enthusiastically
18. See 34-Down
19. Where Lee Harvey Oswald was a lathe operator
20. City where some believe Cain and Abel are buried
21. Warden in drab clothes
23. Take down with a charge
24. Spring event in the Summer Olympics?
25. Setting that makes things right?
27. Less agreeable
30. Be a lush
35. Chicken à la rey?
36. Buzzes, say
38. Tiny amount
39. Was revolting
41. Was a rocker?
43. Tie ___
45. Up
46. Hyperbola parts
50. House meeting place
54. Theoretical
55. Predictor of fame
56. Elasticity
57. School meeting places
59. Photometry unit
60. Be an unhelpful interrogee
61. Lack life
62. Life or death
63. Leaf part

DOWN

1. Go on the fritz
2. Monty Python theme composer
3. Gaps
4. Like cute nerds, in slang
5. "___ did you nothing hear?": Hamlet
6. Stress, to Strauss
7. First-class regulars
8. Keeping buff?
9. Jock: Abbr.
10. Raider in the battle of the St. Lawrence
11. "___ Paw" (Oscar-winning Disney short)
12. "Eyewitness" director Peter
13. Hurdy-gurdy sound
15. Flashed
19. Tuareg rebellion locale of 2012
22. Erase
26. Three-ring setting
27. Some rescue work
28. Neighbor of Rabbit
29. Bunk
31. Foreshadow
32. One not getting benefits, say
33. Make baloney?
34. With 18-Across, software developer's concern
37. Constituent of molding sand
40. Touching scene at an airport?
42. Animation
44. European president who attended Harvard
46. Bank
47. Path
48. One of 64 in a genetic table
49. Piece of work
51. Napoleon, notably
52. Where things may be heating up
53. Molto adagio
58. Bit of sportswear
59. Head

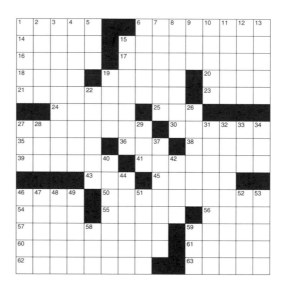

by Kyle Dolan

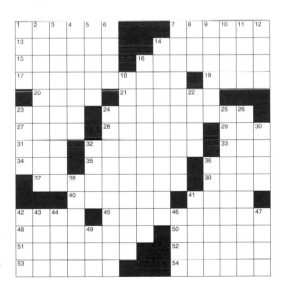

★ ★ ★ **149**

ACROSS

1 Attaché feature?
7 Lawrence who co-wrote "The Empire Strikes Back" and "Return of the Jedi"
13 Seat of Ireland's County Kerry
14 One of the former Barbary States
15 Pride : lions :: ___ : crows
16 "Don't get so worked up!"
17 Ordered pair?
19 ___ running
20 Moving briskly
21 Public record?
23 Not down with anything
24 Deadeye
27 Surprised expression
28 Many old B films
29 Constant critic
31 Leery of being noticed, maybe
32 Decides on
33 Symbol of liberty in the French Revolution
34 Last course, often
35 Domineering men
36 Gridiron cry
37 They deliver on Sunday
39 Ideal world?
40 Sulking peevishly
41 Underattended, say
42 Grocery staple
45 Tub accessory for the head
48 Old-fashioned promotions
50 La to la, e.g.
51 Common gathering in a public square
52 Bet
53 Menelaus' kingdom
54 Menorah inserts

DOWN

1 Bread boxes?
2 Common casino locale
3 One who wants in on the deal
4 Aged
5 Emotionally demanding
6 Dean's "Lois & Clark" co-star
7 Word puzzle popular since the 1930s
8 Bother
9 Unspecific recipe quantity
10 "If opportunity doesn't knock, build a ___": Milton Berle
11 Diploma holder, for short
12 Tiny criticisms
14 Ever since that time
16 Cribs
18 Brainstorming session aids
22 Anti Ballistic Missile Treaty signatory, briefly
23 Flimsy lock
24 1978 disco hit featuring the warning "Don't fall in love"
25 Body of water belatedly added to the course of the Erie Canal
26 Discussed
30 Mafioso foes
32 Bahla Fort site
36 Clicker, of a sort
38 Michael who once led Disney
41 Decrees
42 Omar of TV and film
43 Clutch
44 Memory unit prefix
46 Diplomatic assignment
47 Joins
49 Unsteady walker, maybe

by Patrick Berry

ACROSS

1 It has a close "Kentucky" cousin
16 Tax deferral options
17 Water gun fight?
18 Tumblers
19 Nonprofessional
20 "Thus weary of the world, away she ___": Shak.
21 Burnable medium, briefly
23 Slender runner
25 One may remove grease with elbow grease
30 SC Johnson brand
32 Does a Ludacris impersonation
34 Grid great Greasy
35 Not the least bit
37 "That's expensive!"
39 Sum symbol
40 Rice alternative
42 Stop on Amtrak's California Zephyr
43 Dead player?
45 Key contraction
46 ___ ed
47 Larry of the original "West Side Story"
49 Went nowhere
51 They're usually pixelated on TV
59 Kelp is a natural source of it
60 One who orders trunks to be moved?
61 Member of a drill team?

DOWN

1 U.P.S. deliveries: Abbr.
2 Poor as ___ (destitute)
3 Belly dancers' bands?
4 Native of Caprica on "Battlestar Galactica"
5 Corker
6 Done to ___

7 Alternatives to racks
8 Sawmill supplier
9 Fish in a dragon roll
10 They have bills and appear on bills
11 Renowned boxing gym in Brooklyn
12 Outer limits
13 Diomedes speared him
14 Having good balance
15 They were retired in '03
21 Like new notes
22 Freshwater aquarium favorite
23 Many a dama: Abbr.
24 Deck
26 Brand

27 Renaissance composer of "Missa Papae Marcelli"
28 How troglodytes live
29 Clean out
31 DiMaggio and others
33 Fitting decision
36 Wisconsin county or its seat
38 A.L. East team, on scoreboards
41 Really cheap shots?
44 Monthly
48 Spanish royal
49 Attic promenades
50 Book review?
51 Weigh-in section?
52 Woody trunk
53 Korean War weapon

54 Abbr. by Hook or by Cook
55 Drs. often take over for them
56 iPhone talker
57 Fall scene
58 Fundació Joan Miró designer

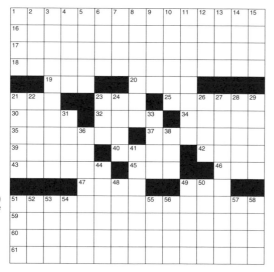

by Martin Ashwood-Smith

ACROSS

1. Vacation destination
6. Spots for thirsty travelers
15. Scooter
16. It's rendered in the kitchen
17. Group studying torts and procedures, typically
18. Psychiatric hospitals
19. Hardly a free spirit?
20. "Thinking back . . ."
21. They often precede showers
23. German port on the Baltic
24. Large bill holder
25. Historical role in Spielberg's "Munich"
26. Mrs. Lincoln's family
27. Cry of surprise
28. Camp accouterments
29. Dandy
30. Stage, as a historical scene
32. Like a ballerina
36. Fox tribe neighbor
37. Operates, as a booth
38. Be useful
39. Cars whose only color until 1952 was bottle green
42. One of the 12 tribes of Israel
43. Just dandy
44. Oscar-winning film based partly on the book "The Master of Disguise"
45. Bowling splits in which the 5 and 10 pins remain
47. Big name in classical education?
49. 1969 role for Dustin Hoffman
50. Recovering

51. It's written with a minus sign
52. Freebie often containing alcohol
53. "To conclude . . ."
54. Extra protection from the elements
55. Source of morning stimulation, maybe

DOWN

1. Harder to see through, say
2. Queen or her subject?
3. Opportunity for a singer or comedian
4. The Shroud of Turin and others
5. Car that offered Polar Air air-conditioning
6. Disobeys standing orders?
7. New York's ___ Cultural Center, promoter of Hellenic civilization
8. Requiring greater magnification
9. Some world leaders
10. Pregnant, maybe
11. Some C.I.A. doings
12. Yellow
13. Inveighed (against)
14. Changing places
22. Bygone station name
26. Put to waste?
28. Some Quidditch equipment
29. End of story?
31. "Don't worry about it"

32. Herb whose name is derived from the Latin for "to wash"
33. One employing trompe l'oeil effects
34. Pets
35. "Now, look here!"
37. It serves as a reminder
39. Footwear similar to klompen
40. Childish retort
41. Terrible time?
42. Reach, in a way
43. ___ Gleason, Tony winner for "Into the Woods"
45. Like wigwams and igloos
46. Have some catching up to do
48. Captain's place

by Kevin G. Der

ACROSS

1 Fast-paced alternative to Scrabble
12 Lance cpl.'s org.
15 It has a Page Navigation menu option
16 100 sawbucks
17 Cop car, to a CBer
18 Inhibiter of free speech
19 Exchange some words?
20 Follower of Bush or Clinton
21 Many an Israeli
23 Part of some bargain store names
24 Do-or-die situation
27 ___-to-be
28 Green on a screen
30 Texas' ___ Duro Canyon
31 High style of the 1700s
32 Oppenheimer's agcy.
34 Vocal trio
36 1983 song with the lyric "Let's leave Chicago to the Eskimos"
40 Women, poetically, with "the"
41 Nonverbal equivalent of "You have got to be kidding me!"
43 Cannes neighbors?
44 Financier Kreuger called the Match King
45 Start another tour
47 "Man!"
50 Alternative to nuts?
51 Like 36 of this puzzle's answers
53 Grease monkey's pocket item
55 Formal identification
57 Mix for a mixer
58 Draw to an end
59 Spanish gentleman
60 Professional organizers?
64 Fidelity offering, briefly
65 Feature of 007's car
66 Cornerback Law and others
67 Beyoncé alter ego

DOWN

1 Katharine Lee ___, "America the Beautiful" lyricist
2 Court wear, maybe
3 "I swear, man!"
4 Have an edge against
5 Its website has lesson plans, briefly
6 Vintage fabric
7 Get set
8 Sharp knock
9 Org. whose members look down in the mouth?
10 Its flag has an eagle in the center: Abbr.
11 Some foreign misters
12 Wear that was one of "Oprah's Favorite Things" four times
13 Circumnavigator's way
14 "Transformers" actress, 2007
22 Impugn
24 Call from a tree
25 Tenor ___
26 Trio in Greek myth
29 Round houses?
33 Bow no longer shot
35 Hits with wit
36 2007 book subtitled "Confessions of the Killer"
37 John's place
38 Simple winds
39 "The Twilight Saga" vampire
42 "A Severed Head" novelist, 1961
46 Itinerary start
48 Thing taken to a slip
49 Ulcer treater
52 Mad bit
54 Beau chaser?
56 Endings of rock names
58 One way to crack
61 1977 Steely Dan title track
62 One side in some chalk talks
63 One might show muscles, in brief

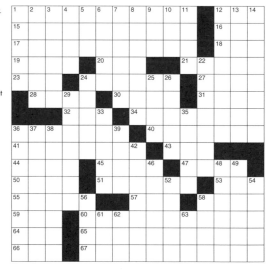

by David Steinberg

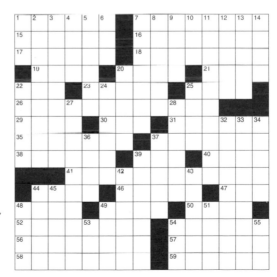

ACROSS

1 Frigid
7 Question at the door
15 Miss out on a board
16 "'Sup?"
17 Subject for a golf lesson
18 Emphatic approval
19 Petition
20 51-Down and others: Abbr.
21 Nighttime
22 Hunky-dory
23 Clobbered
25 Birds in a clutch
26 Group that no one on earth has ever joined
29 Sun disk wearer, in myth
30 Petition
31 "That's quite enough!"
35 Abridged
37 "What's it gonna be?"
38 Feature of a certain bandit
39 20-Down, e.g.
40 Nut
41 What a nonconformist ignores
44 "___ magnifique!"
46 Big employer in Hartford, Conn.
47 Canal checker?: Abbr.
48 One who's trustworthy?
49 Doesn't just grab
50 Green shade
52 Public, as views
54 Instruments played with mizraabs
56 "I'd like you to leave"
57 Nips in the bud
58 Bank guards?
59 Ambush locale in Episode 1 of "The Lone Ranger"

DOWN

1 "Cute" remarks
2 Thallium sulfate, e.g.
3 Figure out on the street?
4 Stick with it
5 One way to pay
6 Civic leader?
7 "Beg pardon?!"
8 Shop alternative
9 Takes credit?
10 Gabriel or Giorgio
11 Basic library stock
12 Iron-pumper
13 Australia's ___ Rock
14 Lose a lot?
20 Nissan ___
22 Italian friend
24 Question in a long-distance relationship
25 Humble dwellings

27 Civil engineering safety feature
28 Square, in old slang, as indicated by forming a square with one's hands
32 1969 hit with the repeated lyric "Big wheel keep on turnin'"
33 So that one can
34 Takes some hits
36 Red states
37 Humble dwellings
39 Short trunks
42 Possible protein shake ingredient
43 Sample in a swab test
44 Weber per square meter
45 Turn red, say
48 Drill bits?
49 Away from port

51 Christopher Columbus Transcontinental Hwy.
53 Kind of port
54 Pouch
55 Frequent form request: Abbr.

by Ian Livengood

154 ⭐ ⭐ ⭐

ACROSS

1 Body that doesn't remain at rest?
7 Having way too much on one's plate
14 It's not normal
16 Dismissive confession follower
17 Start liking a lot
18 Rare electee
19 ___ B
20 Ingredient in an Americano
22 Like Fabergé eggs
23 Repeated battle cry
25 Megadyne fractions
27 Chef DiSpirito
29 Dog it
30 Texts, e.g.: Abbr.
34 "The Valley of Amazement" novelist, 2013
36 Org. for female shooters
38 Inuit knife
39 Writer of the ethnography "Germania"
41 Get out of the blasted state?
43 What isn't the small print?: Abbr.
44 Suffocating blanket
46 Get off the drive, say
47 Food factory stock
49 Ninny
51 Utter
52 20th-century treaty topic
55 Priceline possibilities
56 Release
59 2012 Pro Bowl player Chris
61 Once-common "commonly"
62 Game that can't be played

64 She wrote "The Proper Care and Feeding of Husbands"
66 "Spread the happy" sloganeer
67 Queen's weapon
68 Producing zip
69 Strips at a pageant

DOWN

1 Given a 20 for food, say
2 Drink that often makes a person sick
3 Road hog
4 Record label abbr.
5 Johns of Britain
6 John of Britain
7 Recife-to-Rio dir.
8 Bible
9 Like Huns
10 Refusal to speak

11 Flatten, as a rivet
12 Throw out
13 Keep from
15 Demonstrate a wide range on a range?
21 Gone private?
24 Early CliffsNotes subheading
26 Restin' piece?
28 Energy bar ingredients
31 "You guessed it . . ."
32 Like some diets that avoid pasta
33 People people
35 Ninny
37 Lincoln and others
40 Diesel discharge
42 Primary and secondary, briefly
45 Bunches
48 Habitual high achiever?
50 Label stable

53 C.D.C. concern
54 "Phooey!"
56 Some heavy planters
57 Like some flags: Abbr.
58 Not full-bodied
60 "Modern Gallantry" pen name
63 Swimming gold medalist Park ___-hwan
65 Key component: Abbr.

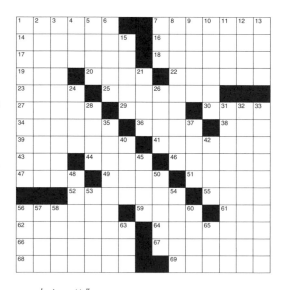

by James Mulhern

ACROSS

1 "No more wasting time!"
16 Pixar, e.g.
17 Was just getting started
18 Some foreign friends
19 Union ___: Abbr.
20 Breathers
21 "Dawson's Creek" star James Van Der ___
22 It's a state
24 Unduplicated
25 ___ Toy Barn ("Toy Story 2" setting)
26 Parked cars
28 A Kennedy
29 Fix
31 Makes a fuss over, with "on"
33 What Sports Illustrated's annual Swimsuit Issue has a lot of
35 Marker's mark maker
39 Bottom line?
41 Cruise
42 Professional org. with a "healthy" balance sheet
45 Musical instrument for a geisha
47 MASH unit
48 Pioneering map publisher William
50 1998 film in which Donny Osmond has a singing role
51 One on the staff?
52 Thin as ___
54 Romanian capital
55 Albert's sitcom co-star
56 Numbats
59 Washington report starter
60 Charm

DOWN

1 Caribbean capital, to locals
2 Cloisonné, e.g.
3 Sets things straight
4 Trash talk
5 "Dream Caused by the Flight of a Bee Around a Pomegranate a Second Before Awakening" artist
6 Tribe of Chief Shaumonekusse
7 It hangs around trees
8 Immobilized
9 Needing
10 Grp. that's got your number?
11 Texting ta-ta
12 Many Rwandans
13 Defensive reply
14 Nitpick
15 Gave a boost
22 Practice test?
23 Square things
26 Setting for "Ocean's 11"
27 Actor Alain
30 Strain
32 Home for E. B. White's Wilbur
34 Pose as
36 "Live más" sloganeer
37 Classic song that begins "When my baby / When my baby smiles at me"
38 "CSI" star William
40 Few of them were made after 1929
42 Source of the word "admiral"
43 One of two in a rumba
44 Pineapples: Sp.
46 Prepares, as some mushrooms
49 "If I ___ Have You" (2001 Best Original Song Oscar winner)
51 Kind of star
53 "Leading With My Chin" memoirist
55 Air force?
57 Slip into
58 Grp. with the 1971 gold album "Pictures at an Exhibition"

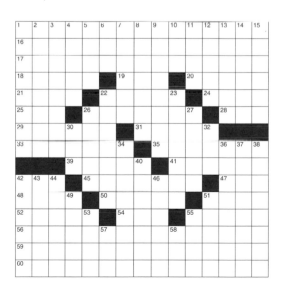

by Chris A. McGlothlin

ACROSS

1 Her 1994 memoir has the chapter "Desert Storm"
12 Plant visitor
15 What watts and volt-amperes have
16 Elementary education, briefly
17 High interest?
18 Choice for a portrait
19 U.K. honours
20 What you may open the door for
21 Aftermath
22 Fun time
23 Toddler coddler
24 Display options, briefly
25 Serpent with a Zulu name
26 Zany
28 On track to win
31 Use pumice on, perhaps
33 He wrote of a "vorpal blade"
35 Gets to a seat, say
36 Member of the German Expressionist group Die Brücke
38 Sky boxes?
39 Exhibit explainer
40 Strawberry, for one
42 Tom Clancy's "Every __ Tiger"
43 Polaris or Procyon
44 Persian language unit?
47 "The Wizard of Oz" farmhand
48 Psychoanalyst Melanie
49 Hometown of the mathematician Fibonacci
50 Much like
51 Words accompanying a low bow

53 X or Y lead-in
54 Uno's alternative
55 Suzanne, e.g.: Abbr.
56 Light insufficiently

DOWN

1 Muddle
2 Great Rift Valley port
3 Dodges
4 Some 27-Down
5 Prefix with culture
6 Like some inspections
7 Danger dinger
8 Old Sony format
9 Come together
10 Cock-a-leekie eater
11 Incubator
12 Sent out in waves?
13 Composer of several "Gnossiennes"
14 Man's name that sounds noble

21 Cooperation exclamation
23 "__ With the Long Neck" (Parmigianino painting)
24 Pro athlete in purple and gold
25 Cary's "Blonde Venus" co-star
26 Dispenser of Duff Beer
27 Desk set
28 Made no mistakes on
29 No breakfast for a vegan
30 TV antiheroine for 41 years
32 One whose shifts shift
34 Development site
37 Warrant
41 Handle
43 Subject to change

44 Screw up
45 Business fraudster Billie Sol __
46 General who won 1794's Battle of Fallen Timbers
47 Navigates a switchback, in part
48 Severinsbrücke's city
49 One may be fingered
51 "Revolution" or "Hound Dog" starter
52 Port named after a U.S. president, informally

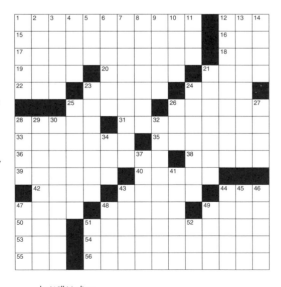

by Will Nediger

ACROSS

1 Drill command to rifle carriers
12 Bit of nonsense famously replacing "strangers in the night"
14 1979 ABBA single
16 Emblem of a pharaoh
17 Hooey
18 Show with an early episode titled "Crate 'n' Burial"
19 Dragon roll ingredient
20 Like grade skippers
22 N.Y.C.-based grp. with its own police department
24 Potential fire hazard
26 Philatelic collectible
27 Littermates compete for them
29 Not had by
30 3ty chore
32 Like Lesbos and Lemnos
34 Patriotic chant
36 Synthetic fiber used in bicycle tires and bulletproof vests
39 Fourth-brightest star in the sky
43 Big Green rivals
44 John P. Marquand's "The Late George ___"
46 Family name in "Look Homeward, Angel"
47 Part of a U.S. president's name that's Dutch for "neighbors"
49 Something one might hang in a street
50 Davis of the screen
51 Nabokov heroine
52 Throughout, in verse

54 Suffix of saccharides
56 Prefix with saccharides
57 Is guilty of petitio principii
61 Got a +2 on
62 500m or 5,000m competitor, say

DOWN

1 Florida food fish
2 Permanent data storer
3 "Your Movie Sucks" author
4 One of Utah's state symbols
5 Paste holder?
6 Passeport detail
7 It helps produce a kitty
8 Fivers
9 Longtime first name in TV talk

10 Century-starting year
11 Nobody's opposite
12 Wretched
13 Code broken by some singers
14 Startled reactions
15 John with an Oscar and a Tony
21 Turn off a lot
23 Solution for toys in the attic?
25 Common standard for model railroads
27 Twinkling topper
28 Flip
31 Spot that may be on the environment, briefly
33 Fig. that's in the neighborhood
35 Query after a wipeout

36 Food stuck in preparation
37 Lost
38 Witchy women
40 Worse for wear?
41 Not printed up?
42 Container for a round
45 Like much baby food
48 "I would ___ surprised"
50 Plague
53 Actress Jennifer of "Pride and Prejudice"
55 Sonic creator
58 More than nibble
59 Snap targets, for short
60 Mooring rope

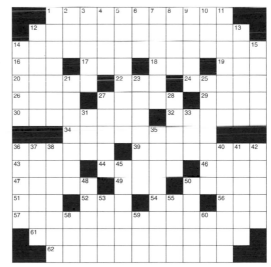

by Ned White

158 ⭐ ⭐ ⭐

ACROSS

1 Things millions of people have received in history?: Abbr.
4 Snap
15 Dieter's beef?
16 Foreigner hit in the musical film "Rock of Ages"
17 ___ poco (soon: It.)
18 Western way
19 Guy
21 Youngest player to qualify for an L.P.G.A. tour event
22 Ain't fixed?
23 Ticket number?
24 Lock combinations?
25 Jewish community org.
26 Running back's target
27 Five minutes in a campaign itinerary, maybe
29 Physics class subj.
30 Chestnut, say
31 2013 Spike Jonze love story
34 Piece in a fianchetto opening
36 Squalid
38 Yo-yo
39 Play with someone else's toy?
43 "Check it out!," in Chihuahua
44 Induces a shudder in
45 Hominy makers extract it
46 One attached to a handle
48 Decks
49 Something a baton carrier might pick up
50 ___ passu (on equal footing)
51 Head, for short
52 This point forward
53 Sri Lankan export

56 Day of the week of the great stock market crash, Oct. 29, 1929
57 It once had many satellites in its orbit
58 Prefix with -gram
59 Prized cuts
60 Nutritional inits.

DOWN

1 Biblical figure famously painted nude by Rembrandt
2 Certain temple locale
3 Not likely to blush
4 Steep-sided inlet
5 It may be on the line
6 Nickname on old political buttons
7 Watchmaker's cleaning tool
8 Threesome needed in Wagner's "Ring" cycle
9 Bar ___
10 Call routing abbr.
11 Peewee
12 Useful item if you 39-Across
13 "Three Sisters" sister
14 Fool
20 Tree with burs
24 Shipping choice
25 Protest vehemently
27 Low-priced American vodka known affectionately (and ironically) as "Russia's finest"
28 Brewers' hot spots
31 Music genre of Poison and Guns N' Roses
32 Poet arrested for treason in 1945

33 Golden Globes nominee who was a Golden Gloves boxer
35 River through Silesia
37 Reddish remnant
40 Quit working
41 Austrian neighbor
42 "___ alive!"
44 Curb
46 Health store snack ingredient
47 "Inside the Actors Studio" channel
49 Nancy Drew never left hers behind
50 Honeycomb maker
51 "I'm game"
52 Left or right, say
54 "No kiddin'!"
55 "The Power to Surprise" sloganeer

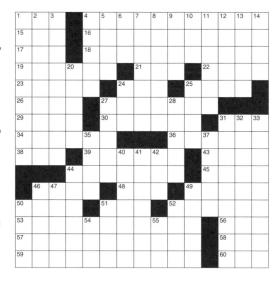

by Doug Peterson and Brad Wilber

ACROSS

1 Bivouac, maybe
9 Presses
14 Classic parental advice to bored children
16 Needle
17 Line of suits?
18 1970s NBC courtroom drama
19 Tacoma-to-Spokane dir.
20 Lupin of fiction
22 Scheming
23 ___ finger
26 Bond phrase
27 20-Across, e.g., informally
28 Gramps, to Günter
30 Wise
31 Standard offspring
32 Wordsworth or Coleridge
35 String bean's opposite
36 Phrase from Virgil appropriate for Valentine's Day
38 Favorites
39 Handy work in a theater?
40 Gifts of flowers
41 Carly ___ Jepsen, singer with the 2012 album "Kiss"
42 Yamaguchi's 1992 Olympics rival
43 Agent of psychedelic therapy
44 Unhinged
46 Pig leader?
50 Spanish name suffix
51 Dr. Seuss title character
53 Liquor letters
54 ___ Vedra Beach, Fla.
56 Entrepreneur who's well-supplied?
59 Full-length

60 Going nowhere
61 Cold forecast
62 "Clever thinking!"

DOWN

1 Adrien of cosmetics
2 Valuable chess piece, to Juan Carlos
3 Like horses
4 P.G.A. stat
5 Cool ___
6 Magical opener
7 Fate personified, in mythology
8 Delivers a romantic Valentine's Day surprise, maybe
9 Total
10 Root word?
11 TV listings info
12 Forever
13 Informal goodbye
15 "Don't stop now!"

21 Quiet break
24 Sticks figures?
25 Building materials?
29 Base letters
31 Home of Lafayette College
32 It was used to make the first compass
33 Dodger's talent
34 Policing an area
35 Broods
36 Fictional island with a small population
37 Prefix with -graph
41 Paris's ___ La Fayette
44 Some U.N. votes
45 Skateboarding trick used to leap over obstacles
47 Like Humpty Dumpty
48 Me.-to-Fla. route

49 The Friendly Islands
52 First name in blues
55 Wine container
57 "All the same . . ."
58 ___ de guerre

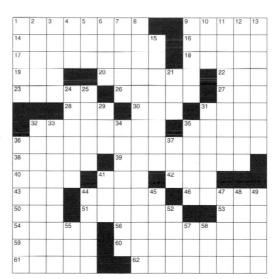

by Bruce Haight

160

ACROSS

1 Position papers?
10 Joneses
15 Vanity case?
16 When Epifanía is celebrated
17 Picayune
18 Not barred
19 Low prime, in Paris
20 Newfoundland, in Naples and Nogales
22 Grp. that suspended Honduras from 2009 to '11
24 Messages using Stickies, say
25 Certain guy "ISO" someone
28 Emmy-nominated show every year from 2006 to '09
32 Suffix with 18-Across
33 Just-once link
35 Beta testers, e.g.
36 Steely Dan's title liar
37 One blowing up a lottery machine?
38 Prozac alternative
39 Winnebago relative
40 Odds and ends
41 Clan female
42 Mexican president Enrique ___ Nieto
43 Clear
44 Crane settings
46 Van follower, often
47 Japanese guitar brand
49 Toy type, for short
51 Flippers, e.g.
55 Members of a joint task force?
59 "It's ___ wind . . ."
60 Dole
62 Green with five Grammys

63 Writer of the graphic novel "Watchmen"
64 Home to the Villa Hügel
65 Outdoor contemplation location

DOWN

1 Didn't spoil
2 Sun or stress
3 MSG ingredient?
4 Certain DNA test
5 Follows a physical request?
6 ___ vez más (over again: Sp.)
7 Photoshop addition
8 Mention on Yelp, say
9 Aspire PC maker
10 Tycoon Stanford
11 Bridge opening option, briefly
12 Managed to get through
13 Where to read a plot summary?
14 Totally out
21 Overnight activity
23 Iconic "Seinfeld" role
25 Eighth-century Apostle of Germany
26 Old collar stiffeners
27 Engagement parties?
29 Company that added four letters to its name in 1997
30 Sides in a classic battle
31 Longtime Cincinnati Pops conductor Kunzel
34 Pavement caution
36 One of a silent force?

44 Longtime name in banking
45 Its seat is Santa Rosa
48 Lawyer on "Ally McBeal"
50 No modest abode
52 2009 Grammy winner for "Make It Mine"
53 Farm block
54 "Mr. Mom" director Dragoti
56 Cross
57 Purpose of many a shot
58 Old carbine
61 End to end?

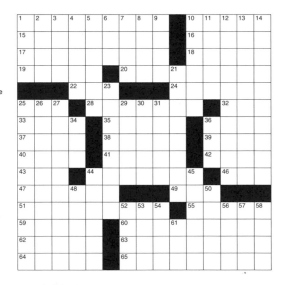

by Julian Lim

ACROSS

1 Freight hopper
6 Much-hailed group
10 Pretreater target
14 Slab strengthener
15 Days long gone
16 End of an Asian capital's name
17 Queen's Chapel designer ___ Jones
18 Stamp act?
20 Like some unhealthy relationships
22 Not so normal
23 Be cognizant of
24 Lamebrain
26 Certain letter attachment
27 Unpleasantly surprised
29 ___ Altos, Calif.
30 Provider of early projections
34 Catchphrase that encourages extravagance
35 Sky hooks?
36 "___ fly through the air with the greatest of ease"
37 DQ offerings
38 Worker who handles your case?
42 Originate
43 With this, you'll probably manage
46 Squared away
48 Panhandler, of a sort?
50 They run out of clothing
52 Stand
53 Fill-in
54 Make cuts, say
55 It would "make other cars seem ordinary," per ads
56 Brewery apparatus
57 Breaks down
58 Teammate of Robinson

DOWN

1 Many folk bands
2 Girl's name that means "born again"
3 Stand
4 Holiday travelers?
5 One with a thing for laughter?
6 Spiral-shaped particle accelerators
7 1998 purchaser of Netscape
8 Head piece?
9 Bob in the Songwriters Hall of Fame
10 Bandies words
11 Swingers
12 Another time
13 18th-century Hapsburg monarch Maria
19 Las Vegas block?
21 Put forward

25 Needs
27 Snarky comments
28 Overbearing types
30 Buildings often segregated by floor
31 Reserved
32 Worker also known as a cordwainer
33 Scams
34 Leaves from the Orient
35 Big name in outdoor art
39 Made slow progress
40 Nabokov's longest novel
41 Furry toys
43 Canadian ranger
44 Rounded items?
45 Tarsus location
47 Change
49 Get behind something?
51 Lightly tease

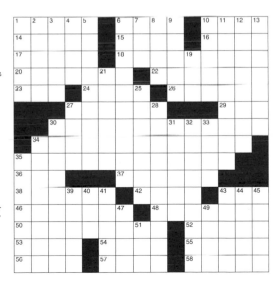

by Patrick Berry

ACROSS

1 Ones who think things are good as gold?
11 Like metals used by 1-Across
15 Feared sight on the Spanish Main
16 Obama's favorite character on "The Wire"
17 Like some parents
18 Big long-distance carrier?
19 Coastal fish consumers
20 Much may follow it
21 Composer of the opera "Rusalka"
23 Deal with
25 People might pass for them, for short
27 High line in the Middle East
28 Small cell
30 Brand of body washes
32 Grp. with the Office of Iraq Analysis
33 Art that uses curse words?
37 Volt-ampere
38 Takes the plunge
39 Peak transmission setting of old?
41 Declines, with "out"
42 Fall apart
44 Score abbr.
45 First name of Woodstock's last performer
46 Split second?
47 Golden, in Granada
49 Hit with skits, for short
51 Get off the drive, say
55 No-gooder
57 2012 baseball All-Star Kinsler
59 Some plans for the future, briefly
60 Rackets

61 High spirits?
64 Land capturer, in literature
65 "Bummer"
66 Tied
67 Whip wielder

DOWN

1 Vaulted areas
2 Tall order at a British pub
3 Big picker-upper?
4 Frequent Monet subjects
5 Projection in the air, for short
6 Kind of bust
7 "___ a man in Reno" ("Folsom Prison Blues" lyric)
8 Well-trained boxer, maybe
9 Punk rocker Armstrong with a 2012 Grammy

10 Reached 100, say
11 Near to one's heart
12 First drink ever ordered by James Bond
13 Do-gooder
14 Composer called a "gymnopédiste"
22 Woe, in Yiddish
24 Symbols of might
26 Scuzz
29 Facebook connections in Florence?
31 Start sputtering, say
33 Aid in fast networking
34 One getting messages by word of mouth?
35 Site of the 1992 Republican National Convention
36 Very small (and very important) matter
37 Like some missed field goals

40 Weapon in "The Mikado"
43 Telejournalist's item
45 Part of many a training regimen
48 Plant in subsequent seasons
50 "Swing Shift" Oscar nominee
52 In the back
53 Game stew
54 Locale of London Stansted Airport
56 "Good ___ A'mighty!"
58 Side in an Indian restaurant
62 Certain sorority chapter
63 Tapping grp.

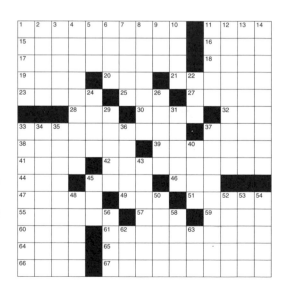

by Evan Birnholz

ACROSS

1 Modern-day locale of ancient Nineveh
5 People down under?
11 Exceeds the speed limit?
14 Exceed the speed limit, maybe
15 Company with an Energy Boost line
16 Minim
17 Terse admission
18 It'll keep a roof over your head
20 Fall, in a way
21 Like a good lookout
22 Bouillabaisse seasoning
23 They soar at the opera
25 When to do a pressing job
26 Mitochondrion-made material, briefly
27 Back, to a shellback
29 Investments since 1975
38 What a tropical tourist definitely doesn't want to bring home
39 It helps you let go
40 Many of them play at the Olympics
41 Some Windows systems
42 Shakespeare sonnet mentioning Philomel's mournful hymns
43 Title for Liszt
46 Gigantic
52 Text with Numbers
54 Patent
55 Carlito's way
56 Street view
58 First name in popular shorts
59 Bond bit
60 Coors Field player
61 Almost never

62 Really dirty
63 Try again
64 Salk Institute architect Louis

DOWN

1 From Galway, say
2 Cuts into a pizza, often
3 Sailing through
4 Last thing seen by a proof reader?
5 Some Wall Street contracts
6 Go on ___
7 Exist abroad?
8 Applies polish to?
9 Flew
10 Squad cmdr.
11 R&B group with the 1972 hit "Back Stabbers," with "the"
12 Proselytizers push it

13 Pickle, e.g.
19 Finder's query
21 Like some helmets and shields
24 Couldn't hit pitches
27 Singer who's a Backstreet Boy's brother
28 Sir James Galway, e.g.
29 Dodgers' foes
30 Hindu hero
31 Legions
32 Suffix with Edward
33 It's around 6 on the Mohs scale
34 "The Lion King" lion
35 Get to
36 "Let me ___!"
37 Philatelic goals
43 When the first dogwatch ends
44 It's not a cheap shot

45 Bombers' locale
46 Spelunker's aid
47 Conjure
48 City with major avenues named Cincinnati and Columbus
49 First name among socialites
50 It means nothing
51 All gone
53 Mann's man
57 Ill-wisher
58 Thai pan

by Martin Ashwood-Smith

ACROSS

1 1987 #1 hit with the line "Yo no soy marinero, soy capitán"
8 Throwback
15 Samsung Galaxy Note rival
16 Go-ahead for un hombre
17 Forward to some followers
18 Curt chat closing
19 Where Melville's Billy Budd went
20 Hubble sighting
22 Jesse Jackson, for one: Abbr.
24 Like some double-deckers
28 One's own worst critic?
32 Put off
34 Dayton-to-Toledo dir.
35 Subjected to venomous attacks?
38 Four roods
40 Pawnbroker, in slang
41 Travel safety grp.
42 Modern device seen on a bridge
45 L.A. law figure
46 Take a little hair off, maybe
47 To date
49 Den delivery
52 Beats by ___ (brand of audio equipment)
53 One picking up speed, say?
55 They're game
59 Sack dress?
63 Dish often served with a tamarind sauce
65 Disc protector
66 Carrier with a pink logo
67 Like some stockings
68 If it's repeated, it's nothing new

DOWN

1 Turkey tip?
2 Burlesques
3 Moderate
4 Norton Antivirus target
5 Tina Turner's real middle name
6 Welcome message to international travelers
7 Danza, e.g.
8 Invite to one's penthouse
9 Proof of purchase
10 Ghanaian region known for gold and cocoa
11 Needle or nettle
12 Having five sharps
13 ___ milk
14 III, in Rome
21 Novel groups?
23 They make quick admissions decisions, for short
25 Ink
26 Come by
27 Openly admitted, as in court
28 They sometimes lead to runs
29 Straighten out
30 Italian brewer since 1846
31 Blood members, e.g.
33 Fund
36 Spirit
37 Emmy category, informally
39 Food brand originally called Froffles
43 Photog
44 Cry with a salute
48 Ignored
50 Fade out
51 Like loose stones
54 Decides
56 ___ Drive, thoroughfare by the Lincoln Memorial in Washington
57 Modern posting locale
58 Produced stories
59 .doc alternative
60 Bird: Prefix
61 The Clintons' degs.
62 Cousin of "verdammt"
64 Suffix with official or fan

by Ian Livengood and J.A.S.A. Crossword Class

ACROSS

1 Cause for squirming
9 Container for Rip Van Winkle
15 TV show that debuted on 11/3/93 (and start of a parent's distressed cry?)
16 Furnishing in many a tearoom
17 Officer's "gift"
18 Lemony, for example
19 Roles, metaphorically
20 ___' Pea
22 "The king of terrors," per Job 18
23 Anklebones
25 In the company of
27 Guilty pleasure?
31 Poetic member of a Greek nonet
32 Having a gaping hole, say
33 Org. in "Breaking Bad"
36 Setting for "The Shining"
37 Bogart role
39 TV show that debuted on 9/22/04 (middle of the cry)
40 Corporate giant co-founded by Thomas Watson
41 Jackie with acting chops
42 Sit on it
43 TV show that debuted on 1/5/70 (end of the cry)
47 Greek hunter trained by Chiron
49 Language that gave us "slogan," originally meaning "battle cry"
50 Dreaded sort?
51 Outside: Prefix
53 Noted septet
57 Trojan rivals

59 Transfer, as wine
61 Merino, Suffolk and Dorset
62 Like Christmas candles, typically
63 "Says who?," e.g.
64 So-so

DOWN

1 It may come with a bite
2 Pet project?
3 "Etta ___" (old comic strip)
4 Worked up
5 Turner of pages in history
6 Put on a key?
7 Isolate, somehow
8 Burnsian "ago"
9 Govt. agency that supports competition
10 Presented

11 See (to)
12 Thing often controlled by a remote
13 Drops
14 Not in Germany?
21 Ending with dog or jug
24 Flurry
26 Word on a biblical wall
27 Certain playoff game
28 Zodiac symbol
29 Requirement for special handling?
30 Swiss standard
34 To be in ancient times?
35 Subj. line alert
37 Chucklehead
38 Alexander who directed "Nebraska"
39 Guiding light

41 Pledge, e.g.
42 Literary inits.
44 Marco Rubio, for one
45 Straight
46 Will Smith flick of 2004
47 Subject of a celebration on the last Friday in April
48 Chisel
52 Lead-in to Apple
54 Trix alternative?
55 Inter ___
56 Ending with inter-
58 Retired boomer
60 Texter's "No way!"

by Matt Ginsberg

ACROSS

1 Cooler idea?
10 Home to the Great Mosque
15 It included a moonwalk
16 Spirit of St. Petersburg?
17 One stocking bars
18 West African capital
19 Old sitcom sot
20 Pimienta's partner
21 Many instant message recipients
22 "Sketches" pseudonym
23 Bad-tempered
25 Compress, as a file
26 Turn the air blue
28 Where many games can be viewed
29 Prefix with data
30 Motor problems
32 Fat-derived
34 Havana highball
37 Recite mechanically
38 Swank
40 Word before red
41 Beech house?
42 Quarter of zwölf
44 Tables in western scenes
48 Word after red
49 Like time, inexorably
51 "___ I forsook the crowded solitude": Wordsworth
52 Walters portrayer on "S.N.L."
54 Dance piece?
55 Thé addition
56 Produce sentimental notes?
57 Big-name web crawler
59 "The Asphalt Jungle" revolves around one

60 Like Francisco Goya
61 "Breaking Away" director
62 She "made a fool of everyone," in song

DOWN

1 A. J. ___, author of the best seller "The Know-It-All: One Man's Humble Quest to Become the Smartest Person in the World"
2 Director of "The 40-Year-Old Virgin" and "This Is 40"
3 Turn positive, say
4 Some Yale degs.
5 Nellie who wrote "Ten Days in a Mad-House"

6 Martini accompanier?
7 Uses a drunkometer, e.g.
8 Provençal spreads
9 100-at currency unit
10 It was run in the 1980s–'90s
11 Abbr. for the listless?
12 Tab alternative
13 Big name in allergy relief
14 It's flown in
21 ___ Anne's (pretzel maker)
23 Ultra ___
24 Quick missions?
27 Slightly biased?
29 Like some finishes
31 Hole in one on a par 5 hole
33 "No ___ is worse than bad advice": Sophocles

34 Bahrain, Bhutan or Brunei
35 Clearing
36 Popular line of footwear?
39 Endurance race, briefly
40 Cardiff Giant, e.g.
43 Cry for another piece
45 Starfish setting
46 Some opera passages
47 Parlor piece
49 Word on a restroom door
50 Loose
53 Thing twitched on "Bewitched"
55 River known for the goldfields in its basin
57 Sign on an interstate
58 "___ Tarantos" (1963 film)

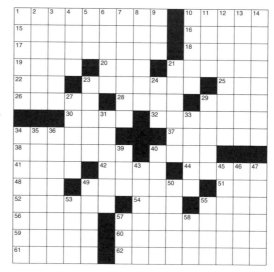

by David Steinberg

ACROSS

1 Did some above-average work
6 Doesn't just tear up
10 One way to get the beat going?
13 Master, in Mysore
14 Hostiles
16 "Well, well, well!"
17 He may be trying to unload crates
20 "Am ___ France?": King Lear
21 Jeans reinforcer
22 They're easily fleeced
23 Chinese dish eponym
24 See 39-Across
25 Magazine industry's equivalent of a Pulitzer
27 Not nixed
29 Composition of some wreaths
31 Living or dead follower
32 Yom Kippur War setting
34 Dam designer: Abbr.
35 Vet
36 Mutating, highly resistant microbe
39 Lang. in which "friends" is 24-Across
40 Start of an intermission?
41 Boo Boo Bear's co-creator
42 "___ name I love" ("America" lyric)
43 Shop spinner
44 Campus letter
45 Fence alternative
47 Old paper parts
49 Monitor option, for short
52 "___ back!"
53 Kind of training done by music majors

54 The shorter you are?
55 Tend to work without a net
58 He proclaimed "I shook up the world"
59 Gervasi who directed 2012's "Hitchcock"
60 Shake in an opera house
61 Year Charles IX was born
62 Rectangular paving stone
63 Unlikely bruiser

DOWN

1 Test pilot's protection
2 Mecca or Medina
3 1985 Ralph McInerny novel
4 Support
5 Longtime airer of "Any Questions?"
6 Place for a delivery

7 Withdrawing words
8 Withdrawing
9 Range of sizes, briefly
10 Mathematics branch associated with fractals
11 Establishing by degrees
12 Jockey Turcotte
15 Many nods
18 Biathlon need
19 Cádiz condiment
26 Twin Cities suburb
28 Jazz player Malone
30 Places for quick operations, briefly
32 Speaks to Shakespeare?
33 Not domestically
35 "In principio ___ Verbum"
37 "Tell ___ story"

38 Things to play with matches?
43 Its natives are called Loiners
46 Master's seeker's hurdle, briefly
48 Shell accessory
50 Holders of many selfies
51 With no sparkle
55 Flight for someone 8-Down
56 Small power sources
57 The Rams of the A-10 Conf.

by Alan Olschwang

ACROSS

1 Like some methods of detection
10 Winter athletes' pull-ups?
15 Without requiring scrutiny
16 Last name in the skin care industry
17 Indication that one wants to get smacked
18 Producer of "whirlybirds"
19 How the descriptions of most things usually end?
20 Cast
21 Like many taxis
22 Bathhouse square
23 N.B.A. team starting in 1988
24 A line, e.g.
27 A lines, e.g.
28 "Essays in Love" writer ___ de Botton
29 People everywhere
32 Since 2010 it's had a shield on its back
33 Buckles
34 Jack for Jacques?
35 Two or three in a row, say
37 Texas state tree
38 Prevent from having anything?
39 What cookies are often baked in
40 Stung
42 Swiss bank depositor?
43 Spare change collector
44 Spare change collectors
45 Vineyard, in Vichy
48 Song of exultation
49 Sexy
51 Failed in a big way
52 Seaweed used in home brewing
53 Some men's sizes
54 One controlling drones

DOWN

1 Relative of a haddock
2 Uplifting company?
3 Bad way to finish
4 Classic two-seaters
5 Blissful
6 Without incident, say
7 Lacking a point
8 A teller might update it: Abbr.
9 Connection between Obama and Robinson?
10 Member of the marmoset family
11 Cold discomfort, of sorts
12 Poppycock
13 Found new tenants for
14 Polar bearers?
21 They're often accompanied by "Hava Nagila"
22 Penalty for some overly prolific posters
23 Rope and dope sources
24 Body bags?
25 Title 54-Across of film
26 Skin behind a slip, perhaps
27 Less likely to have waffles
29 Like supervillains
30 Grape, Cherry or Strawberry lead-in
31 A lot of the time?
33 Need for life
36 Staples of Marvel Comics
37 Cayenne producer
39 Velvety pink
40 Annual winter honoree, briefly
41 Modern two-seater
42 Murphy of "To Hell and Back"
44 "Zzz" inducer
45 Something to buy into
46 Device
47 Miracle on Ice loser of '80
49 Crab house accessory
50 "___ Wed" (2007 Erica Durance movie)

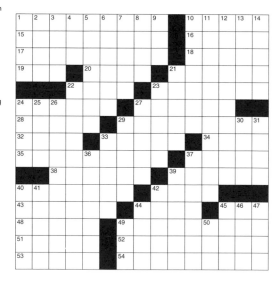

by Ed Sessa

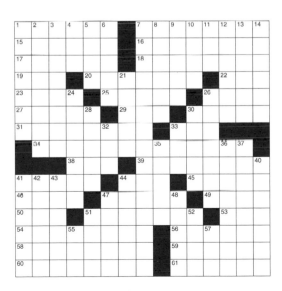

★ ★ ★ **169**

ACROSS

1 Spa supplies
7 Sir Henry ___, pioneer in steelmaking
15 Sulky
16 Getting-off point
17 Household
18 Drink made with tequila, rum, vodka, gin, bourbon, triple sec, sweet-and-sour mix and Coke
19 Contractor's fig.
20 Edward who was dubbed "The Dark Prophet" by Time magazine
22 Invoice nos.
23 Actor/director Schreiber
25 Standouts
26 2014's "The ___ Movie"
27 Contribute
29 Mauna ___
30 Figure skater Kadavy
31 Breaks away from a defender
33 Feature of many a Duchamp work
34 Follow every rule
38 N.B.A.'s Gibson
39 Became tiresome
41 Formal dress option
44 Bush beast, briefly
45 "A Midsummer Night's Scream" author
46 What can help you toward a peak performance?
47 Barbed spears for fishing
49 Classic work in Old Norse
50 Many Ph.D. candidates
51 Assesses
53 End: Abbr.
54 One learning how to refine oils?
56 ___ Mouse
58 Renaissance woodwind
59 Fasts, perhaps
60 Nonviable
61 Engage in horseplay

DOWN

1 Skype annoyance
2 Very unbalanced
3 Had the itch
4 Sustainable practices grp.
5 Durability
6 Anagram of "notes," appropriately
7 Funny or Die web series hosted by Zach Galifianakis
8 Semicircular recess in Roman architecture
9 High rolls
10 Pollster Greenberg
11 High rollers
12 Big name in colonial Massachusetts
13 Cabinet department
14 "The natural organ of truth": C. S. Lewis
21 Well-pitched
24 Tourist
26 1961 Michelangelo Antonioni drama
28 Away from
30 High rollers' rollers
32 Popular sandwich, informally
33 ___ usual
35 Dances onstage
36 "Hmm, ya got me"
37 More sympathetic
40 Most smart
41 Paper-clip, say
42 Pizza chain since 1956
43 Raise by digging
44 Some T.S.A. confiscations
47 Enemy of Cobra
48 Shrub that produces a crimson-colored spice
51 Comic Mort
52 Kind of bread
55 Abbr. on a letter to Paris, maybe
57 National Adoption Mo.

by Brendan Emmett Quigley

ACROSS

1 Passed in a blur, say
7 Develops gradually
15 Smoking
16 Change-making
17 Where to look for self-growth
18 Obsolescent storage device
19 Historic first name in W.W. II
20 Locale of three presidential libraries
21 Fried
22 One often behind bars
24 Ditch
25 Doesn't carry on
26 Oxygen's lack
27 Rescuer of Princess Peach
28 Near: Fr.
29 Churchyard gravedigger
30 Signs of things to come
34 Truckloads
35 Hard to grasp
36 Remains after the aging process
37 Opposite of 28-Down
38 Santa's reindeer, e.g.
39 Some sharp words
43 Lou's "La Bamba" co-star
44 Concord concoction
46 Many a "Meet the Press" guest, informally
47 Swindler's moola
48 Hiked
49 Former panelist on "The View" in 2007
51 Many a worker at Union Pacific headquarters
52 Like Enterprise vehicles

53 Fired up?
54 Best, as friends
55 One of Leakey's "Trimates"

DOWN

1 Decorated band along a wall
2 "Reality leaves a lot to the imagination" speaker
3 He directed Bela Lugosi in "Bride of the Monster"
4 High rollers, in casino lingo
5 Cheap, shoddy merchandise
6 Financial statement abbr.
7 Outdoor wedding settings
8 Alchemist's offering
9 Green party V.I.P.?

10 Three Stooges creator Healy and others
11 Concourse abbr.
12 Personalize for
13 Picture
14 Troopers' toppers
20 Almanac info
23 Large pack
24 Get set to take off
27 What an 18-Across's capacity is measured in, briefly
28 Opposite of 37-Across
29 Message sometimes written below "F"
30 Regular embarkation location
31 Series starter
32 Left
33 "¿___ se habla español?"
34 Did an entrechat

36 Flier
38 Voice lesson subjects
39 Protection for flowers in bud
40 Socially dominant sorts
41 Dirty rat
42 Biggest city on the smallest continent
44 Diving bird
45 Mammoth
47 Cookout irritant
50 ___ root (math quantity)
51 Bungler

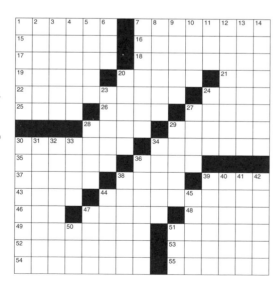

by Greg Johnson

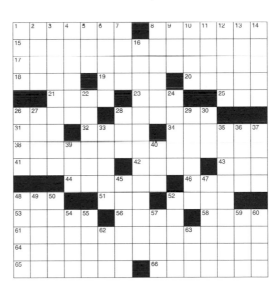

ACROSS

1 Those who respond to pickup lines?
8 Drags
15 Central Florida daily
17 Part-time jobs for college students, say
18 Disbelieving, maybe
19 Major-leaguer from Osaka who threw two no-hitters
20 Trap
21 Haddock relatives
23 Constellation described by Ptolemy
25 Part of 56-Across: Abbr.
26 Conductor with a star on the Hollywood Walk of Fame
28 "A Chorus Line" lyricist Ed
31 Iran's Ayatollah ___ Khamenei
32 Year the Angels won the World Series
34 Brit's cry of surprise
38 See 16-Down
41 Standard
42 Extreme piques
43 "I'll ___"
44 Old letter opener: Abbr.
46 Upper regions of space
48 Org. of which Tom Hanks is a member
51 Mauna ___
52 Shaving brand
53 Slip preventer
56 Terminal announcements, for short
58 Writer William
61 Mobile creator
64 Go mad
65 Demanded immediate action from
66 Superlatively bouncy

DOWN

1 ___ Nostra
2 Aligned, after "in"
3 Relatively low-risk investments
4 Actress for whom a neckline is named
5 ___ 500
6 Unspoiled places
7 Meh
8 First of two pictures
9 Start to color?
10 Range parts: Abbr.
11 Symbols of timidity
12 Modern message
13 Fictional teller of tales
14 Wasn't alert
16 Hijackers who captured 38-Across
22 "What's the ___?"
24 First name in '60s radicalism
26 Old club
27 Flourish
28 Connected people
29 Ready
30 Nothing
33 Eastern European capital of 2 million
35 Screw up
36 Sport with automated scoring
37 River of W.W. I
39 Dickens boy
40 Ballpark dingers: Abbr.
45 Positioned well
47 English hat similar to a fedora
48 Where flakes may build up
49 ___ nothing
50 Simple sorts
52 Musical grp.
54 Fires
55 Western setting for artisans
57 They may be heavy or open
59 Bee ___
60 Formerly, old-style
62 Nautical heading: Abbr.
63 Part of 56-Across: Abbr.

by David J. Kahn

172

ACROSS

1 It's made from an ear and put in the mouth
12 Highlander's accessory
15 1967 hit by the Hollies
16 One may have a full body
17 Copied the page?
18 They often land next to queens: Abbr.
19 Prefix with flop
20 They often land next to queens
22 Cross quality
23 Move a whole lot
25 Backward
26 Fame
29 Spice stores?
31 Enigmatic
34 Nanny, in Nanjing
35 Question after a surprising claim
36 Party bowlful
37 Supply one's moving address?
38 Network point
39 Now whole
41 Orphaned lion of literature
42 Knit at a social function?
43 Brownie alternative
45 "Veep" airer
46 Pinch-hitter
49 Smallest member of the Council of Europe
52 See 7-Down
53 Withdraw
54 It's between Buda and Pest
57 After
58 Forum setting
59 180
60 Target of a spy

DOWN

1 Herder from Wales
2 Live warning?
3 Voice lesson topic
4 Bulldogs play in it: Abbr.
5 86
6 Rush target
7 With 52-Across, something in a gray area
8 Himalayan production
9 Golfer Aoki
10 Ayn Rand, e.g.
11 Higher-up?
12 Target
13 Every second
14 Jam
21 Product of some decay
23 O's is one more than N's
24 Comb composition
26 Like some pitches
27 Orders
28 Locals call it the "Big O"
30 Where spades may be laid down
31 End of a song often sung by inebriated people
32 Shark's place
33 Polar Bear Provincial Park borders it
37 Minestrone ingredient
39 Repetitive
40 Bunch
44 Self-congratulatory cries
46 Not just wolf down
47 "I'd love to help"
48 Part of Che Guevara's attire
49 Junior in 12 Pro Bowls
50 Highlander of old
51 Period sans soleil
52 Magazine fig.
55 Half of nine?
56 U.S.P.S. assignment

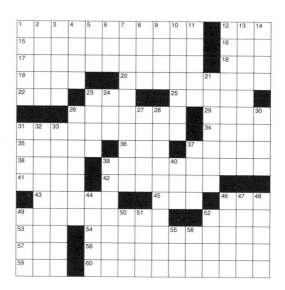

by Barry C. Silk

ACROSS

1 Romania and Bulgaria, once
16 Frank Loesser show tune
17 It might cover an oil spill
18 Doing the rounds?
19 Sporting goods chain with the slogan "Get outside yourself"
20 Potsdam pronoun
21 Peculiar: Prefix
22 Start-up helper: Abbr.
24 Puce at Pompano Park
26 Shoving matches?
29 Relative of one tulipe
31 "Frasier" role
33 Match cry
34 Pooh-pooh
38 "You're probably right"
40 Mojo
41 Sister co. of Virgin
42 Middle square, maybe
43 Sea of ___ (view from Crimea's eastern coast)
45 Chart, in Cádiz
48 Sol mates?
50 Frost-covered
52 Crook's place
54 Many activists' concerns: Abbr.
56 One given up for good?
61 "What a sight for sore eyes!"
62 Its islands are not surrounded by water
63 Unease

DOWN

1 Some defensive weapons, in brief
2 "Love and Death on Long Island" novelist Gilbert
3 Lead-tin alloys
4 Unmarried, say
5 Activist Guinier
6 Some claims
7 "Cool, dude"
8 Many a backpacker, at night
9 62-Across option north of the border
10 Go a couple of rounds
11 Preweighed, in a way
12 Very rarely heard instruments
13 Long shift, perhaps
14 Ending to prefer?
15 Young or old follower
23 Rich person's suffix?
25 Alternative to .net
27 Rural parents
28 Cry of pleased surprise
30 Songwriters Hall of Fame member who wrote "April Love"
32 Get-up-and-go
34 Doo-wop syllable
35 Body part detecting odeurs
36 One getting rid of possessions?
37 "Third Watch" actress Texada
39 Hester Prynne wore one
44 Labor Day arrivals, e.g.
46 Conf. whose membership increased by two in 2011
47 Melodic
49 Not leave the house
51 Prefix with second
53 Sticks in the brig?
55 Utah senator who co-sponsored a tariff act
56 Potential serial material
57 "___ in Full" (Tom Wolfe novel)
58 Security figure: Abbr.
59 Abrupt transition
60 Some picnic supplies

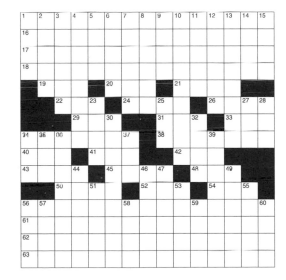

by Martin Ashwood-Smith and Joe Krozel

174

ACROSS

1 "That's crazy, dude!"
5 Drive to drink, e.g.
15 It's best to stay out of its way
16 Debut Peter Tosh album, and a rallying cry for pot smokers
17 Scheme for the start of a sonnet
18 Opinion leader?
19 Pioneer of New Journalism
21 "r u there?," e.g.
22 Unpolished pro?
23 Stationary
24 Cro-Magnon orphan of literature
25 Head turner
26 Rihanna or Sharon Stone
28 Big name in late-night TV
29 See 25-Down
30 Dandy
31 Ripped
32 U.S. Open champion whose last name is a toy
34 Artist and chess player who said "While all artists are not chess players, all chess players are artists"
38 The end?
39 It takes time to cure
40 McDonald's denial
41 The end
44 It involves hand-to-hand coordination
46 Souls
47 Wish-Bone alternative
48 Lodging portmanteau
49 1967 Calder Trophy winner at age 18
50 ___ Epstein, baseball V.I.P. known as "Boy Wonder"
51 Last name in "Star Wars"

52 Singer with the 1996 triple-platinum album "Tidal"
55 Panache
56 Where Jason Kidd played college hoops
57 Rap's ___ Yang Twins
58 1996 Rhett Akins country hit
59 Store whose shoe department has its own ZIP code (10022-SHOE)

DOWN

1 "Yes?"
2 Certain chili
3 Third degree for a third degree?
4 One may prefer them to blondes
5 Bit of ballet instruction
6 Like Tickle Me Elmo
7 "My treat"
8 Parent company?
9 Internet traffic statistics company
10 Pleasant cadence
11 Strong arm
12 Joint
13 Buckle
14 Forever in the past?
20 Up-to-date
24 Like some seamen
25 With 29-Across, nest egg choice
27 Cockerdoodle, e.g.
28 "Oh goody!"
31 Clipped
33 Young foxes
34 Certain gumdrops
35 It was home to two Wonders of the Ancient World
36 Earn a load of money, in modern lingo
37 Some kitchen detritus
39 Impressive range

41 Tool
42 Fortify
43 Oxygen user
44 Imitated chicks
45 Carnival items served with chili
47 Yellow-brown shade
50 Fictional home five miles from Jonesboro
51 A through G
53 Duck Hunt platform, briefly
54 Historical figure a.k.a. Marse Robert

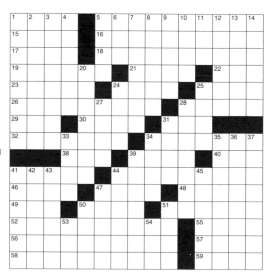

by Ashton Anderson and James Mulhern

ACROSS

1 Retreat
9 "3 O'Clock Blues" hitmaker, 1952
15 "Obviously . . ."
16 Uses, as a chaise
17 Particle ejected from an atom during ionization
18 Home of Bwindi Impenetrable National Park
19 "Star Wars" villain name
20 Identify
21 Celebration of the arrival of spring
22 Blew out
24 Eastern hereditary title
26 Specks
27 Things worn at home?
31 Like some details
32 Maddeningly surreal
33 "Girls" home
34 Some adoption candidates
35 Address found online
36 Ones unlikely to drag their feet
38 ___ Ruess, lead singer of Fun
39 Weep
40 Order of ancient Greeks
41 There might be a battery of them
42 Rid (of)
43 Matt's onetime "Today" co-host
46 Runs the show, for short
47 Like prosciutto
48 Way over the top
50 Head of the Catholic Church when Luther's "95 Theses" was posted

53 Daddy Warbucks's henchman
54 "Gracious me!"
55 Completely safe, as a proposition
56 Lecture series with well over a billion views

DOWN

1 Century starter?
2 Something in that vein?
3 Line outside a club, maybe
4 Frode
5 Leaves of grass
6 Ran
7 High-level appointee
8 It has all the answers
9 Alternative to cords
10 Bowls, e.g.
11 Mauna ___
12 ". . . and who ___?"
13 Network connection
14 Part of a moving cloud
20 Foe of the Vikings
22 Tour parts
23 Bigwig
24 High beams
25 Orders in a restaurant
27 Millionaires and billionaires
28 Theodore Roosevelt's domestic program
29 Rapper ___ Blow
30 Elite
32 Part of a TV archive
34 Model introduced in the 1990s
37 Target of a 1972 ban
38 "Breakfast at Tiffany's," for one
40 Plain-spoken
42 Took in

43 Routing aid: Abbr.
44 Big Apple neighborhood next to the Bowery
45 "Christians Awake," e.g.
47 Semaphore signals, e.g.
49 Asian path
50 Hog-roasting locale
51 Planet whose inhabitants age backward
52 Pair of Dos Equis

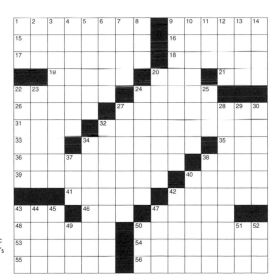

by Peter Wentz

ACROSS

1 Popularity boost due to a certain TV endorsement
12 Rebel in a beret
15 "A thousand pardons"
16 Athlete in a shell
17 Diet, e.g.
18 "Collages" novelist, 1964
19 Arab spring?
20 Mexicans roll them
21 Composers of some rhapsodies
23 Business of 41-Down: Abbr.
24 Wear for Hu Jintao
25 Mythical abode of heroes slain in battle
29 "Each of us bears his own Hell" writer
30 Part of a drag outfit
31 Relatives of black holes
34 Cousin of an agave
35 Dispatch
36 To you, in Toulouse
37 Place for rank-and-filers in the House of Commons
39 Ozone menace
40 Pungent panini ingredient
41 Gets started
42 They often provide illumination in galleries
44 Arm with many vessels, maybe
45 Like angels
46 Palooka
47 Throws for a loop
51 Shakespeare sonnet that begins "So am I as the rich, whose blessed key"
52 Parts of some alarms

55 Fleece
56 White whale's whereabouts
57 Bath setting: Abbr.
58 People sampling mushrooms, say

DOWN

1 Druid, e.g.
2 Spanning
3 Theme of several theme parks
4 Piltdown man, say
5 Dot-dot-dot
6 Casualty of the Battle of Roncesvalles
7 Old dynasts
8 Some spam senders
9 The Negro R. runs through it
10 "Fantasy Island" host
11 Stray mongrels
12 Chancellery settings

13 Where Nord, Nord-Est and Nord-Ouest are departments
14 Arp contemporary
22 "Interesting . . . but museum-worthy?"
23 Org. whose logo has an eagle and scales
24 Opposite of gloom
25 King of Kings
26 1987 Lionel Richie hit
27 21st-century pastime for treasure hunters
28 Leonov who was the first man to walk in space
29 Balboa's first name
31 Alternative to shoots?
32 A cube has one
33 ___-Soviet

35 Like many a purple-tinged moorland
38 "Fur Traders Descending the Missouri" painter, 1845
39 Creator of "30 Rock"
41 Its parent is Liberty Mutual
42 Opposite of agitato
43 Pizza topping
44 Pizza topping
46 Bart and Lisa's bus driver
47 Sacs studied by 58-Across
48 Parts of a sob story
49 Latin 101 word
50 Phishing loot: Abbr.
53 Orange's org.
54 Periodic dairy aisle offering

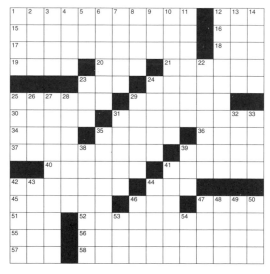

by Mel Rosen

ACROSS

1 "Definitely, dawg!"
10 Art enabled
15 Reading room
16 Timeline segment
17 Reward for knocking 'em dead
18 Moving supply
19 Bare peak
20 Before retitling: Abbr.
21 "It"
22 Drop
24 Name dropper's phrase
26 Cousin of -kin or -let
27 Unpaid babysitters, maybe
29 "Property Virgins" cable channel
30 "Out!"
31 It's often described by horses
33 Regard
34 "And ___ the field the road runs by": Tennyson
35 Common loss after a breakup
37 Rush
39 Clipper feature
41 It can be painful to pick up
43 Radio racket
46 Parentheses, e.g.
47 Slight
49 Subject of the 2011 book "The Rogue"
50 Grp. seeking to improve No Child Left Behind
51 "Pensées" philosopher
53 It might mean "hello" or "goodbye" to a driver
54 Woodchuck, e.g.
56 Bradley with five stars
58 Musician who co-founded Nutopia

59 Popular type option
60 "The Pentagon Papers" Emmy nominee
62 Verbal equivalent of a shrug
63 Something awful
64 A couple of rounds in a toaster?
65 Rain forest, e.g.

DOWN

1 Subtle trick
2 Easy chair accompanier
3 Philanthropic mantra
4 Blue symbol of Delaware
5 Prefix with Germanic
6 The Congolese franc replaced it
7 Crest

8 What's often on wheels in an airport
9 Some punk
10 Parts of many chamber groups
11 Pacific port
12 Visually uninspiring
13 15-Across frequenter, maybe
14 "Add ___ a tiger's chaudron, / For the ingredients of our cauldron": Shak.
21 "No more guesses?"
23 Blots
25 Astronomical distance: Abbr.
28 It's associated with Chris Rock and 30 Rock
30 Occupy
32 Destroys insidiously
36 Pales
38 More than nod

39 Artificial
40 Relative of a throw
42 Country
44 Hero-worship
45 Learn to teach?
48 Capital on the Niger
51 Some preppy wear
52 Left Turn Only and others
55 A leader and follower?
57 A little blue
60 It can make you squiffy
61 Monopoly quartet: Abbr.

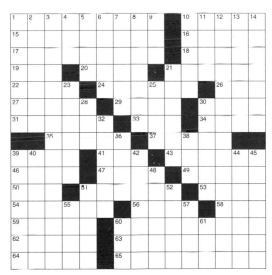

by James Mulhern

178 ★★★

ACROSS

1 Simpler
16 Sequential
17 Harry Potter series part
18 Can't take
19 One of a familiar septet
20 Rocks on the Rhein?
21 Gabriel García Márquez's "Cien ___ de Soledad"
22 Weapon in old hand-to-hand combat
23 Figures in "Teutonic Mythology"
25 "Vous êtes ___"
26 Alaska's ___ Fjords National Park
27 Candy pioneer H. B. ___
28 Abbr. in many a military title
29 Small skillet
31 Abbr. before a date
32 Big Chicago-based franchiser
33 1958–'61 political alliance: Abbr.
35 March on Washington grp.
38 Dirgelike
42 20-Across in English
45 Blush
47 Not a good person to entrust with secrets, informally
48 And moreover
49 Answer (for)
50 Goya figure
51 Part of a plowing harness
52 Problem for Poirot
53 Quickly imagine?
55 Swiss city that borders France and Germany
56 Spotless

59 Boos, e.g.
60 "Different strokes for different folks"

DOWN

1 Either of two Holy Roman emperors
2 Better
3 "Get cracking!"
4 White-bearded types
5 Some budget planners, for short
6 Gambling inits.
7 Putting one's cards on the table, in a way
8 Package for sale, say
9 Principal port of Syria
10 "___ out?"
11 Strongbox
12 Raiding grp.

13 Robin Hood and his Merry Men
14 Otherworldly in the extreme
15 Decent
22 "Portraits at the Stock Exchange" artist
24 Look that's not liked
26 ___ party
30 ___ York
32 Seattle's Space Needle or St. Louis's Gateway Arch
34 Something that often follows you
35 Greta of "The Red Violin"
36 Hardly any
37 Immediate, as relatives
39 Seeps
40 Actress in "Ferris Bueller's Day Off"
41 Decorate fancily

42 Bothered
43 Broadway hit with the song "I Wonder What the King Is Doing Tonight"
44 Telescope part
46 Mezzo-soprano Regina
51 Must
54 Blanched
55 Inexpensive writing implements
57 ___ price
58 Bad computer?

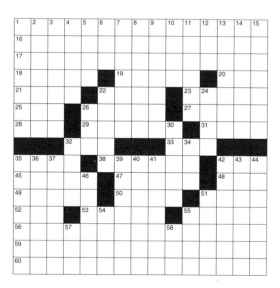

by Stu Ockman

ACROSS

1 Take it easy
8 Vostok 1 passenger
15 Try
16 Supermodel Lima
17 Scale with the highest reading at midday, usually
18 More than startle
19 Show horse
20 Juniors' juniors, briefly
22 Those, to José
23 Organ part
25 Classic Jaguar
26 Latin word in legal briefs
27 Princess Leia was one in "A New Hope"
30 Bamboozled
32 It's nothing new
35 Hot shot?
37 Germany, to Britain
39 It helps you focus
40 Unlocked area?
42 Expenditure
43 T-shirt sizes, for short
44 Allstate subsidiary
46 One who deals with stress well?
48 Hat, slangily
49 Reuben ingredient, informally
53 Completely dry, as a racetrack
54 Rub it in
56 Org. with the New York Liberty
57 BlackBerry routers
59 "This statement is false," e.g.
61 Strong and regal
62 Elvis hit with a spelled-out title
63 Gallery event
64 Sharp-pointed instruments

DOWN

1 Sucker
2 Where French ships dock
3 Like many academic halls
4 Help
5 "Cupid is a knavish ___": "A Midsummer Night's Dream"
6 Biographical data
7 Love letters
8 One foraging
9 Drinks stirred in pitchers
10 [Back off!]
11 Put on
12 Complain loudly
13 Obsessive need to check one's email or Facebook, say
14 Cons
21 U.P.S. cargo: Abbr.
24 Tennis smash?

26 Puzzle solver's complaint
28 Punishment, metaphorically
29 Hypothetical particle in cold dark matter
31 Turn down
32 Five-time U.S. presidential candidate in the early 1900s
33 School handout
34 Colorful party intoxicant
36 Shrill howl
38 "Just wait . . ."
41 Cream, for example
45 Changes for the big screen
47 Short jackets
50 "Watch ___ amazed" (magician's phrase)

51 It takes two nuts
52 Campaign issue
53 Nike rival
54 Mil. bigwig
55 Like sour grapes
58 Long in Hollywood
60 ___ Halladay, two-time Cy Young Award winner

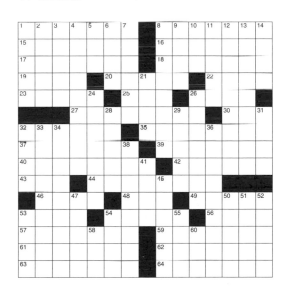

by Joel Fagliano

180 ☆ ☆ ☆

ACROSS

1 "Friday the 13th" setting
5 Cry accompanying a slap
15 Green leader?
16 Office addresses?
17 Tragically heartbroken figure of myth
18 Some cocktail garnishes
19 Noted nominee of 2005
21 Stumped
22 Bit of audio equipment?
23 Controversial thing to play
25 Stats. for new arrivals
27 Base's opposite
29 "That's true — however . . ."
33 Locale for the Zoot Suit Riots of '43
36 Fashion clothes
38 Team unifier
39 They created the Get Rid of Slimy Girls club
42 Brand with a "Wonderfilled" ad campaign
43 Nail
44 Beginning of some tributes
45 Just beginning
47 Longtime rival of 42-Across
49 Midwest terminal?
51 Reality show documenting a two-week trade
55 "A veil, rather than a mirror," per Oscar Wilde
58 Line outside a gala
60 Dreaded message on a returned 32-Down
61 Reverse transcriptase is found in it
64 "To End ___" (1998 Richard Holbrooke best seller)
65 Q&A query
66 Barker in a basket
67 One endlessly smoothing things over?
68 Cross state

DOWN

1 Fencing material
2 Europe's City of Saints and Stones
3 Battlefield cry
4 Abstention alternative
5 "Let ___ Run Wild" (B-side to "California Girls")
6 Physical feature of Herman on "The Simpsons"
7 Home to Main Street, U.S.A.
8 The Hardy Boys and others
9 He called his critics "pusillanimous pussyfooters"
10 With flexibility in tempo
11 Reagan-___
12 Harkness Tower locale
13 Pueblo cooker
14 Red giant that disintegrated?
20 Round windows
24 Brand named after some Iowa villages
26 High (and high-priced) options for spectators
28 Rocker ___ Leo
30 Sci-fi villain ___ Fett
31 They may be made with koa wood, briefly
32 Course obstacle?
33 Elasticity studier's subj.
34 It's canalized at Interlaken
35 Boatload
37 Boatload transfer point
40 Mann's "Man!"
41 Eagle of Delight's tribe
46 Group with the 1963 hit "South Street," with "the"
48 Obsolescence
50 Moisturizer brand
52 Cry accompanying a high-five
53 Treasured strings
54 Politico caricatured by Carvey
55 Start of Egypt's official name
56 ___ Belloq, villain in "Raiders of the Lost Ark"
57 Modern farewell letters
59 Air
62 Wood problem
63 Title for knights on "Game of Thrones"

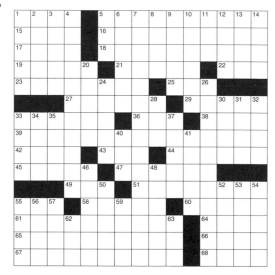

by Evan Birnholz

  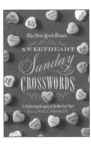 
  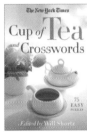 

Answers

1

```
VOLS  COPTO  SLAV
AVOW  INLAW  HIVE
NAVI  GEESE  AVES
FLEVE  ABE  EVICT
   REVEL  RAVEN
KISLEV  VIRGIN
OWL  REVIVAL  WHO
LOAD  NIVEN  LION
ANNE  SCANT  ALPO
STEEL  ANE  MILES
    MIGRATION
SPA  MOI  INN  BAD
TORPEDO  ANIMATE
UPTOYOU  NICEJOB
DESISTS  SEALANT
```

2

```
 TAMP  SWAP  RASP
SARAH  TODO  UTAH
THEREGOESMYBABY
DOW  WIKI  AIDES
SEEN  DESSERT
 AFTERMIDNIGHT
DOLLS  ESE  NEAR
RHO  ABS  INC  TRA
EONS  AAS  BATTY
WHEELINTHESKY
 NOTEPAD  ASAP
TWEEN  ERGO  BRA
SINGINGTHEBLUES
ANNA  ASEA  EANS
HEEL  BARR  YOGA
```

3

```
CHOO  ETHIC  DOS
HASH  LAREDO  RNA
ARTI  ATARIS  ELY
 LOST  PROMISES
BREAKER  MONDAY
LORNA  EPI  STEVE
TDS  TBTEST  ONES
  LETITSNOW
ATTA  WEEUNS  RCA
THRUM  DRE  ASIAN
HEARYE  SAMEOLD
LOCATION  GALL
EMI  HELENA  DOTH
TEN  OILCAR  OBIE
ENG  SOAKS  MONY
```

4

```
TAPE  GAPE  NALA
NEIN  ALOT  MOTOR
USAINBOLT  ATTIC
TONGA  USUALFARE
 POMPS  BLARED
 BASIN  SARI
SEAS  BOSC  ARTSY
PAR  USBPORT  ATE
ARSON  LYLE  ULEE
 IRAE  DANSK
MILLER  MOORE
USERSFEES  IPADS
GETIT  USHEREDIN
GROGS  RAIL  NINA
YENS  OINK  SOAP
```

5

```
GRUB  AILS  JIHAD
LISA  KNEE  ONONE
ATMS  IFAT  STATE
MACINTOSH  HEXED
 LIAR  CUR
TOXIC  MECHANIC
ADASH  NRA  GLO
MICKEYMOUSECLUB
PUT  EEK  NAOMI
 MOCCASIN  TROPE
 HUH  USES
SEDER  MUCKRAKER
EVICT  ELLE  LOVE
GEEKS  ANEW  EKED
ANTSY  DAIS  SOLO
```

6

```
CATTY  DRIVE  PAP
OMAHA  RADAR  ONE
RUNAWAYJURY  GEE
ASKING  ANI  DOWN
LES  ELF  NOSES
 BREAKOUTSTAR
SETA  TIN  SUPINE
AXONS  LEA  DICTA
FEUDED  ESQ  SKID
ESCAPECLAUSE
 HITCH  PAT  SHE
LAUD  LOG  FATHOM
ALP  TAKEOFFRAMP
ZOO  ARENA  FUMET
YEN  BERET  SEEDY
```

7

A	H	O	R	A		B	A	S	I	C		D	L	I
R	A	T	E	R		E	T	H	N	O		O	I	D
C	L	E	A	R	T	H	E	A	I	R		O	C	T
O	A	R			M	A	I			O	S	H	E	A
	L	I	N	E	A	R	T	H	I	N	K	I	N	G
		C	N	N			I	S	A	A	C	S		
S	T	P	A	T		S	O	T	O			K	E	V
I	H	E	A	R	T	H	U	C	K	A	B	E	E	S
B	R	A			W	I	T	H		S	A	Y	S	O
	A	N	C	H	O	R			C	T	R			
A	C	U	T	E	A	R	T	H	R	I	T	I	S	
S	I	T	A	R			U	A	E			N	U	T
S	A	O		M	I	D	D	L	E	E	A	R	T	H
A	N	I		E	R	R	O	L		S	H	E	R	A
Y	S	L		S	E	E	R	S		A	I	M	A	T

8

H	I	D		A	G	E	G	A	P		O	H	M	E
A	M	O		R	O	C	O	C	O		M	I	C	A
W	H	E	R	E	O	H	W	H	E	R	E	H	A	S
K	O	R	E	A		O	N	O		A	G	O	N	Y
			G	M	C		S	O	N	I	A			
	R	E	G	A	L	E		I	N	S	P	O	T	
O	E	D	I	P	U	S	R	E	X			E	W	E
R	A	G	E	S		T	A	G		P	L	E	N	A
E	T	E			R	A	N	G	E	R	O	V	E	R
M	A	D	M	A	X			S	E	E	P	E	D	
		E	L	S	I	E		C	S	I				
A	L	E	R	O		D	V	R		A	N	D	U	P
M	Y	L	I	T	T	L	E	D	O	G	G	O	N	E
F	R	A	T		A	E	R	A	T	E		O	T	S
M	E	L	S		T	R	Y	S	T	S		M	O	O

9

A	S	T	R	A		E	I	D	E	R		C	A	B
L	I	R	A	S		L	D	O	P	A		O	V	I
A	G	A	S	P		F	I	R	E	P	O	W	E	R
W	H	I	T	E	S	M	O	K	E		P	E	R	T
	S	T	A	R	E	A	T		B	E	R	T	H	
			S	T	N		O	D	I	N				
S	P	I	C	E	S		B	I	R	D	B	A	T	H
E	A	C	H		H	O	U	S	E		A	L	S	O
C	L	E	A	N	O	U	T		A	I	R	B	A	G
		N	O	T	I		P	M	S					
A	C	I	N	G			T	R	O	O	P	E	R	
W	A	N	E		G	R	E	E	N	L	I	G	H	T
F	U	L	L	C	O	U	R	T		A	E	R	I	E
U	S	A		A	G	E	N	T		T	R	E	N	D
L	E	W		M	O	S	S	Y		E	S	T	E	S

10

O	A	K		B	R	A			S	C	O	F	F	S
B	E	I		M	A	X	I		C	O	L	L	I	E
G	I	N		W	I	L	T		I	N	D	E	N	T
Y	O	G	I		D	E	S	K		S	E	X	E	S
N	U	A	N	C	E		R	A	N	T	S			
		R	U	H	R		A	L	C	A	T	R	A	Z
L	O	T	S	A		N	I	K	O	N		I	R	E
U	S	H	E	R		A	N	A		T	A	C	O	S
M	S	U		L	O	G	I	N		I	S	H	O	T
P	A	R	M	E	S	A	N		I	N	C	A		
		A	M	O	N	G		D	E	A	R	M	E	
M	A	Z	D	A		O	M	N	I		P	D	A	S
S	M	U	D	G	E		E	C	O	N		I	N	T
R	E	L	E	N	T		N	A	T	O		I	D	O
P	R	U	N	E	S		A	S	S		I	M	P	

11

G	S	A		O	P	E	R	A		A	N	A	I	S
O	W	L		M	O	P	U	P		H	E	N	R	I
W	I	L	D	G	E	E	S	E		H	A	T	E	D
E	T	U	I		S	E	E	M		R	I	F	E	
S	C	R	E	W	Y		A	R	P		N	U	B	
T	H	E	T	A		W	I	N	E	H	O	U	S	E
		R	A	I	N		P	A	C	K	E	T		
	W	I	N	G	E	D	H	O	R	S	E			
T	A	I	P	E	I		U	R	S	A				
W	I	N	O	R	L	O	S	E		O	B	I	T	S
E	R	N		S	E	N		S	H	U	M	A	I	
E	L	I	S		E	R	I	N		R	B	I	S	
Z	I	P	U	P		W	I	S	E	C	R	A	C	K
E	N	E	R	O		A	T	B	A	T		C	H	E
S	E	G	E	R		Y	A	N	K	S		K	I	L

12

O	R	C	S		B	L	E	S	S		F	O	U	R
M	I	R	E		L	E	D	U	P		L	A	Z	E
A	G	E	R		A	N	I	S	E		I	R	I	S
H	O	P	E	T	H	A	T	H	E	L	P	S		
A	R	E	N	A			S	I	D	E	B			
		P	A	B	L	O			T	O	S	C	A	
O	N	A		S	P	R	I	N	G	S	O	P	E	N
P	A	P	P		G	E	N	O	A		K	I	D	D
E	T	E	R	N	A	L	C	I	T	Y		K	E	Y
L	E	R	O	I			R	E	E	C	E			
		C	L	O	C	K			A	U	J	U	S	
	A	L	E	X	A	N	D	E	R	P	O	P	E	
C	O	L	A		B	R	I	E	R		O	N	O	R
A	N	T	I		O	T	T	E	R		L	E	N	T
B	O	O	M		W	A	S	P	S		A	S	E	A

13

```
J E T S   . R A T E D G .   H O P
E A R P . A P O G E E . . E R R
D R A F T D O D G E R . . R I O
I S M . W A H D . . . C M O N
. . . D I R T Y D A N C I N G .
C A N O N S . . I D E S T . . .
E X A M . . S A N E R . C A D
D E M O L I T I O N D E R B Y
E S E . O R A L S . . B A L E
. . D U R A N . . T A B B E D
D U N K I N D O N U T S . . .
I R A E . . R O T A . . S A S
M G M . D O U B L E D U T C H
L E E . O N S I T E . N A T O
Y D S . S T A T E S . I N ? D
```

14

```
B O P S . T S A R . S T A R R
E B A N . E L I A . P A T I O
A E R O . R A M S . E N V O Y
G R E G O R Y S P E C K . . .
L O N . P I S . V I S A G E
E N T R E E . O G E E . M I D
. H A R R I S O N S F O R D
F E E S . N A R . . R U D Y
A R T H U R S M I L L E R .
I I I . T A T A . E Y E P I T
R E C O A T . U S E . R O W
. S H A R O N S S T O N E
A L O H A . O N C E . O P I E
L O R E N . P Y L F . D N A T
F L E A S . E X E S . D E N S
```

15

```
C H A T . S P F . F A Z E S
H O B O . F L U E . E X A L T
O N E O F O U R S . R E P L Y
M U L T I . T O S I R . S A X
P S I . S C O R E P A D . .
. . N E H I . . O R I G I N
M A C S . G R A N D O P E R A
A L O T . E D U . P T A S
S A L E S E V E N T . E T N A
T I N E A R . A I R Y . .
. . M I D Y E A R S . S R A
J A I . L E A R N . B A B E S
A L A M O . W A G O N F U L S
C A G E R . S T E W . T R E F
K N O T S . O L E . A G E S
```

16

```
J E S T S . M I T E . P S I S
A L O H A . I B E X . L I N T
M I L A N . L E A P . E D N A
. I D R A T H E R B E I N
C I D . P E D . O L E . B E D
H O N K I F Y O U L O V E .
A W A I T . U S E . I N K S
N A S T . F I N E D . P E N A
G N A T . U N C . B E F I T
. M Y O T H E R C A R I S A
A M P . R U E . H A D . T H Y
W I L L B R A K E F O R
A S I A . A V E S . M A J O R
K E N O . M E N U . E V A D E
E R G S . A N T S . N E R D Y
```

17

```
E D I C T . A R C S . A B A B
D A N N O . H U I T . L E N A
G R A N O L A B A R . I A T E
A L P . T A B L O I D B U Z Z
R A T I O N . E S P R I T .
. . D O D O . . O S I E R
C A S E . S A M U E L . F L U
E S C A L A T O R C L A U S E
L A O . I T S A G O . P L E D
S P O C K . . E T R E . .
. B L E N D S . O A X A C A
Y O Y O D I E T I N G . D O S
E N D S . T R A D E M A R K S
O T O E . E M I L . A T E I N
W O O D . S A N E . N A P E S
```

18

```
W O L F . O H A R E . D A V E
E R I E . N I N E R . F N O E
B E L L . A L I N E . L E G S
. L I T T L E L E A G U E
C C S . D E S . O X Y G E N
A R E O L A . F I N E S .
R E D H E R R I N G S . B I G
A D A M . U N O . C O D A
T O N . R I D I N G M O W E R
. C O N E S . R E E L E D
S T R O B E . S E A . S S E
H O O D O R N A M E N T .
A T A D . T E N O N . A R A B
K A R L . I R A T E . P A P A
E L S E . A F T E R . E Y E D
```

19

```
G L O M   T I B I A L   A D S
A U D I   O R A N G E   W O W
S A D D L E S H O E S   A B E
H U M M E D   I N S P I R E
    A A A   H A L T E R T O P
M A N Y   D E I   S R I
I P O   T E A R S   G A W K S
S P U R O F T H E M O M E N T
O S T E O   H O P E D   L E E
    C T N   S O T   C L E M
B I T O H O N E Y   J A I
E N S N A R E   F A U L T S
B S A   C R O P C I R C L E S
O E R   H I N T A T   U B E R
P T S   E S S A Y S   S E N S
```

20

```
S N A P   I W O N   C A P N
R U E R   N E R O   J O L L Y
S T R O N G A R M   E N I A C
  C A M E O S   P U T T Y
T A T   S T E P P E   A T O P
V S O P   L I O N S C L U B
S E R I F S   C O N E   E T S
    U L T R A H I G H
U S N   A R E S   B A S T E S
S P E A K E A S Y   T E X T
E L B E   S L O U G H   S P Y
  A U N T S   P L E A S E
I S L E Y   U P P E R D E C K
C H A I R   N E I N   E R T E
E Y E D   E T E S   N A S A
```

21

```
S L A V   D R A W O N   W B A
A E R O   E E Y O R E   E L L
M A G I C M A R K E R   B O G
    L O O M   O C C U R
D R E A M T E A M S   L A S E
R O O   M E D I C I N E M E N
A N N A   M I N O R
M I S S M I S S I S S I P P I
    C A N O F   C E O S
M O D E S T M O U S E   D R E
I R A N   S E R P E N T I N E
M A N D M   H A V E
I N C   M U C K E T Y M U C K
C G I   E M P I R E   P R A Y
S E N   S P A R E D   T I L L
```

22

```
L A P I S   C I A O   Y A P S
P R I M E   R O M E   O R E L
S E E Y A L A T E R   U R S A
    O N E M A N   S L I C K
A C D U C T S   B M O V I E
S H O R E S   C H A I S E
H I S S   D O U B L E D U P
E N V   G O O D B Y E   E N O
S K I S L O P E S   E R I E
    D I A P E R   M A S C O T
S T A N D S   T E N P I N S
L O N G E   L I E S T O
U T I L   H A S T A L U E G O
G A Y E   E M I R   E S S E X
S L A T   T A T A   R E P L Y
```

23

```
A R S   A P B S   S U B W A Y
T A U   C H I C   E L A I N E
T I N B A D G E   E A R N I T
I N B U D   I N O N   B B S
C H A R S   D E M   O R A T E
S A T I   K E V I N B A C O N
  T H E S E A   T I O   K N T
    S O B   G E S
O O P   N A H   D E S P O T
O N I O N B A G E L   I P O S
H E N R Y   H O S   S T E N T
  N B A   A A R E   N O N N A
K O A L A S   G R E E N B A Y
I T L L D O   E V E R   A G E
R E L Y O N   D E L T   R E D
```

24

```
C O L A   C R E S T   B O N G
R A I D   C I N C O   A M O R
O R Z O   S P E R M W H A L E
P S A L M   M I C A   N A G
    P I G G Y B A C K I N G
M E T H A N E   E T O N
A B O   M A S C   O J O S
T A K E I T T O T H E B A N K
E Y E S   Q U O I   W I I
    M O E T   B R E A S T S
R I V E R P H O E N I X
A V E   C O E N   O I N K S
F O G M A C H I N E   O O O H
T R A M   H A N O I   M A K E
S Y N E   S T E R N   S H O D
```

25

```
T W A . R A F T . R O B B E N
E A T . E I R E . I L O I L O
A L T . P R E S I D E N T O F
. L E D A . E S S O . Y I P E
P O N Y C A R . A F T . N E E
F W D E K L E R K . W A G S .
C I E . T I E . S O X . . . .
. N E L S O N M A N D E L A .
. . . I T S . A D O . I L L .
. T A T A . A P A R T H E I D
B A N . Y E S . P E R U S E S
A R N O . C O O T . I N O N .
S O U T H A F R I C A . V A T
S T A R E R . S N A G . E T A
I S L A N D . O G L E . R E X
```

26

```
W I N G . Z I T I . A B O D E
E S A U . A P E D . B R U I N
B A N E . P A N T S U I T E D
A B A S H . N O A H . O T T O
P E N T U P A N G E R . H A W
P L A S M A . . P A P E R S .
. . . . R E F S . G A R Y . .
. P I N T M E A S U R E . . .
. P O S E . O Z M A . . . . .
S O W H A T . . M E S S R S .
O P E . P O N T L E V E Q U E
A T R A . T O R A . A R U B A
P U N T R E T U R N . V I A L
E N A C T . E N V Y . E S T E
R E P O S . S K A T . S H O D
```

27

```
A F L A C . M Y B A D . B U T T
L L A M A . A E R I E . L E E
L I V I N G L A R G E . I N N
S P A . O U T S . J U N C O
. H O R A T I O A L G E R .
X A N A D U . S K Y E . . .
T W I R L . P O L E . F O B
R O C K E T S R E D G L A R E
A L E . H A G S . I B I Z A
. . I D O L . A V A L O N .
P R E M I U M L A G E R . .
L O U P E . E T T A . A R F
A I R . C H I V A S R E G A L
G L O . U M B E R . I M A G E
E S S . T O M E I . P U R E E
```

28

```
O B E Y S . R I D E . S K I P
H A V O C . E M I R . M E S A
M N I G H T S H Y A M A L A N
S E L A . N E O . A L L O T
. M B U T T E R F L Y . . .
G O K A R T . L E I . G A M
A N I T A . L E I L A . R P I
V C R S . X A C T O . T E A L
E L K . M E R G E . T H E R E
L E G . I N A . P L E N T Y
. I A M A M E R I C A . . .
A M B L E . B I N . L A U D
V I S F O R V E N G E A N C E
E L O I . A I R S . E M I L E
R E N E . G A T E . R O M A N
```

29

```
S A C S . J I M I . V O D K A
H U L U . F R O S . I T R I P
O D I N . K I L L E R B E E S
G E O D E . N T E S T . S L O
I N S A N E A S Y L U M S .
. . E T C . . A U S T . . .
R B I . R A D I C A L S I G N
A R N O . R E D O S . E Z I O
W I C K E D W I T C H . E F T
. T U R N . . A A A . . . .
. B A D M O O N R I S I N G
B O A . W A H O O . R I D E R
I S T H I S G O O D . A I R E
F L E A S . O L I O . N O V A
F O S S E . D A L I . S T E T
```

30

```
O F F E R . P L U S . C O P .
N O L T E . E O N S . E R O S
T R E A T . P H O N E C A L L
H A W . I O T A . V I L L A
E S S . R H O N E V A L L E Y
G O O S E S . A I D . Y D S
O N L Y . 3 E R I E S . . .
. G O N E B A L L I S T I C
. . C A L M L Y . E R A S
F A R . S O B . F A M I N E
S T O N E W A L L E D . S I P
T O M E I . O U Z O . H S T
O N E A N D A L L . P A S T E
P A R T . A C L U . T W E E T
. L O O . B E S S . S E A R S
```

31

J	I	V	E		J	A	Z	Z		H	O	K	U	M
U	B	E	R		A	G	E	E		A	C	U	R	A
M	A	R	S		I	N	N	S		D	E	R	A	T
P	R	A	T	T	L	E		T	W	A	D	D	L	E
			R	O	W	B		M	T	A				
H	O	T	A	I	R		A	N	D		R	A	P	S
A	D	O	U	T		G	L	A	S	S		N	A	T
B	I	L	G	E		R	O	T		T	R	I	P	E
I	L	L		R	H	O	N	E		R	E	G	A	L
T	E	S	H		I	K	E		B	U	S	H	W	A
			A	O	K		Y	A	R	N				
B	L	A	T	H	E	R		H	O	G	W	A	S	H
L	E	F	T	S		A	T	Y	A		E	C	H	O
A	T	R	I	A		N	S	E	C		B	L	I	N
H	O	O	E	Y		T	O	S	H		B	U	N	K

32

H	D	T	V		T	U	D	O	R		P	U	P	S
A	R	O	O		I	R	A	N	I		A	P	I	A
L	I	N	C	O	L	N	M	E	M	O	R	I	A	L
S	P	E	A	R		P	A	I	R	I	N	G	S	
		B	E	D	E		L	E	T		T	E	A	
J	E	T		C	I	V	I	L	R	I	G	H	T	S
A	M	A		K	E	E	N			Z	O	E		
M	I	K	A		M	L	K	J	R		D	A	W	N
	E	T	D		E	P	O	S		I	I	I		
I	H	A	V	E	A	D	R	E	A	M		R	N	A
N	E	S		U	S	E		G	R	A	B			
A	T	T	A	C	K	A	D			R	E	M	I	X
W	E	A	R	E	F	R	E	E	A	T	L	A	S	T
A	R	N	E		O	M	A	N	I		O	M	A	R
Y	O	D	A		R	E	N	D	S		W	A	W	A

33

	W	O	R	D		W	O	O	D		W	O	O	T
C	I	D	E	R		A	B	L	E		E	B	R	O
O	L	D	I	E		T	E	E	M		M	E	M	O
R	E	E	N	A	C	T	S		I	M	A	R	E	T
D	E	R	I	D	E		E	A	S	E	D			
			N	E	D	S		B	E	N	E	A	T	H
C	A	B		D	A	V	I	S		S	I	C	K	O
O	W	E	N		R	E	S	E	T		T	I	T	O
R	E	V	E	L		L	E	N	I	N		D	S	T
K	E	Y	W	E	S	T		T	E	E	S			
			S	T	E	E	P		R	U	P	I	A	H
C	A	R	W	A	X		L	I	S	T	E	N	T	O
O	G	E	E		U	P	A	S		R	E	T	R	O
O	R	N	E		A	L	T	A		A	D	R	I	P
K	O	O	K		L	O	O	K		L	O	O	P	

34

S	T	A	B		U	H	O	H		M	A	C	H	O
T	R	U	E		S	O	L	O		A	L	L	E	N
A	I	R	T	R	A	V	E	L		G	E	E	S	E
L	E	A	S	E		I	D	U	N	N	O			
L	D	S		P	E	A	C	E	K	E	E	P	E	R
			P	E	N	N		M	E	T		A	M	A
L	I	F	E	L	I	N	E			O	A	T	E	N
I	R	I	S		D	O	L	C	E		B	R	E	D
K	A	B	O	B		F	A	C	E	C	A	R	D	
E	N	O		L	O	S		R	O	W	S			
D	I	N	N	E	R	T	A	B	L	E		S	H	E
			A	E	N	E	I	D		R	A	P	I	D
N	I	C	A	D		T	I	M	E	S	H	A	R	E
C	A	C	T	I		C	E	L	L		A	D	E	N
O	N	I	O	N		H	U	B	S		B	E	D	S

35

S	T	E	M		I	L	K	S		S	I	T	U	P
P	A	P	A		N	O	A	H		C	O	W	L	S
A	C	I	D		F	O	R	A		R	U	I	N	S
S	O	C	C	E	R	M	A	M	B	O		S	A	T
			A	V	A	S	T		A	L	O	T		
S	A	P	P	E	R			S	P	L	I	T	U	P
N	T	H		R	E	A	C	H		S	N	A	R	E
A	E	O	N		D	R	O	O	P		K	E	G	S
F	I	N	E	D		C	L	E	A	R		B	E	T
U	N	E	A	R	T	H		R	I	G	O	R	S	
			B	R	A	N		D	I	A	N	A		
P	S	I		S	T	R	U	C	K	D	U	M	B	O
A	L	L	O	T		O	B	O	E		C	O	A	T
R	A	B	B	I		L	A	N	E		H	A	R	T
S	T	O	I	C		L	I	S	T		O	N	T	O

36

A	C	T	S		L	A	D	Y		P	O	R	C	H
L	O	O	P		E	L	I	A		A	D	I	E	U
E	M	I	R		A	M	O	K		R	O	B	O	T
C	A	L	E	N	D	A	R	Y	E	A	R			
			E	L	S		A	D	D		I	M	P	
I	M	O		C	H	U	C	K	Y	E	A	G	E	R
S	A	R	A	S	O	T	A			S	I	N	A	I
A	R	C	S		T	E	N	P	M		D	I	N	O
A	S	H	E	S		D	I	A	M	E	T	E	R	
C	H	I	C	K	E	N	Y	A	R	D		E	R	S
S	Y	D		I	O	U			T	S	P			
		C	A	N	A	R	Y	Y	E	L	L	O	W	
G	A	T	O	R		N	O	I	R		A	E	R	O
O	H	A	R	E		C	O	P	E		T	A	C	O
P	A	R	K	A		E	K	E	D		O	R	A	L

37

```
H O D S . B A S K . J O J O .
A N O N . I L I E . S O D O I
J K R O W L I N G . B O S U M
J P M O R G A N . M A H A L O
. Z O E S . S E C . L A N .
E X J E T . . L A H T I . .
A R B . E A T S I N . E N V Y
R A F T . C R O C I . A G E E
L Y L E . H A N K E R . E R S
. E N J O Y . . A B R A M .
P O T . J O S . M O N A . .
I N C A P S . J M B A R R I E
N E H R U . J C D I T H E R S
E L E C T . A T I T . O M I T
. B R O Z . I S I S . P O S E
```

38

```
D U S K . D A S H . A S S E S
U N T O . I T T Y . Z O O M S
S C O R E C A R D . A U N T S
T A L E N T . O R A L S . . .
S P E A R . S P A R E C A S H
. . N A S H . . K A H U N A
A F L . P O O L S . E T A S
C R E A T U R E C O M F O R T
H A N D . T E R R Y . S K Y
E N D O R A . E A R L . .
S C A R E C R O W . T E A S E
. A L E U T . A L A S K A
Y A B B A . R E C C E N T E R
E A R L Y . A R O N . T E E N
S H O E S . L I N E . O R T S
```

39

```
. I T D . G L A Z E D . H U N
M E A . M O D E L A . S O F T
P A R . C A L L I T A W A S H
A S K A . T A I . E N E R O
L E A V E H I G H A N D D R Y
E U G E N E . A B E . E T A
S P E N D . J A I L . O R S O
. . G O T O P R E S S . .
O P I E . H I P S . U S A F B
U R N . G E N . C R I M E A
R E T U R N T O T H E F O L D
. P O L I O . I R A . Y U L E
L A U N D R Y L I S T . N O G
O R C A . T E E T E R . T U G
N E H . . H E R E S Y . S T S
```

40

```
S L I P . U C L A . E L I A S
L I N E . S P A N . T O N T O
U N C L E B U C K . C O D A S
S K I E D . T A K E S I T .
H A S . N O M O R E T E A R S
E G O . A K A . A G E . N O T
S E R B . A S H . R A S T A
. S A Y S A Y S A Y . .
N A S A L . T E E . E D E N
B T W . L O S . A L I . A T E
C H E E S E C U R L S . Y I P
. L A S T D O N . L A T C H
V E R S A . W H A T A J O K E
O T T E R . L I S A . A N E W
L E O N S . S P U D . R A T S
```

41

```
A T O Z . B A R B . G O N E R
C O D Y . B B O Y . O R O N O
I D I G . C H A T T E R B O X
D O N O W . O N E R S . E R I
. . T E A R . I S I T M E .
H A K E E M . E X G O V . .
I C I . A M I D . F O N D U
G A R M E N T D I S T R I C T
H I K E S . G E N L . S O N
. . I C I E R . U R S I N E
P I A N O S . L E A H . .
O R K . R E U S E . J O H N Q
K A R A T E C H O P . L U A U
E N O T E . L E N O . O M N I
D I N E D . A L E X . M E A N
```

42

```
D I D I N . S P R I G . B M W
E Z I N E . O R O N O . Y E A
J O K E S A R O U N D . E R S
A D E . T R E A T . O B I T
. . V I E . M E G A B Y T E
A R S E N A L . A M I E .
C H O N G . A D E L A . L I U
L O U I S A M A Y A L C O T T
U S N . I M A G E . G A V I N
. D A T E . S C A L E N E
B E T H E S D A . M M E .
L A R A . O L I V A . D I M
A S A . A M Y L N I T R I T E
D E C . R E L I C . E A V E S
E L K . E L E N A . D E E M S
```

43

```
M O M A   O R B S   I B I S
S N A R K   R E A M   T A P A
G O T T I   A F R O   A N A T
      F E N C I N G B L A D E
U N C I V I L     L I N
R O L L   N E E D L E C A S E
S T O M P   M U T E   S E X
U F W   S E A B I R D   P E P
L A N   A X L E   S A L S A
A R A B L E A D E R   M I T T
    R U M   L E A N T O S
C R O S S W O R D E S E
Z E U S   O B O E   I S I A H
A N N E   R E V S   S I N G E
R O D S   N Y E T   A N E W
```

44

```
W A L S H   P J S   S C A N T
A M A T I   H A H   U H H U H
D I V A N D I V A   B R A K E
S E E N T O   A R C   I B E X
      Z A N Y   O U T S
    P A T T E R N P A T T E R
I B E   G O A   P I A N O
F R E E T O W N F R E E T O W
W E L S H   G O O   E S E
E A S T E R N E A S T E R
      R E P O   L I R A
B R I O   M B A   E U G E N E
B A D G E   L E A R N L E A R
Q U E E N   E R R   K E N T S
S L A N G   R O T   S T Y L E
```

45

```
D R D O O M   I B M P C
J A R U L E   B R A I D
E V E N E R   E A R N S
D I S C O V E R I N G   I D A
  S S E   D I N E   E T A T
A H I   A W A Y   B L A R E
B E N J A M I N   Q U E L L S
E D G E D I N   F U R C O A T
    L A D   P R I N T
G O F L Y   S H A D   R O D S
E U R O   A M E N   I B E T
I T A   S K U N K   S C A L A
S E N S E I   O L D T I M E R
H A C K I T   M I S S T A T E
A T E A S E   S N L   Y S E R
```

46

```
F I X I T   O B I S   A M A T
E L E N I   F A S T   D I M E
S I N G L E F I L E   A K I N
S E A E E L   T E N   P E C K
    A R N E   T O P T H I S
O D O R   I N K   S R T A
H A N   I N D I A   O O M P H
O T T   T O O L B O X   M O E
H A H A S   N O B L Y   E R R
    E L M S   S O D   A R E A
B A L L E T S   T A C T
E K E D   I O U   G O O G L E
T I V O   F I N G E R N A I L
S T E N   F L I P   N A V E L
Y A L E   S S T S   S L E D S
```

47

```
S T A L E   A S A P   M A S H
T O T E S   R I G A   I D E A
A F O O T   S T I R   A L I S
B U M S A R O U N D   T I N A
      T A N   O N A B E T
G L A Z E D   P A N E
L U N E S   B U R M A R O A D
I L I A   C U R I E   E G G O
B U L L N O S E D   B E R E T
      B O S E   M E L E E S
U P T I C K     A H A
M A N N   B U T T O N W O O D
P R O B   O C H O   B I L B O
E T T U   O L I N   A D D I N
D Y E D   K A N E   G E E S E
```

48

```
C A R D   A T T I C   T S A R
L E E R   F R E D O   H E X A
I R A E   G A M E W A R D E N
N I L S   H I P   L I E U
G E M S T A T E   M E C C A
      C A N   S E E   T O T
M A J O R   G I M M E F I V E
A V I D   R U L E S   A V E S
G O M E R P Y L E   I N E R T
N I P   H I S   A N T
A D A N O   G U M B A L L S
  L A D E   U N U   S O U P
G Y M N A S T I C S   I F S O
P E E N   A I S L E   E A T S
A W R Y   U L E E S   S T Y E
```

49

```
B A D . . C O B B . S M A R T
A L I A . P A R A . C O M E R
B U R G L A R A L . I T A L Y
A M T O O . . I T A . O T I S
. . G E N T D I S T R I C T .
. B O O B O O . C H A O . . .
C U P . . R N A . C L O G S .
A F A R E W E L L T O A R M S
D F L A T . B I O . C A W . .
. . T U B Y . M R B E A N . .
. D E A T H W E D O V E R . .
E R I E . I S A . B E A S T .
E R O D E . S N A K E C H E R
R E L O S . I T S O . T E R I
F D I N A . R E I N . M A P .
```

50

```
B L O W . A D I E U . W O E S
Y O G A . N E S T S . I L G A
F I L T H Y R I C H . L E A N
A R E T O O . T H E C L O U D
R E D . A N G . R A D . . . .
. G R E A S Y S P O O N S . .
C E D E D . S T E I N . V A L
E X A M . S P U R N . P E P E
L I T . G H E N I . A C N E D
S T A I N E D G L A S S . . .
. R A E . E R N . C H A . . .
S P L I T P E A . G E N D E R
I R A S . D I R T Y W O R D S
Z O N E . O N E A L . L O G O
E W E S . G E S T E . O M E N
```

51

```
P R I S M . S L A M . C H E X
S A S H A . C A L I . O I L Y
I T A I N T O V E R U N T I L
. S O R T A . I N S I D E . .
A R C H L Y . J A R . T E M .
W A L K O F F H O M E R . . .
O R I E . O L E G . P I I H .
L A M B . R O U G E . C H A P
. T E A S . O R E M . H E R E
. B U Z Z E R B E A T E R . .
F O G . L A Y . O N R A M P .
S C R U F F . R E D I D . . .
T H E F A T L A D Y S I N G S
O R E O . I O T A . L I A R S
P E T S . G L A M . E I G E R
```

52

```
M I D I . H I K E S . B O T .
I M I N . D O R I T O . A P R
M A S Q U E R A D E P A R T Y
E X H U S B A N D . R B I S .
. E D U C . D E C A N T . . .
M A S S A G E P A R L O R . .
P I T T . I D O S . E L K . .
A D O . M A A N D P A . L E I
A E R . A F R O . A L A N . .
. M A C A R T H U R P A R K .
J A S P E R . A N A P . . . .
A D U E . U R S A M A J O R .
M A R D I G R A S P A R A D E
E G G . M O D E L T . E V E N
S E E . S O U S E . L A S T .
```

53

```
A R G O . S K A T . R I F L E
M O U S E P A D S . O R I O N
B E S T T H R E E . M I S D U
I S (IT) . H E M P . B A S (HT) E S
. E R A T . E N E . . . . . .
(HT) U M B L E . R A I S I N .
I V I E S . M I I D A . C O B
N E X T . (HT)EA AI DL S . L I R A
T A U . N O L T E . M O N T Y
. S P R I N T . C O U G H S .
. A T E . (HT)O O T . . . . .
S C E N T S . A U D I . S E C
T O S C A . O U T O F F I V E
U N P I N . U N I N S U R E D
B E N D Y . R T E S . N I N E
```

54

```
P A I R . W E B . D U A L .
A N N O . S H R U G . A N T E
D O U B L E O R N O T H I N G
R U S T I C . S O O . T O O .
E K E . R O B E . D R S . . .
. J A N U S . Y E N T A . . .
H O P E . D O E . I H O U P E
A N A R C H Y . S W O O N E D
T U S S L E . R H O . Z E R O
. S T E E L . A I S L E . . .
. Y A P . H A H A . A R M . .
S A G . V I A . O P A Q U E .
T W I N E N G I N E P L A N E
U R G E . G E N U S . I B I S
D Y A D . S A T . F A C E . .
```

55

T	A	C	H		M	A	D	A	M		L	E	T	O
S	P	R	Y		A	N	O	D	E		O	X	E	N
K	E	E	P	I	T	D	O	W	N		W	A	N	T
	S	W	E	D	E	S		A	S	S		C	H	A
G	U	T	S	Y			W	R	A	P	I	T	U	P
P	I	E		L	I	T	H	E		I	R	A	T	E
S	T	A	T		B	R	A		G	R	O			
		M	O	V	E	I	T	A	L	O	N	G		
			M	I	X		N	B	A		S	A	S	H
E	A	S	E	S		G	O	U	D	A		S	E	A
C	U	T	I	T	O	U	T			U	P	S	E	T
O	R	E		A	N	I		A	U	D	I	T	S	
L	O	A	M		K	N	O	C	K	I	T	O	F	F
A	R	L	O		E	E	R	I	E		A	V	I	A
W	A	S	P		Y	A	R	D	S		S	E	T	S

56

A	D	A	M		P	A	I	L		G	L	O	O	M
N	A	S	A		A	L	O	U		R	U	M	B	A
T	H	E	R	E	Y	O	U	G	O	A	G	A	I	N
E	L	A	T	I	O	N		E	X	P	E	N	S	E
			S	L	E	W		E	E	R				
M	A	R	I	N	A		R	A	Y	S		M	A	P
O	B	E	S	E		W	O	R	E		C	O	M	A
T	H	E	I	R	F	I	N	E	S	T	H	O	U	R
T	O	S	S		O	L	G	A		R	I	N	S	E
O	R	E		D	O	T	E		L	A	P	S	E	D
			B	E	D		D	E	E	D				
S	T	L	U	C	I	A		A	G	E	G	A	P	S
T	H	E	Y	R	E	G	R	R	R	R	E	A	T	
A	R	N	I	E		R	I	T	E		E	R	I	E
B	O	O	N	E		A	C	H	E		W	O	R	M

57

L	A	D	E	N		S	E	M	I	S		V	A	L
A	S	O	N	E		T	R	A	D	E		E	M	U
H	I	G	H	T	R	E	A	S	O	N		R	I	M
R	A	G	A		B	A	S	S		D	O	D	G	E
			I	N	S	I	D	E	E	D	E	E		
P	R	E	C	I	S				A	N	T			
L	A	B	E	L		A	M	I	D		O	M	I	T
U	S	A		L	O	W	B	L	O	W		A	P	E
S	A	G	E		P	E	A	K		H	O	R	S	E
			A	T	E				P	E	R	S	O	N
O	U	T	S	I	D	E	C	H	A	N	C	E		
P	R	I	E	D		S	L	O	W		H	I	F	I
A	I	L		B	A	S	E	B	A	L	L	S		
R	A	D		I	N	E	R	T		O	R	L	O	N
T	H	E		T	A	N	K	S		A	D	E	P	T

58

S	T	U	D	I	O		B	A	B	Y		L	A	S
A	S	S	I	S	I		A	N	T	E		Y	E	T
H	O	M	E	P	L	A	T	E	U	M	P	I	R	E
L	S	A	T		P	O	I			E	R	N	I	E
			B	A	N	K	M	A	N	A	G	E	R	
R	O	D	M	A	N			A	T	I	T			
O	R	E	O	S		Z	E	R	O		F	E	M	A
B	L	A	C	K	J	A	C	K	P	L	A	Y	E	R
S	Y	N	C		E	G	O	S		A	L	E	R	T
			A	S	T	A			T	I	L	D	E	S
C	E	N	S	U	S	T	A	K	E	R				
A	B	O	I	L			D	I	X		R	A	V	E
C	O	U	N	T	E	R	E	X	A	M	P	L	E	S
T	O	S		A	R	A	L		C	O	M	B	A	T
I	K	E		N	A	P	E		O	N	S	A	L	E

59

K	A	M	P	A	L	A		H	A	M		C	C	S
I	G	O	O	F	E	D		E	L	I		L	O	N
T	I	C	K	L	E	D		N	U	T	C	A	S	E
T	O	S	E	A		A	T	M		A	R	E	A	
			C	O	M	M	O	N	S	T	O	C	K	
E	S	S	O		L	O	O	F	A	H				
T	I	C	K	E	D	O	F	F		E	R	A	S	E
E	N	T	I	R	E		D	E	A	R	I	E		
S	E	V	E	N		M	C	L	I	N	T	O	C	K
				I	S	O	M	E	R		A	O	K	S
T	I	C	K	E	T	B	O	O	T	H				
U	L	N	A		U	S	N			A	U	D	I	E
R	I	O	T	A	C	T		B	U	T	T	O	C	K
B	E	T		I	C	E		O	P	E	N	T	O	E
O	D	E		D	O	R		S	C	R	E	E	N	S

60

T	O	F	U		S	A	N	K	A		E	S	Q	S
A	P	E	D		C	A	I	R	N		A	Q	U	I
H	E	A	D	T	O	H	E	A	D		R	U	I	N
I	N	S	E	R	T		C	U	R	B		E	E	L
T	E	T	R	A		T	E	T	E	A	T	E	T	E
I	D	S		C	E	O			A	M	A	Z	E	S
			G	E	L	A	T	O		K	E	D	S	
		B	O	D	Y	D	O	U	B	L	E	S		
C	O	L	T			S	A	T	E	E	N			
O	N	E	T	W	O		D	E	G		M	A	W	
M	A	N	O	A	M	A	N	O		A	N	I	M	E
E	D	D		N	A	V	I		S	T	O	L	E	N
N	A	S	H		H	A	N	D	T	O	H	A	N	D
O	T	I	S		A	N	J	O	U		I	N	D	Y
W	E	N	T		S	T	A	N	D		T	O	S	S

61

```
S H A F T █ B L I P █ P R E T
A I D A N █ O O N A █ L A L A
P H I N T S O F T H I E V E S
S E N T █ P I T H █ N A I V E
█ █ A G I N █ E M U S █ █ █
█ L O S I N G P A T I E N T S
S E L I G █ L I N T █ O B E
U C L A █ Y O U R S █ T W I X
M A I █ L A N G █ H A I R Y
P R E S E N T S O F M I N D █
█ █ W I K I █ I D O L █ █ █
A T T I C █ P O L I █ G I G I
J U M P A T T H E C H A N T S
A T E E █ V O I R █ S T O O L
R U N S █ G E O S █ T E N S E
```

62

```
H U L A █ H O F F █ S L O T H
O H O S █ O R A L █ C A N W F
S U C K S ᴮᴮ Y O U █ A F T E R
P H O E N I X █ ᴮᴮ A L O V E R
T A X I █ H E R E █ G A E A
O P E N A R E A █ S E E M S ᴮᴮ
M A N █ ᴮᴿ O R N O T ᴮᴮ █ I T O
B R I D E ᴮᴮ █ C H E S S S E T
S T A R █ E W E S █ C H E T
█ █ Y P R E S █ A P R █ █
ᴮᴮ H O N E S T █ B R I E F E D
G O M E R █ B O R N ᴮᴮ W I L D
U M A S S █ A R I A █ I S S A
N O R S E █ R I T Z █ T H E Y
```

63

```
R A D S █ C A P E D █ P S S T
E S A U █ I V A N I █ E T T A
D O A N D R O I D S D R E A M
O F E L E C T R I C S H E E P
█ █ A B L E S T █ C A L L A
C O M M I E █ █ A S P █ █
E R U P T █ B U M P █ S P I N
R A T █ S A M P L E D █ O D E
F L E A █ D I C K █ A D U L T
█ █ R I D █ T N O T E S █
A L A R M █ P I G O U T █ █
W E C A N R E M E M B E R I T
F O R Y O U W H O L E S A L E
U N I E █ H E I D I █ O R Y X
L A D D █ R E P E N █ N E A T
```

64

```
S A D █ P A E A N █ █ B A C K
A B E █ E R A T O █ R E P R O
L O S █ D U S T S W E E P E R
I R K █ A M Y █ T I M █ O D E
V I T A L █ V A R I A T I O N
A G O G █ L I R A █ I A N █
T I P S █ E R E █ N U T S
E N C █ SUN MON TUE WED THU FRI SAT █ M I D
█ E A Z Y █ O C D █ M E D E
█ L E A █ E N Y A █ O N E A
S W E E T E N E D █ O C T A D
K I N █ S R A █ I M F █ B I B
U N D R E A M E D O F █ O S O
L E A N N █ E L E V E █ O L D
L Y R A █ L O S E R █ K E Y
```

65

```
A L C A P P █ O H M Y █ S Y L
M O O S H U █ F A R E █ C O E
F L O O R M A T H I S █ A U G
M A P █ E I R E █ C R A G
█ B A C O N F A T H E R S
I C H O K E D █ I R A I S E █
N O O N █ A S I F █ A H S
T H R O W I N T H E T O W E L
O A S █ H S I A █ D A R E
█ B E G O O D █ A N N O Y E D
H I S P A N I C R O O M
U T E S █ A C H T █ M A C
M A N █ H E R S H E Y B A B Y
O N S █ E V A C █ L E O N A S
R T E █ X E N A █ P T B O A T
```

66

```
B M W █ N A M A T H █ L S A T
B A H █ I S I D R O █ S T I O
S C O T L A N D Y A R D A G E
█ B S A █ S U T R A █ G I S
N E W Y O R K P O S T A G E
A T H E N A █ L A G E R
T H O █ K S T A R █ E R S
█ A P P E N D A G E
█ O M B █ K O A L A █ J E D
B Y E A R █ F R I E N D
E S T R E E T B A N D A G E
O R T █ C A N O E █ E N A
C L A S S I F I E D A D A G E
T I R E █ M I L N E R █ R E S
A N S A █ S N E E R S █ P D Q
```

67

```
A R C H . I S L E S . B A D E
S O H O . S A U T E . A R I A
T W I S T E R C H E C K E R S
I S P . R E D . . P U E N T E
. M B A . I O U . T R A Y S
C L U E M O N O P O L Y
A I N T . R E F I N E . N E O
F A K E I D . . S T E E L S
E R S . G E O R G E . V I A L
. S O R R Y O T H E L L O
R E M I T . R E O . A R S
E L I C I T . D O N . I D A
B A C K T O B A C K G A M E S
E T R E . C O L O R . S O U P
L E O N . K A P P A . I N X S
```

68

```
A D A P T T O . I N K P O T S
R E N E W E D . D E C O D E S
T A N G O E D . E G A L I T E
S R A . W R S . S A B I N E
A N A L Y S T . P I E H O L E
M O R A . H E A V E . N O N
B O O M E R A N G E F F E C T
I S M . L O T T E . A B A R
T E A S E T S . A R T I C L E
. A V A . E E L
. A F L A R E . S T K . T R I
F L O U T E R . A U C T I O N
I S O T O P E . K R I S T I N
B O L E R O S . E N T A I L S
```

69

```
C A W . S P R Y . P U S H I T
A V E . Y O Y O . E S P A N A
R I A . S W E D I S H F I S H
L A S S . B A S T E . R P I
S T E A M E R . B O R O D I N
J E L L Y B E A N S . N O R I
R D S . B O A S . C A S E S
. C A N D Y C O R N .
S T R A D . E A V E . E G G
T W I N . H O T T A M A L E S
P O S T M A N . E L E M E N T
E T S . A B Z U G . A V E R
T O O T S I E R O L L . A R I
E N L I S T . G R I P . T I N
R E E S E S . E Y E S . E C G
```

70

```
W O L F M A N . N A M F L O W
I N U T E R O . A R I G A T O
M O N S T E R . R E T S N O M
P R E M I U M . N A T . D E B
. I M P . M I S E R .
S K A T E . V I A . N O T S O
L O C H . J A R . J S B A C H
O A T . A T R I A . C A Y
G L O S S Y . O R B . E I N E
S A R A H . A R K . P U T T S
. D I A L S . S A G .
A C C . A B U . I N S E C T S
P H A N T O M . M O T N A H P
E A S E S I N . S W E E P E A
D R A C U L A . X X X X X X X
```

71

```
D R U G S . M U S S . A B B A
N I G H T . O H N O . C O L T
A B H O R . S A I D I T N O T
. S I T S U P . M O N T E
C A N T F O O L . B E R E T S
O R A T E S . A L L . T O T
M I S O . A R M A D A .
B E T W E E N Y O U A N D M E
. N A N T E S . Y E A R
H A T . G I S . C A M A R O
O S W A L D . T A L K I N T O
W H A L E . M O V E I N .
D O N T S C A R E . T U R B O
A R G O . S P A R . A T A R I
H E S S . A S H Y . S E G A L
```

72

```
R I A T A S . S H A M . F B I
A N T E U P . W O V E . A L F
R H O N D A . (1) B A N D I T S
E A U . I N I . O R S O N
BIT BIT C R O O K S . I A N
. H U B . E P I C . T R I P
A P O L O . B O N E S . E C O
F I V E O . A R D . T O T E S
T E E . K I N T E . E L U D E
A R R S . G A S X . A I R
. E I N . (2) (3) (4) M O N T E
. S A T I N . S A P . F I R
WAY WAY WAY WAY S T O P . M I N I N G
N I E . M E D E . O P O R T O
E N D . E D E N . M E R E S T
```

(1) ARMED (2) CARD (3) CARD (4) CARD

73

O	J	S			T	A	B	L	E		I	K	E	A
P	U	P		S	H	R	I	E	K		S	I	L	L
A	D	O		M	I	N	C	E	G	A	R	L	I	C
L	I	N	G	E	R	I	E			D	A	N	Z	A
		G	R	A	T	E	P	A	R	M	E	S	A	N
O	L	E	A	R	Y	S			W	A	I	L		
N	A	B	S			F	O	U	R		O	B	E	
C	H	O	P	B	A	S	I	L	L	E	A	V	E	S
	E	R	B		U	N	I	X			N	E	A	T
		A	S	I	S		R	E	B	I	R	T	H	
C	R	U	S	H	P	I	N	E	N	U	T	S		
L	A	N	C	E			O	B	V	I	A	T	E	S
A	D	D	O	L	I	V	E	O	I	L		A	V	A
P	I	E	T		M	I	L	O	R	D		T	I	N
S	I	R	S		P	L	U	T	O		E	L	K	

74

C	A	R	O	B		R	E	P	S		T	V	A	D
A	G	A	P	E		O	X	E	N		H	I	K	E
M	O	D	E	M		M	E	T	E		E	D	A	M
P	R	O	N	O	U	N	C	E	A	B	L	E		
S	A	N		A	G	E		K	O	M	O	D	O	
		U	N	H	Y	P	H	E	N	A	T	E	D	
A	L	I	A	S		H	E	R	D		A	M	O	
P	O	N	E		Q	U	A	Y	S		S	P	U	R
P	E	T		O	U	R	S		T	I	E	R	S	
T	W	E	L	V	E	L	E	T	T	E	R			
S	E	R	I	E	S			R	E	L		A	H	A
	P	E	N	T	A	S	Y	L	L	A	B	I	C	
H	E	L	D		I	L	L	S		A	R	E	N	T
E	R	A	T		N	E	A	T		L	E	I	G	O
M	A	Y	O		G	E	M	S		L	A	S	E	R

75

A	H	E	A	D		G	P	A		A	S	S	O	C
V	A	L	S	E		A	R	T		T	U	L	L	Y
O	B	E	L	I		Z	O	O		R	H	O	D	A
W	A	C		G	E	E		P	O	I		W	G	N
I	N	T	E	N	D			N	A	P	O	L	I	
N	E	R	D		S	H	A	P	E		A	N	O	D
G	R	O	G			E	R	R		E	I	R	E	
	A	M	A		C	D	R	O	M		S	H	Y	
E		A	R	R	O	W		N	O	F	E	E		F
A	L	G		A	R	I		T	O	R		U	S	E
R	U	N	N	I	N	G		O	N	E	M	P	T	Y
S	P	E	E	D	S			B	E	A	T	E	N	
H	I	T	S		I	M	A	G	E		F	A	R	M
O	N	I	T		L	I	B	R	A		I	K	E	A
T	E	C	S		K	A	S	E	M		A	E	O	N

76

C	O	N		A	R	C		A	T	H	O	M	E
H	M	O		W	O	O	D		S	H	A	R	E	S
A	N	T		L	O	C	O		S	I	S	A	L	S
R	I	T	E		F	O	W	L	E	S		N	E	E
M	A	O	R	I	S		N	O	N	W	A	G	E	S
		W	I	T		A	C	E	T	I	C			
S	P	O	N	G	E	B	O	B		L	E	T	T	S
U	A	R		E	D	A	M		O	L	D	H	A	T
F	I	R	S	T	S		F	L	A	P		E	X	E
I	D	Y	L	S		B	O	O	K	A	T	R	I	P
		A	B	O	A	R	D		S	E	E			
C	O	P	Y	E	D	I	T		T	S	E	T	S	E
A	B	O		T	E	N	E	T	S		S	H	A	Q
V	A	U	L	T	S		R	O	A	M		E	M	U
E	M	C	E	E	S		S	I	R	I		R	O	I
S	A	H	A	R	A		L	S	D		F	S	P	

77

M	A	L	I	A		A	L	A		A	B	C	S
U	C	O	N	N		T	O	M	E		D	U	A	L
G	R	A	V	Y	T	R	A	I	N		D	I	C	E
S	O	M	E		R	I	N	S	E	S		C	H	E
		S	Q	U	A	S	H	R	A	C	K	E	T	
C	A	C	T	U	S			O	T	O	S			
I	S	H		I	T	A	L	O		N	E	R	D	
T	H	A	N	K	S	G	I	V	I	N	G	D	A	Y
E	Y	R	E		A	N	I	M	E		A	C	E	
		L	O	E	B			P	R	A	N	K	S	
D	R	E	S	S	I	N	G	R	O	O	M			
W	E	S		L	O	O	I	E	S		S	O	B	A
E	T	T	E		T	U	R	K	E	Y	T	R	O	T
E	R	O	S		A	N	T	E		M	E	Z	Z	O
B	O	N	E			S	H	Y		A	L	O	O	P

78

P	A	S		I	S	P	S			E	T	A	S
O	D	E		R	I	A	A		C	L	A	S	P
T	H	E	B	R	O	W	N	B	O	M	B	E	R
S	O	Y	A		U	N	D	E	R		S	A	Y
	C	A	L	Y	X		B	I	K	O			
		L	O	W	M	A	N		R	A	S	P	
A	M	S		H	A	N	G	G	L	I	D	E	R
S	A	P	P	O	R	O		A	B	O	V	E	
S	T	A	S	H		A	S	P	I	R	E	S	
N	E	W	Y	O	R	K	J	E	T		E	R	S
S	Y	N	C		A	L	A	M	O	S			
		H	A	N	A		I	P	A	N	A		
E	E	W		M	I	X	I	N		H	A	S	P
S	N	A	K	E	S	O	N	A	P	L	A	N	E
P	Y	R	E	X		N	O	R	A		C	E	L
Y	A	N	G			S	T	Y	X		P	R	E

79

```
M E T A L ▢ G E O M ▢ L A V S
A S O N E ▢ R E A R ▢ A L I T
S Q U I D M A R K S ▢ N O V A
O U T L A I D ▢ ▢ M Y D E A R
N E S ▢ ▢ N E W S I E S ▢ ▢
▢ S Q U A R E T A C T I C
H I R E E S ▢ E T H ▢ A R N O
G R A N D ▢ L A S ▢ A P E R S
T A G S ▢ S O T ▢ A L E X E I
S Q U I R T C H A S E R ▢ ▢
▢ ▢ T H E I S T S ▢ R C A
A C T I O N ▢ T E A S E R S
D R O Z ▢ G R E A T S Q U A T
D O M E ▢ E E O C ▢ P I N T O
S P E D ▢ L A N K ▢ S N E E R
```

80

```
C A V E ▢ T E M P T ▢ T A C T
U T E S ▢ I R I S H ▢ A T O E
R E S T ▢ B A T T E N D O W N
R A P S ▢ I S T ▢ S E A M E D
E W E ▢ M A E ▢ F I R ▢ I R E
N A R C O S ▢ E N D U S E R
T Y S O N ▢ P E A ▢ L T D
▢ ▢ C O N F U S I O N ▢ ▢
▢ N E O ▢ B I G ▢ L A S E D
S O D A C A N ▢ C A R O L E
C M I ▢ I D S ▢ R A Y ▢ P E S
R I B B E R ▢ T A N ▢ B R A C
I N L A L A L A N D ▢ L A Z E
P E E R ▢ F A T A L ▢ O N A N
T E S T ▢ T R I T E ▢ C O R D
```

81

```
G O B A D ▢ A M A S S ▢ M A W
P R O T O ▢ N U B I A ▢ A M A
S T R A T ▢ I F A T F I R S T
▢ D R E A M T ▢ S E N A T E
T H E I D E A I S ▢ S U E R
A T L ▢ U R L ▢ T I M I D L Y
D E L I ▢ ▢ R E T A G ▢ ▢
▢ N O T A B S U R D T H E N
▢ S L A K E ▢ T I E R
M I N O L T A ▢ C O D ▢ N I H
A M E N ▢ T H E R E I S N O
S G T M A J ▢ A L B E R T
H O P E F O R I T ▢ J E E R S
E N A ▢ T H A T I ▢ A N I O N
D E Y ▢ A N T I C ▢ Y E N T L
```

82

```
C E D I L L A ▢ E S I A S O N
O P E N O U T ▢ N A S T A S E
R A M B L E R ▢ G R A M M A R
N U I ▢ A G E S A G O ▢ O K D
E L L E ▢ O S A G E ▢ M A A S
R E L Y ▢ ▢ T G I ▢ J A N N
S T E E D S ▢ O N I O N S ▢
▢ B E A M ▢ G I G I ▢
▢ C O V E R T ▢ I S A Y S O
▢ B O L O ▢ A W E ▢ C O H N
D E N T ▢ K N I T S ▢ S U R E
E N D ▢ P A D T H A I ▢ L I N
E G O T I S M ▢ A B A L O N E
M A R I N E R ▢ N E M E S E S
S Y S T E M S ▢ E R A S E R S
```

83

```
B U B B A ▢ W A N D ▢ E B O N
A A R O N ▢ A T T U ▢ T O R E
A W A R D O F T H E S T A T E
▢ D E E P E N ▢ H A T E S
P B S ▢ S I R ▢ D S O ▢ E G O
A A H S ▢ E S C A P E P L A N
S H A P E ▢ ▢ U S E B Y
▢ A W A Y W I T H W O R D S ▢
▢ D E E R E ▢ X E R O X
I S M E L L A R A T ▢ S E R E
M T A ▢ A L S ▢ B U S ▢ S T S
P A R E S ▢ G A S H E S ▢
A L I G H T I N T H E D A R K
L A N A ▢ I R A E ▢ A G G I E
A G E D ▢ P E T S ▢ R E E D Y
```

84

```
C A T ▢ R O M A N C E ▢ B C D
A R R ▢ E X E D O U T ▢ A L E
P T A ▢ C O L O R T V ▢ N E E
T I N F [OIL] ▢ [OIL] L A M P
A C C O S T S ▢ T R A I N E R
I L E S ▢ U L T R A ▢ M A N E
N E S S ▢ B R [OIL] E R ▢ E S T D
[L] I K E W A T E R A N D O I [L]
A [WE] ▢ A [T] A T I [ME] ▢ U [R] I
S H Y ▢ H O T [2] B A G ▢ T A B
T E A ▢ O D E ▢ S I R ▢ L T R
P E R I O D ▢ ▢ T O L I F E
A L E C ▢ L A Y E R ▢ O N I T
S I N E ▢ E L A T E ▢ W E N T
S E A [1] ▢ R A Z E D ▢ [3] S K I
```

(1) WATER (2) WATER (3) WATER

85

```
C H A D S   M U R K   A D D S
H U L O T   A S I A   F E A T
I R E N E   N U M B   O M N I
S T E E L I E R   U P R O A R
    E L L   P E K O E
O W L   A L P   M I S S T E P
F E A R   D U M B   E A U D E
F I V E G O L D E N R I N G S
T R A C E   S S R S   D I F T
O S S E T I A   S Y S   S R O
    S A C R A   N Y C
S H A S T A   L A C R O S S E
N O R I   R U I N   I R A T E
O H N O   U S E D   A N G E L
B O O N   S O N Y   C Y S T S
```

86

```
I D A H O S   A F T E R A L L
A R R A N T   T I A M A N I A
N U C L E A R E N G I N E E R
  G O O G L E   S T R O N G
    S I E N N A   A L E E
D R J   G R E E N A L G A E
I K E S   V A R I G
P O T E N T I A L E N E R G Y
  A I R E D   D O P E
  R I F L E R A N G E   Z A P
B A R A   I N A R U T
E C A R D S   V A R I E S
G E N E R A L D I S A R R A Y
F M I R A T E S   S I E R R A
M E S S T E N T   O L D S A W
```

87

```
E R N E S T   V I C   C H I C
G E I S H A   O W A   O O N A
B U R O A K   C O S   N A T L
E N V   R E B A   S H E R R Y
R I A   P A U L I N A   S U P
T O N O E N D   T A R G E T S
  N A T   I A N S   D O N H O
    H A P P Y 2 0 1 4
C A V E R   E E L S   I R T
H E I R E S S   A U S T E R E
I R A   W A T U T S I   C I A
M A D M E N   B E A M   I R R
E T U I   D U O   N E A T E N
R O C K   A K A   N O N A M E
A R T E   L E T   A N G L E D
```

88

```
I B A R S   A L L   A F L A T
R E C A P   D U O   M O O C H
M A C H I N E S V   A R A C E
A R E   N O L T E   T O N E R
  U P L A T E   C H I N E S E
O P T I C S   S H A V E R S
D O E T H   M O I R E S
A N D I   W A L L M   E M U 3
    G E A R E D   P L A N K
  F R A N C I S   D E F T L Y
G L U T T O N   D E A F T O
R O S I E   A C O R N   R O E
O R S O N   T H E R U L E S B
F E I N T   E A R   T O S E A
E T A P E   D I R   S A S S Y
```

89

```
B Y O B   S P U N   P A R S E
H O V E   O G L E   E T A I L
A H E M   B A I H S P O N G E
T O R I I   R A T   B O N N
T H I N G A M A B O B   U F O
Y O T E A M O   P A S T O R
    O T I C   S H O R E
  N I C K E L O D E O N
N I E C E   T O M B
O R W E L L   B L I N K A T
S K I   T I M E S S Q U A R E
E S S A   M E N   S T R E P
B O S S Y P A N T S   J A N E
A M U S E   L U A U   O T O E
G E E N A   Y I P E   B E T S
```

90

```
Z I P S   M E S   I N T E L
A S E A   I I T A S   N O O N E
P L A Y   T O N H   D I R G E
P E C   B A N A I   E S T E R
A S H T O N   N N A P E E L
  F O O T E D Y E I
D R U B S   A H   R H E S U S
O O Z E   B R E L O   Q U A Y
E N Z Y M E   A A   C U B E D
    A T M S B R O A D
  P A T C H O F   A D L I B S
S A R A H   R A I C E   V A T
P R O T O   S U T E   J I B E
E S S E N   E L E R   E D E N
D E E R E   T M S   B E L T
```

91

```
J A C O B   C O D A   B A B A
A R O M A   A S A P   A F E W
G E O G R A P H Y B   S T A R
S A P   B L E A T   P I E T Y
      L A T H   O S I E R
E M B E R   O W N U P   N S C
V O L T A I R E   M E M O I R
A D A M   O N L Y U   A O N E
D E C E I T   L I P S Y N C S
E L K   B A D G E   H A T E S
    E R A S E   L O O N
F O Y E R   C A D R E   C U E
E V E N   C A R I B B E A N C
M A D D   O N I N   O W E T O
A L P S   S T A G   X E N O N
```

92

```
H O G   A D A M   L A R S O N
A N E C D O T E   A M A N D A
C A N O E I S T   D O T E O N
K N E W   T E E   D I C E R S
    R E F   A R F   H R S
S T A R E S   L A C E S
C A T S U P   G O D O T
H O E   D O T T E D I   R E A
      P A I R S   U N B E L T
      B E L L A   P E O P L E
  V A N   P J S   D R E
D O T A G E   A T M   Z A H N
A I M L O W   Y O U D O T O O
P L A T T E   N U T R I E N T
S A N Y O S   E T T U   D E E
```

93

```
L O B S   H I S T   T H E S(2)
A C R E   I N T O   A B A T E
S T A N   G U A M   L E T U S
H A N S C H R I S T I A N
A N D E R S E N   R A M O N A
T E S L A     B U S   F I X
      E V I C T E D   C A K E
H A N S E L A N D G R E T E L
O N E S   L E S S E E S
S K A   T E N     L A M E R
T H R O W S   P A N O R A M A
    B R O T H E R S G R I M M
A B E A R   A T T Y   I T I S
T I E T O   N E O N   T A T E
(1)B R E W   K R O C   Z I T S
```
(1) HOME (2) WITCH

94

```
F I G   J O N     A S S U M E
I N O   A V E C   S L U R R Y
E V A   M I M I   T E N S E R
N E W K I D O N T H E(3) A D E
D R A I N     D U E T S
S T Y X   S H E B   O O Z E
      W H E R E   B U X O M
B U T C H E R(2) P A R T I E S
A T S E A   A Q A B A
A Z U L   L U N E   D R E W
    L A N D O   S U E D E
I C E(1) B U S T E R M O V I E
D O N A L D   E L O I   E B B
A P O G E E   S E A R   A L I
S E W E R S   A R K   L E T
```
(1) BLOCK (2) BLOCK (3) BLOCK

95

```
S A L A   F E D U P   J P E G
E M I T   I L O S E   O A S T
R O B E   V I T A E   H Y P O
U L Y S S E S S G R A N T
M E A T Y     E S Q   O N E
    S N E A K   U N P I N
P R S   E L G I N B A Y L O R
H O H O   S I N A I   C A B O
A D A M S A N D L E R   Y E N
S I D E A   S A L A D
E N O   B I T   V E I L S
  W O O D R O W W I L S O N
D E B I   E A T E R   M O P E
E N O L   A C T I I   A L E E
W A X Y   S K O R T   R A Z R
```

96

```
P I S M O   B U R Y   E R G O
A M P E D   A R E A   P E E K
W H A T S B L A C K W H I T E
N O M E   E L L A   E E N S Y
      O S A Y   L O A M
A N D R E(EA) D A L L O V E R
L E E   T Y R O   H E R E T O
A M A J   D U D   A C I D
N O L O S S   S O A R   A D O
    T H I S N E W S P A P E R
  A D I A   A K I N
V E R N E   R A G E   K I E V
A S U N B U R N E D P A N D A
M A N E   N O I R   A R D E N
P U T S   O W L S   W A Y N E
```

97

```
R O A S T █ S N I T █ █ C O O P
E C L A T █ H O N E █ █ R U B E
H E L L O R H I G H W A T E R
A L F █ P A H S █ R I F T █
B O O M █ T H E W A L T O N S
S T R A I T █ █ E N D █ S E E
█ C R E A S E █ █ J E S T
█ S H R E D D E D W H E A T
O L I O █ A N Y H O W █ █
M U D █ E S S █ E R E C T S
G R E A T W H I T E █ L A R K
█ A C T A █ L A Z Y █ T U E
S O W H A T E L S E I S N E W
A L A E █ H O B S █ P R A T E
K E Y S █ S N E E █ S A P O R
```

98

```
B A N G █ O J S █ A R T I E R
E L E A █ H I T █ S E N T R A3
W A S S O B B Y █ C O N S E N T
I M T H E R E █ F I R █ A C H E
T O L E D O █ A R I G O T T O W
C R E D █ T I D Y █ █ D R O M E
H T S █ U H O H █ S M E A R E D
█ P S E U D O C O U P █
A R C H E R S █ H A M M █ P T L
R E H A B █ E M M A █ B L U E
C A R R Y O K I E █ N O L A N S
A D I A █ B E N █ C D R A T E S
D I S O B E Y █ J A P A N E S E
E N T H U S E █ A G O █ C A I N
█ G A S S E D █ R E P █ H U N S
```

99

```
█ S H E E S H █ N E P A L I
S H A R P E I █ I N D I A N A
T U R N I N G T H E T R I C K
P T A █ H O I █ D I A █
█ T K O █ S N E L L █ P O S
C L I C █ T O T I E █ O V I D
A E R O █ R O A S T █ N E V E
T R I M M I N G T H E T R E E
█ E E K █ █ A Y E █
M A C █ D E L █ O L E █ S S T
I D O L I Z E █ M A L A C H I
S I L I C O N █ A G E D O U T
T E L L I N G T H E T R U T H
S U I T █ E T H A N █ E R I E
█ X E S █ S H U N T █ M S N
```

100

```
A K I M B O █ A L P A C A S
R E L O A D █ I C A N T L I E
[MAD]E L I N E █ T A X I F A R E
I N F █ D R E S D E N █ U N I
L E A N █ L A I R █ [MAD]D E N
L A M F █ A R [MAD]A █ S E I S
O R E G █ N O [MAD] █ A S W A S
█ L A D Y [MAD] █ O N N A █
█ A B E T S █ [MAD]R E █ V I S A
█ R O C A █ S W A T █ F C O L
A I N T █ █ S C O T █ S E R I
[MAD]A M █ S T A R E A T █ D E A
E D O N E I L L █ M I A T A S
U N T U R N E D █ I N H E R E
S E S T E T S █ S A [MAD]A M S
```

101

```
W A D S █ T H A N █ D A S H
O M I T █ H O H O S █ I B I S
O M O O █ E L E N A █ P E R T
F O R W A R D M A R C H █
█ E S M E █ O A T S █
S R O █ C O M P A N Y H A L T
H I P P O S █ L U G █ O T O E
A V E R T █ Y E S █ K N I S H
R E N E █ K E N █ I A G R E E
P R E S E N T A R M S █ E R E
█ R O S E █ E P E E █
█ R E A D Y A I M F I R E
I S N T █ D I O D E █ I M A C
M I C E █ S A G E T █ L A S H
P R O D █ G A R Y █ E X P O
```

102

```
C H I P █ S T O C K █ P I L E
L E N O █ I A D L E █ A D O S
A A R P █ A R O A R █ D O R M
P R E D A T O R Y █ A R N I E
█ I C E S █ C O S E T █
C A R V E R █ W O R K █ B I N
A G U A █ G A U Z E █ U N E
R O B █ W O O D R O W █ Y A W
O R I █ A D I E T █ S I N E
M A N █ W I N D █ C U T T E R
█ S L A N G █ █
T A T A S █ O R I G I N A L S
O N E S █ E V A D E █ C R O P
O K I E █ T E T O N █ E C R U
L A N D █ C R A F T █ S H E D
```

103

```
P I G S ■ A V I A T E ■ C A F
A M O K ■ N A S S A U ■ R I O
C U B I S T R E P O R T E R S
S P I C E ■ Y E S ■ A I D E S
■ ■ A N G ■ ■ A S P I R E
P O M P O U S A S S I S T ■
O R A ■ R E P L I C A ■ R A W
P S I ■ ■ V O I L E ■ I C E
E O N ■ C A R B O N S ■ S H E
■ S T A R K I S T N A K E D
A T T I L A ■ ■ S A D
S U R L Y ■ G A S ■ I D I O M
S L E E P E R C E L L I S T S
E S E ■ S E A N C E ■ C L O G
T A T ■ O L D E S T ■ T E E S
```

104

```
■ S C A R C E ■ F A C A D E
■ O H I O A N ■ A M A Z I N
■ D O N T T A L K A B O U T
M A S T S ■ M O E ■ A R R I D
A P E ■ Y E A ■ P L E N T Y
Y O U R S E L F W E ■ S A L E
A P P A L L ■ S O A R ■ L E D
■ G O L F ■ O P E L ■
A R P ■ B O B S ■ O D I S T S
S E A T ■ W I L L D O T H A T
I D I O C Y ■ O A S ■ R N A
A R D O R ■ A M Y ■ W H I N Y
■ A F T E R Y O U L E A V E
■ F O O D I E ■ P O R T E R
■ T R O O P S ■ S T E E L Y
```

105

```
C H E ■ G R A M S ■ E P S O M
H E M ■ C E L I A ■ R O U T E
A Y E ■ H E L L I F I K N O W
M Y R I A D ■ ■ D A T E S
P O I N T ■ I M S T U M P E D
S U L K ■ A D I O S ■ O O Z E
■ ■ S H R E D ■ I N T R A
G A S ■ B E A T S M E ■ S A D
O U T G O ■ E L U D E ■
O T O E ■ A E R O S ■ D E A R
D O N T A S K M E ■ F I R M A
■ E E R I E ■ J E T S E T
I H A V E N O C L U E ■ A C T
R O G E T ■ U P E N D ■ T H E
K E E N E ■ T A N K S ■ Z E D
```

106

```
J A M B S ■ P A R T ■ R A F T
A L E R T ■ A R I E ■ A C A I
R I G O R ■ S O B E ■ (4)E C T
■ N O N A M E S ■ T R I O
S E I (1)H E D A Y ■ J I B E S
I N H A S T E ■ E M I R ■
A G A R ■ W N W ■ O N E O N
M E D ■ S O A P B O X ■ K O S
■ L A B O R ■ A R N ■ M A M A
■ R O K S ■ U S U R P E D
K A R A T ■ P I S (3)N G I N E
A N U T ■ C R O S S E R ■
B I B I ■ L I N E ■ S E I K O
O T I S ■ A N I L ■ C E C I L
B A K (2)■ P T A S ■ O N E N D
```

(1) ZEST (2) LAVA (3) TONE (4) DIAL

107

```
M I L K ■ J U I C E ■ T E A
E P E E ■ U P B O W ■ S L U G
A S A N ■ S L A V E ■ K E R I
D O N T S T A R E ■ P E C A N
■ S N I T ■ C A D ■
C S A ■ O N E S T O P ■ F A V
I A M S O ■ T I M E T O G O
D R I N K S A L L A R O U N D
E A G L E E Y E ■ D E R E K
R H O ■ R I S O T T O ■ S S A
■ L E S ■ O I L S ■
A R C E D ■ P L O T L I N E S
L A I D ■ F L I N T ■ N O T A
E S A U ■ E E N I E ■ E W O K
■ P O P ■ W A T E R ■ W I N E
```

108

```
■ B O A R S ■ F E R B E R
B R U N E I ■ C O R D E L I A
R A T E D X ■ O P E D P A G E
A V A N T I ■ L E S ■ O C H
N E C T A R ■ O N C D ■ K T S
D R T ■ P O O R ■ A E R O B E
■ D E N E B ■ S T E P I N
E S P O ■ R Y N ■ E S T D
M E A N I E ■ N A G E L
M A R G I N ■ U V E A ■ D P S
A G T ■ I C B M ■ T S T R A P
R H E ■ L O B ■ A Y E A Y E
S E R E N A D E ■ T O R P O R
K E E L O V E R ■ A N S E L M
I N E S S E ■ N E E D A
```

109

```
N O H A S S L E . A S T R A L
P R E M O L A R . B E W A R E
R U N A L O N G . B E A T I T
. . . Z E T A . J A Y . E S S
T A K E A H I K E . A D D T O
U S A . . S S G T S . A X O N
B O T O X . . S T A I R . . .
B U Z Z O F F . A M S C R A Y
. . . A X I O N . H Y E N A .
S N O W . G R E A T . . E N D
K O L A S . M A K E L I K E A
I T D . I D S . I N A N . . .
B A N A N A . A N D S P L I T
U R A N U S . S T A T U A R Y
M Y G O S H . T O Y S T O R E
```

110

```
T A L E . S Q U A B . A C D C
A L E X . O U N C E . D O R A
P I N T . P A T E G U R N E R
A S T O R . D O S . R E G A L
S T O R A G . . I G N O R E .
. . . T H E M . S T E A L . .
B M W S . T A N K S . L E A K
A I R . . Y O U . . . S K I
A X I S . T O W N S . J E A N
. . T A S E R . K A L E . . .
C O L L E G . . G A Z E B O
O R A T E . T U B . S E V E R
A B R I D O O F A R . B I G A
T I G E . A F O R F . F T A L
S T E R . F U S E D . L E N S
```

111

```
E C O . R O C . D J S . N E S
M A C . O N A . R E Q U E S T
I N H A L E R . Y O U L O S E
T E S T L A B . S P I N N E R
. . . O S L O . A R A L . . .
R A I M I . N A C R E . I T S
O R R I N . C L O D S . G E T
C R O C . L O O P Y . N H R A
K A N . S O P U P . N U T R I
Y U M . C L Y D E . I M S A D
. . A G A L . R O B B . . .
P H I L L I P . H O L E D U P
R U D O L P H . E M E R I T I
O N E W O O D . A P T . V A T
M S N . P P S . D H S . A H A
```

112

```
L I S T O N . A H S . F U L L
I N H A L E . F O E . O N E A
E L I X I R . R E R O U T E S
L I F E O F [PI] . D E A R E S T
O N T V . R M O N T H S . .
W E S A Y . (1) A W A Y . T F A
. . D U B . E N D . P E A L
A R T E M I S . S E W E D U P
R O A R . K E G . D A R . .
M D S . S I D E 2 . C S P O T
. . M A G N U M [PI] . E R N O
E L A S T I C . R M O V I E S
B A N I S T E R . A R F N A S
A V I A . O R O . C I R C L E
N A A N . P S Y . K N E E L S
```

(1) SQUARED

113

```
D A D E . J U M P . N E W A T
I T O N . O R C A . A C E L A
S W O R D H I L T . P O T O K
C O B A I N . I T A . T H E E
O R I G A M I . I G L O O . .
S K E E . U N D . R A N O F F
. . D E I C E R . T E D D Y
S E A . I R A N H I T . S R I
P U R S E . S I E G E S . .
A R M P I T . M A O . E L S A
. Y E O W S . S T R E E T S
N O W A . O C D . N I P S A T
S N A K E . R A R E C A T C H
F E S T S . O N Y X . S E E M
W A H O O . D E E T . T R Y A
```

114

```
A H E M S . N U F F S A I D
R A D I O S . A S I A N F L U
C H A N U K A H M E N O R A H
S A M I S E N . . B U O Y S
. . . E K G . C O T . . .
C H A O S T H E O R Y . M E A
A O R T A . T W A . F I S H
C H A R L O T T E B R O N T E
T U B A . O S H . A T S E A
I M S . C H A I N S M O K E D
. . K O S . S A T . . .
A S N A P . R I B C A G E
C H C H C H C H C H A N G E S
L A I L A A L I . L A B R A T
U N S O R T E D . S C A R S
```

115

```
P S S T . P A W S . M U S K Y
O M A N . A G E E . O P I N E
T I L T . P A R E . A L L E N
A L I . W A T E R S N A K E .
T E N S I L E . . K E N .
O D E O N . S T R A D D L E D
. . R E S . O A T . E R A
W H A T S I N T H E B O X E S
O B I . G E E . S E T .
W O R D I N E S S . S I T U P
. O N E . I C E C U B E
. F I R S T L I G H T . S O D
M A S A I . A S H E . T S A R
R I N D S . T O E S . A L T O
S N O O T . E N D S . B E S S
```

116

```
. A T V . I L L . A U S T I N
B L A C K T I E . S B A R R O
A G G R I E V E . H O W A R D
B O G . A M E R I C A N P I E
A R E A . . P A T . P T A
R E D S K E L T O N . R E A R
. P O L I O . C O R N
C H E C K E R E D P A S T
S U C H . S M E A R .
M I N T . W H I T E S A L E S
O M G . S H E . . T I N E
P I R A T E R A D I O . B R A
P A I S A N . M O N O G R A M
E M E T I C . S I X F L A G S
T I R A D E . O N S . O S E
```

117

```
J U M P . E W O K . O M A R S
A F A R . C O R E . H A S A T
Y O G I . L O B E . B R I N E
. M A I D E N V O Y A G E
E N C A M P . O A T . G E L
C O L L I S I O N T H E O R Y
R O O . E L S . S E T .
U N G E R . K A T . R A J A H
. D E A . G A S . E C O
T I P O F T H E I C E B E R G
O D O . I L E . E L O P E S
T I T A N I C S I N K S
A D A G E . K N O T . T U F T
L I T E R . L A T E . O K I E
S T O R Y . E G A D . N E X T
```

118

```
G O O N . J O T . E A C H
A M N O T . A W E . T Y C H O
W A L S H . R E X . H E R O S
P R O W E S S . T S E L I O T
. W E N T . P A I D .
. A R I A . S E N D
C O T T O N Y . I L O S T I T
H U H . O K E . M U S . H A Y
E T E . F A S T O N E . E M P
S H O T . T H I N K . R O S E
S O H O T . A C E . D U R O C
G U E R R E . . C A N A D A
A S A . O L D P R O S . N E S
M E R . T H R O U G H . K A T
E S T . I T E M S . S D S
```

119

```
S C H I R R A . G R I S S O M
E R O D I N G . N O R E P L Y
V A M O O S E . A C E T A L S
E V E N . S A S K . C A T
N E S T S . T H E D I E .
. E D E R . T O R R I D
M A C . N O T O K . O K A P I
A L A . S H E P A R D . C A P
T O R S O . S H O A L . E D S
S U P E R C . I N G E
. E E Y O R E . R E T A G
C O N . O E D S . M E R L
A T T E M P T . E N T E N T E
L O E S S E R . W H E R E O N
M E R C U R Y . S L A Y T O N
```

120

```
B O L A . A L M A . H U L A S
E L A L . N O E L . U T I C A
R I T E . G A R B . S A F E S
E V E R Y O N E O F T H E .
T E X T I L E . M E L . B A S
. P A R S . D E C E N T
M A R N E . C U T E . O L G A
C L U E S H A S E X A C T L Y
C O N S . I R A N . M O S E S
O N S T A R . N O R A .
Y E A . C E O . C A N T A T A
. F O U R S Y L L A B L E S
P E T R I . C O O L . A G E S
A T E A T . A G C Y . L A N E
C A R L Y . R A K E . L E S S
```

121

S	A	N	T	A	N	A		N	E	T	F	L	I	X
C	H	U	N	N	E	L		O	X	I	D	A	T	E
A	I	R	T	A	X	I		S	P	R	A	Y	E	R
L	T	S		G	U	M	S	H	O	E		A	M	O
D	U	E	T		S	O	L	O	S		T	W	I	X
E	N	R	O	N		N	O	W		G	R	A	Z	E
D	A	Y	L	I	L	Y		S	P	L	A	Y	E	D
		K	E	Y			D	I	P					
E	T	A	I	L	E	D		I	Q	T	E	S	T	S
N	O	T	E	S		I	N	C		Z	Z	T	O	P
C	O	E	N		I	V	I	E	S		E	U	R	E
A	S	I		A	M	O	E	B	A	S		N	N	E
M	O	N	S	T	E	R		A	M	I	S	T	A	D
P	O	T	O	M	A	C		T	O	R	P	E	D	O
S	N	O	C	O	N	E		H	A	I	R	D	O	S

122

A	C	T	F	I	V	E		O	F	F	C	A	S	T
F	A	I	R	B	A	N	K	S	A	L	A	S	K	A
F	H	E	E	A	S	S	O	C	I	A	T	I	O	N
A	L	G	O	R	E		M	A	N	X		M	P	G
B	E	A	N	S		P	O	R	T		M	O	J	O
L	A	M	S		B	U	D	S		L	O	V	E	S
E	S	E		B	R	N	O		R	O	O			
	E	S	P	R	I	T	D	E	C	O	R	P	S	
		A	I	M		R	A	M	P		L	I	D	
S	K	O	R	T		H	A	S	P		N	O	L	O
A	A	H	S		S	A	G	E		J	A	W	E	D
I	B	M		Z	E	R	O		D	U	P	I	N	G
D	O	Y	O	U	W	A	N	N	A	D	A	N	C	E
H	O	M	E	L	E	S	S	S	H	E	L	T	E	R
I	M	Y	O	U	R	S		C	L	A	M	O	R	S

123

F	A	W	N		A	B	B	A		T	A	S	K	S
E	C	H	O		H	E	A	R		I	R	E	N	E
M	E	A	T	T	H	E	R	M	O	M	E	T	E	R
A	S	T	A	R		T	R	Y	M	E		T	W	A
		H	R	A	P		S	A	G	A	L			
P	L	A	Y	M	E	O	R	T	R	A	D	E	M	E
S	A	P		S	O	X	E	R		P	I	S	A	N
E	S	P	O		N	Y	T	O	L		A	I	N	O
U	S	E	A	S		G	I	N	O	S		H	O	T
D	O	N	T	E	V	E	N	G	O	T	H	E	H	E
		S	H	E	E	N		P	I	E	S			
C	T	N		K	E	A	T	S		L	Y	C	E	E
W	H	E	R	E	S	T	H	E	R	E	M	O	T	E
T	A	X	E	R		E	U	R	O		A	R	A	L
S	I	T	E	S		D	R	E	W		N	E	T	S

124

N	A	S	T	Y	G	R	A	M		N	A	P	E	S
I	N	T	H	E	R	E	A	R		O	R	R	I	N
P	A	R	A	S	A	I	L	S		B	O	O	N	E
S	L	O	W		S	D	I		G	O	A	T	E	E
		S	T	P		Y	S	I	D	R	O			
S	R	O		U	S	U	A	L	L	Y		T	E	D
C	A	M	E	R	A	S	H	Y		S	T	Y	L	I
A	D	A	P	T	T	O		F	S	H	A	P	E	D
N	A	H	A	L		P	R	O	P	O	N	E	N	T
F	R	A		E	Y	E	E	X	A	M		S	A	O
		B	A	D	E	N	D		M	E	T			
S	T	E	P	I	N		Z	I	A		E	S	A	U
M	I	A	T	A		P	O	O	L	H	A	L	L	S
U	L	C	E	R		E	N	T	O	U	R	A	G	E
G	E	H	R	Y		D	E	A	T	H	S	T	A	R

125

S	T	I	L	L	D	R	E				A	L	B	A
C	O	N	E	H	E	A	D	S			M	E	A	N
A	R	C	T	A	N	G	E	N	T		O	A	T	S
R	E	L	I	S	T	S		O	R	I	E	N	T	E
F	A	U	N	A	S		T	W	I	N	B	I	L	L
A	D	D	O	N		J	E	T	P	L	A	N	E	
C	O	E	N		G	A	L	I	L	E	E			
E	R	S		D	E	S	E	R	E	T		L	O	B
		D	E	T	O	X	E	D		J	O	N	I	
	S	T	E	A	R	N	E	S		T	A	M	E	S
T	H	E	O	R	E	M	S		L	I	M	B	I	C
Y	E	S	D	E	A	R		S	A	N	T	A	N	A
P	A	S	A		L	A	B	O	R	P	A	R	T	Y
E	T	A	T		Z	E	N	G	A	R	D	E	N	
A	H	S	O			L	E	O	N	T	Y	N	E	

126

W	H	I	P	I	T		S	P	A	C	E	J	A	M
H	A	M	E	L	S		C	O	C	A	C	O	L	A
A	M	P	S	U	P		H	I	T	S	O	N	G	S
T	R	U	T	V		O	M	N	I	S		K	O	S
S	A	D	O		N	A	U	T		P	Y	R	E	
U	D	E		K	I	T	T	Y	K	E	L	L	E	Y
P	I	N	C	E	N	E	Z		H	D	A			
G	O	T	O	V	E	R		M	A	G	N	U	M	S
		R	I	T		T	A	K	E	O	N	M	E	
J	O	H	N	N	Y	C	A	K	E	S		D	M	X
A	N	A	S		O	X	E	N		G	E	M	S	
R	E	V		H	E	L	P	S		G	O	R	G	E
J	O	E	B	O	X	E	R		M	O	N	G	O	L
A	N	N	E	R	I	C	E		F	A	Z	O	O	L
R	E	S	T	S	T	O	P		A	T	O	D	D	S

127

```
M A D E M I N C E M E A T O F
E C O N O M I C W A R F A R E
L O S A N G E L E S T I M E S
S P E C I A L I N T E R E S T
█ S T E M S █ █ I S S █ █ █
█ O D E █ F F F █ T R E E
S T U R M █ B E E F S █ A X L
M O R S E C O D E S I G N A L
O J S █ N I L E S █ L A K M E
G O A L █ M A X █ T V S █
█ U G A █ P I E R O █
C O M M E R C I A L R A D I O
F R E E T R A N S L A T I O N
C H A N S O N S D E G E S T E
S E T S O N A P E D E S T A L
```

128

```
P I Z Z A C R U S T █ B L A B
A R I O N A S S I S █ F O R A
C I P H E R T E X T █ F O R T
A S S A M █ D A R K █ K I T
█ N O G O █ M A N C A V E
P S A █ N O O N █ P E L T E R
H O C K E Y M O M █ W E T L Y
O L E N █ A P L U S █ A H A B
N A T A L █ H O T P O T A T O
E R I C A S █ S E C T █ T E X
B A C K L I T █ D A T A █
O R A █ A N O N █ O L D I E
O R C A █ B R O O D M A R E S
T A I L █ I T A L I A N A R T
H Y D E █ N A M E S N A M E S
```

129

```
B L U E C R A B █ L O W F A T
O I L S H A L E █ B R O O C H
N O N T I T L E █ J I L T E E
D N A █ T O R T R E F O R M
█ C L A W C R A N E █
P A T R O N S A I N T █ A S A
E B O O K █ N E C █ R C A S
T A R N I S H █ S H T E T L S
A C M E █ M A O █ R A I T T
L I E █ V E L V E T E L V I S
█ F A L L E N H E M █
E L D O C T O R O W █ V F W
C O U G A R █ B R A S S E R A
O R S I N O █ I M R U I N E D
N I E N T E █ D E T E N T E S
```

130

```
S Q U A B B L E █ J A M C A M
E U P H O R I A █ O R I O L E
T I P S H E E T █ K I D U L T
B B S █ M A L I C E █ E L S E
A B A S █ K O T O █ H A D T O
I L L I N █ W U N D E R B A R
L E A N O N █ P I E R █ E R S
█ S O U P █ C L O P █
S E A █ G T O S █ L I T O U T
E X Q U I S I T E █ C A N S O
A T U N E █ S U C H █ S E T T
G R I P █ D E C A Y S █ M I A
R E V I S E █ K R A T I O N S
A M E L I E █ U T T E R R O T
M E R E S T █ P E T P E E V E
```

131

```
█ D A R E S S A L A A M █
█ C O N T A C T L E N S E S █
W H A T S T H E B I G D E A L
R O S H █ A N T E █ F R I A
A L I E N T O █ I N F █ K N T
P E D R O █ O S T E O P A T H
S R O █ N U K E █ A R E T E S
█ T O P S E C R E T █
S A R D I S █ T O S S █ O Y E
P R E S S E S O N █ E R T E S
E F S █ E T O █ C H E E T O S
N A T E █ B R E A █ T A M A
T R Y T O S E E I T M Y W A Y
█ F L A S H I N T H E P A N █
█ E S T A T E S A L E S █
```

132

```
B U T T D I A L E D █ G I B E
O N A R A M P A G E █ U N O S
T I D A L B A S I N █ M O B S
S T A P L E R █ S A C █ N S A
█ P A C T S █ L O V E L Y
I C E █ S I M I █ I N A P E T
N A N S █ L E T S █ A S I D E
B R I E F E N C O U N T E R S
A D D E R █ T O R N █ S C U T
D E B T E E █ M E I N █ E N S
S A L O O N █ S L O O P █
O L Y █ N A M █ O N S E R V E
R E T D █ C A S S I O P E I A
T R O Y █ T A K E S A S E A T
S S N S █ S M A R T P I L L S
```

133

C	A	S	H	B	A	R	S	■	K	A	R	S	T	S
O	S	C	A	R	W	A	O	■	N	I	I	H	A	U
N	O	I	F	S	A	N	D	S	O	R	B	U	T	S
G	N	A	T	■	I	D	I	O	C	Y	■	T	A	S
R	E	T	■	S	T	R	U	C	K	■	M	I	R	E
A	M	I	G	A	S	■	M	I	I	■	O	N	Y	X
T	A	C	O	S	■	O	P	E	N	E	D	■	■	■
S	N	A	P	E	■	N	E	T	■	D	E	V	A	S
■	■	A	S	M	A	N	Y	■	G	R	A	C	E	■
H	A	P	S	■	A	B	T	■	P	A	N	G	E	A
O	N	I	T	■	N	O	O	N	E	R	■	A	D	O
O	Y	L	■	A	C	U	T	E	R	■	A	B	E	T
T	H	E	T	R	U	T	H	W	I	L	L	O	U	T
C	O	U	R	T	S	■	A	L	L	I	A	N	C	E
H	O	P	E	S	O	■	■	L	Y	S	A	N	D	E	R

134

A	P	P	L	E	C	A	R	E	■	R	A	N	C	H
D	O	U	B	L	E	D	E	D	■	O	M	A	H	A
I	M	T	O	O	S	E	X	Y	■	M	A	T	E	Y
D	E	T	■	N	A	Y	A	■	O	A	T	E	R	S
A	L	E	R	■	R	A	L	P	H	■	■	D	O	E
S	O	R	O	S	■	N	L	R	B	■	P	O	K	E
■	■	■	S	T	E	T	■	S	A	V	A	G	E	D
Z	E	A	L	O	T	■	■	B	I	N	G	E	S	■
A	L	E	Y	A	R	D	■	T	Y	N	E	■	■	■
P	E	O	N	■	A	E	R	O	■	G	R	I	E	G
C	O	N	■	D	R	E	W	U	■	A	N	N	A	■
O	N	F	I	R	E	■	L	A	N	D	■	T	R	I
M	O	L	D	Y	■	F	O	R	C	E	Q	U	I	T
I	R	U	L	E	■	B	A	D	A	D	V	I	C	E
X	A	X	E	S	■	I	N	S	P	E	C	T	O	R

135

B	O	S	C	O	■	■	J	A	C	K	L	O	R	D
A	X	T	O	N	■	R	E	T	R	I	E	V	E	R
S	N	A	R	E	■	A	B	O	U	T	F	A	C	E
Q	A	D	D	A	F	I	■	N	E	S	T	L	E	S
U	R	I	■	M	E	N	D	E	L	■	■	T	I	S
E	D	A	M	■	L	I	E	S	■	C	H	I	V	E
■	■	■	A	L	I	E	N	■	P	A	I	N	E	D
■	L	I	F	E	P	R	E	S	E	R	V	E	R	■
C	E	L	I	N	E	■	■	U	L	N	A	F	■	■
A	T	L	A	S	■	O	V	U	M	■	S	O	A	P
T	A	G	■	■	P	R	E	M	E	D	■	R	U	E
C	L	E	A	R	E	D	■	D	N	A	T	E	S	T
H	O	T	P	O	T	A	T	O	■	W	H	I	T	E
O	N	I	O	N	R	I	N	G	■	N	A	D	E	R
W	E	I	P	A	I	N	T	■	■	S	W	A	N	S

136

J	U	J	I	T	S	U	■	J	A	Z	Z	A	G	E
E	L	A	T	I	O	N	■	S	H	O	O	T	U	P
T	A	K	E	A	I	M	■	B	O	O	T	E	E	S
S	L	A	M	S	■	A	L	A	R	M	■	D	S	T
F	U	R	S	■	S	P	I	C	A	■	V	I	S	E
A	M	T	■	D	E	P	T	H	■	F	A	R	S	I
N	E	A	T	I	D	E	A	■	S	A	L	T	O	N
■	■	■	A	C	E	D	■	Z	A	N	E	■	■	■
F	I	B	B	E	R	■	H	A	N	G	T	I	M	E
A	P	L	U	S	■	P	A	N	T	S	■	C	O	X
S	A	I	S	■	L	A	N	Z	A	■	B	A	R	T
T	N	T	■	A	U	S	S	I	■	P	E	N	T	E
C	E	Z	A	N	N	E	■	B	U	I	L	T	I	N
A	M	E	R	I	G	O	■	A	T	A	C	O	S	T
R	A	N	K	L	E	S	■	R	E	S	H	O	E	S

137

P	U	D	D	Y	T	A	T	■	■	P	L	A	S	M
I	N	I	T	I	A	T	E	■	C	L	I	C	H	E
L	I	E	S	D	O	W	N	■	H	U	N	T	E	R
L	T	D	■	D	I	A	N	■	A	R	C	A	D	E
■	■	■	I	S	R	■	N	R	A	■	■	■	■	■
A	F	I	R	S	T	■	K	E	L	L	O	G	G	S
N	O	D	U	H	■	J	F	W	I	S	H	R	Y	E
I	R	O	N	■	P	U	L	S	E	■	B	A	R	N
M	I	N	T	J	E	L	L	Y	■	C	O	C	O	A
A	T	T	O	R	N	E	Y	■	C	O	Y	E	S	T
■	■	■	E	A	P	■	B	A	R	■	■	■	■	■
S	P	R	A	W	L	■	T	E	R	N	■	A	S	U
C	O	O	L	I	T	■	H	E	R	C	U	L	E	S
A	L	B	A	N	Y	■	O	N	E	O	R	T	W	O
R	E	O	R	G	■	■	M	E	L	B	L	A	N	C

138

S	G	T	S	C	H	U	L	T	Z	■	C	R	A	B
U	R	A	N	I	U	M	O	R	E	■	L	I	L	O
D	A	T	I	N	G	P	O	O	L	■	U	G	L	Y
S	P	I	T	E	■	I	K	I	D	■	S	H	O	W
Y	E	N	S	■	O	R	S	■	A	C	T	T	W	O
■	■	■	P	A	E	A	N	■	H	E	M	A	N	■
B	I	O	G	A	S	■	T	A	M	A	R	I	N	D
U	N	M	A	T	E	D	■	S	I	L	E	N	C	E
S	T	E	V	E	S	A	X	■	R	E	D	D	E	R
H	E	L	E	N	■	M	R	M	E	T	■	■	■	■
W	R	E	A	T	H	■	A	I	D	■	S	E	T	I
H	A	T	H	■	A	P	T	S	■	P	I	C	O	T
A	L	P	O	■	N	A	I	L	S	A	L	O	N	S
C	I	A	O	■	S	A	N	A	N	T	O	N	I	O
K	A	N	T	■	A	R	G	Y	L	E	S	O	C	K

139

```
B A M B I   M I N I     T S K S
O P A R T   U P O N     U T A H
S A L E S R O O M S     N O L O
C R E A M A N D S U G A R
      S E M     G L O R Y B E
R I T T     R A H     T O O B A D
I C I     B O R O N     F L O S S
M E L T E D C H O C O L A T E
M A T E S     S U D A N     R E L
E X A L T S     M E N     A D D S
D E W L I N E     C A B
    H A R A J U K U G I R L S
P A I L     C E L I N E D I O N
S I R I     K C A R     N E L L E
I S L E     S T N S     A D E L E
```

140

```
P R O A C T I V     B B G U N
H A S N O I D E A     P U L S E
E M M A S T O N E     O G E E S
L E O I     O L D G E E Z E R
P A N S Y     O I L     A C N E
S U D     E V E R S O     P L A T
    E T A T S     P U M A
O B T A I N S   J E Z E B E L
B A A S     A I R E R
I C K Y     D I S B A R     S T U
S K E G     O A F     O C E A N
    B O O K S M A R T     H E R D
M O V I E     B R E A K I N T O
O N E N D     S A N D A L T A N
B E R G S     S T A L L O N E
```

141

```
A L F A L F A     S N O W J O B
T O R S I O N     M A N H O U R
A N A C Q U I R E D T A S T E
D E T O U R     O L I O     H E W
    T O C C A T A     D U D S
B A M     R O I L S     N R A
E N A M E L E D     B O O T E E
E G G E D O N     A L S O R A N
B E N H U R     C L U E L E S S
    A T P     V A L E T     E Y E
R I C A     V E R Y T O P
E R A     A C R E     O N E O F F
H E R E S H O W T O O R D E R
E N T R A I N     I T S D O N E
M A A N D P A     T H E U R G E
```

142

```
    P A N A M G A M E S     P C S
D E T E R I O R A T E     H A L
T E R R E N C E M C N A L L Y
E T A T S     O T I S     L O V E
N E S S     S M E E     F I X E R
        J A M     V I P
A N C H O R A G E A L A S K A
F O R E I G N M I N I S T E R
T R A I N E D E L E P H A N T
A N T S I N O N E S P A N T S
    T N T     E S O
G O B I G     C A N A     A M A T
U P O N     W O R F     S C A R E
S E R G E A N T O R O U R K E
T R A     R I G O R M O R T I S
S A X     B L O O D S T A I N
```

143

```
M A N C A V E     M U G S H O T
E Q U A T O R     U S O T O U R
S U N S E T S     D E T E N T E
H A S H     E A R     R O P E I N
    C A R T O O N     D Y E D
S C R A P     Z A P A T A
P H O B O S     S A M A D A M S
E E L     L E A T H E R     N O T
C R O P L A N D     S O O T H E
    H O T T U B     I N E R T
V A Y A     B I C Y C L E
A G E N D A     K E A     T E C H
R I O T A C T     B R A I L L E
I T W O R K S     Y E S M A A M
G A S M A S K     E D H E L M S
```

144

```
A N G I E     N E W Y O R K
P E R K S     S O L E M N E R
S H E E T     F U N G I C I D E
E R E     T A M P A     A C O W
S U N D A Y W O R L D     E S E
    L U M E N     O L E S
O M A N I S     O W N E R S
R A N D O     C O S T A
O R D E A L     C L O S E D
    E L O I     S T A T E
B B S     A R T H U R W Y N N E
E L A M     E W E L L     T E X
D A L A I L A M A     C H I R P
I N E X C E S S     G U A V A
M C M X I I I     I N L E T
```

145

```
G O O D C A T C H ■ S T O R M
I N S T A G R A M ■ T I N E A
N E W S R E E L S ■ S L E D S
U S E ■ B E A V ■ ■ L I S T
P E G S ■ ■ T I C ■ S Y N C H
■ C O L A S ■ N A O H ■ T A E
■ ■ I N T ■ A L O E V E R A
D J A N G O U N C H A I N E D
A U C K L A N D ■ E V A ■ ■
D I T ■ O T O H ■ D E L O S
S C A M S ■ S O W ■ ■ S T U F
T E L E ■ B R I G ■ T A I
O B O T E ■ O B A M A C A R E
B O N E S ■ V E T O P O W E R
E X E R I ■ A S H K E N A Z I
```

146

```
J U M B O F R I E S ■ S R T A
O N I O N R I N G S ■ U I E S
G U N S L I N G E R ■ G P A S
S M A ■ E D G E R ■ P A S S E
■ ■ P A G O ■ G A R N E T
M O J A V E ■ S T U C C O
E D U C E ■ B O R N T O R U N
W I S E ■ B A R A K ■ A T N O
L E T S P A R T Y ■ S T E P S
■ P E O R I A ■ P I E R C E
O D E T T E ■ M I L D
F I A T S ■ A T O L L ■ D A D
O N C E ■ S M I L E Y F A C E
L A H R ■ S E N T I M E N T S
D R Y S ■ A N Y O N E E L S E
```

147

```
P E T I T F O U R ■ Y A W P S
I R O N H O R S E ■ E N I A C
D O N N A R E E D ■ S E P I A
G I G S ■ E G R E T ■ W E N T
I C U ■ W V A ■ E W E ■ O F T
N A E ■ Y E N ■ M I X T U R E
■ A C H O ■ S T P E T E R
■ M O T H S ■ T E N S E
G A N N E T T ■ B E D S
N I C O L A I ■ E R I ■ B A H
O N O ■ M M M ■ A V A ■ H A Y
C R U Z ■ P E N N E ■ C A F E
C O R E S ■ L I B R A R I A N
H A S T Y ■ A N A S T A S I A
I D E A L ■ G O G E T T E R S
```

148

```
A S I A N ■ D J P A U L Y D
C O N D O ■ G R E A T B E A R
T U T O R ■ L A T C H O N T O
U S E R ■ M I N S K ■ A D E N
P A R K R A N G E R ■ T A S E
■ V A U L T ■ T A B
C R A B B I E R ■ T I P P L E
P O L L O ■ D U S ■ G R A I N
R O S E U P ■ T E E T E R E D
■ T A C ■ A L O F I
A R C S ■ T H E C A P I T O L
M O O T ■ D I X O N ■ G I V E
A U D I T O R I A ■ L U M E N
S T O N E W A L L ■ A R E N T
S E N T E N C E ■ V E R S O
```

149

```
A C C E N T ■ K A S D A N
T R A L E E ■ T R I P O L I
M U R D E R ■ C H I L L O U T
S I D E D I S H E S ■ A R M S
■ S P R Y ■ C E N S U S
W E L L ■ C R A C K S H O T
I S A Y ■ O A T E R S ■ N A G
S H Y ■ O P T S F O R ■ E L M
P I E ■ M A C H O S ■ H I K E
■ P R E A C H E R S ■ E D E N
■ I N A P E T ■ D E A D
E G G S ■ B A T H P I L L O W
P R I N T A D S ■ O C T A V E
P I G E O N S ■ S T A K E D
S P A R T A ■ T A P E R S
```

150

```
C A N A D A B L U E G R A S S
T R A D I T I O N A L I R A S
N A V A L E N G A G E M E N T
S T E M L E S S G L A S S E S
■ L A Y ■ H I E S
C D R ■ S K I ■ S O S P A D
R A I D ■ R A P S ■ N E A L E
I N N O W A Y ■ I T S A L O T
S I G M A ■ O R Z O ■ R E N O
P O S S U M ■ O E R ■ S E X
■ K E R T ■ S A T
O B S C E N E G E S T U R E S
P O T A S S I U M I O D I D E
E L E P H A N T T R A I N E R
D E N T A L A S S I S T A N T
```

151

```
S H O R E ■ H O T E L B A R S
M O P E D ■ A N I M A L F A T
O N E L S ■ S A N I T A R I A
G E N I E ■ A S I R E C A L L
G Y M C L A S S E S ■ K I E L
I B I S ■ M E I R ■ T O D D S
E E K ■ B O A S ■ F O P ■ ■ ■
R E E N A C T ■ L I S S O M E
■ ■ ■ O T O ■ M A N S ■ P A Y
S A A B S ■ L E V I ■ J A K E
A R G O ■ D I M E S T O R E S
B E E T H O V E N ■ R A T S O
O N T H E M E N D ■ A N I O N
T O W E L E T T E ■ I N S U M
S T O R M D O O R ■ L A T T E
```

152

```
B A N A N A G R A M S ■ U S M
A D O B E R E A D E R ■ G E E
T I J U A N A T A X I ■ G A G
E D I T ■ E R A ■ ■ S A B R A
S A V ■ C L U T C H ■ S O O N
■ S E T H ■ P A L O ■ P O U F
■ ■ ■ A E C ■ T E R Z E T T O
I L O V E L A ■ F A I R S E X
F A C E P A L M ■ E N S ■ ■ ■
I V A R ■ R E U P ■ G E E Z ■
D A R N ■ A C R O S S ■ R A G
I T I S I ■ D I P ■ W A N E
D O N ■ T A X O N O M I S T S
I R A ■ E J E C T O R S E A T
T Y S ■ S A S H A F I E R C E
```

153

```
A R C T I C ■ W H O S T H A T
W A H I N E ■ H O W A R E Y A
S T A N C E ■ A M E N A M E N
■ P L E A ■ R T E S ■ D A R K
A O K ■ S M O T E ■ H E N S ■
M I L E H I G H C L U B ■ ■ ■
I S I S ■ S U E ■ S T O P I T
C O N C I S E ■ Y E S O R N O
O N E A R M ■ S U V ■ K O O K
■ ■ ■ P E E R P R E S S U R E
T R E S ■ A E T N A ■ D D S ■
H E I R ■ A W E S ■ L I M E ■
E S P O U S E D ■ S I T A R S
P L E A S E G O ■ A V E R T S
S A N D B A G S ■ C A N Y O N
```

154

```
Z O M B I E ■ ■ S W A M P E D
A N O M A L Y ■ S O S U E M E
G E T I N T O ■ W R I T E I N
A T O ■ S O D A ■ D A I N T Y
T O R A ■ N E W T O N S ■ ■ ■
R O C C O ■ L O A F ■ M S G S
A M Y T A N ■ L P G A ■ U L U
T A C I T U S ■ S O B E R U P
E N L ■ S M O G ■ D E L E T E
D Y E S ■ B O O B ■ S H E E R
■ ■ ■ T E S T B A N ■ I N N S
U N L O C K ■ S N E E ■ O F T
R A I N O U T ■ D R L A U R A
N U T E L L A ■ S T I N G E R
S T E R I L E ■ S A S H E S
```

155

```
L E T S D O T H I S T H I N G
A N I M A T I O N S T U D I O
H A D A L O N G W A Y T O G O
A M I C I ■ S T A ■ L U N G S
B E E K ■ B E I N G ■ S O L E
A L S ■ V A L E T E D ■ T E D
N E U T E R ■ D O T E S ■ ■ ■
A D P A G E S ■ F E L T T I P
■ ■ ■ X A X I S ■ V O Y A G E
A M A ■ S A M I S E N ■ C O T
R A N D ■ M U L A N ■ N O T E
A R A I L ■ L E U ■ G A B O R
B A N D E D A N T E A T E R S
I C A N N O T T E L L A L I E
C A S T O N E S S P E L L O N
```

156

```
B A R B A R A B U S H ■ B E E
E Q U I V A L E N C E ■ R R R
F A S C I N A T I O N ■ O I L
O B E S ■ D R A F T ■ W A K E
G A S ■ M O M M Y ■ L E D S ■
■ ■ ■ M A M B A ■ M A D C A P
A H E A D ■ E X F O L I A T E
C A R R O L L ■ L E A D S I N
E M I L N O L D E ■ K I T E S
D O C E N T ■ E X M E T ■ ■ ■
■ M A N A ■ F S T A R ■ M E W
Z E K E ■ K L E I N ■ P I S A
A L A ■ Y O U R M A J E S T Y
G E N ■ O L I V E G A R D E N
S T E ■ U N D E R E X P O S E
```

157

```
    P R E S E N T A R M S
  D O O B E D O O B E D O O
G I M M E G I M M E G I M M E
A S P   R O T   C S I   E E L
S M A R T   M T A   S H O R T
P A N E   T E A T S   O N T O
S L O P P I N G   A E G E A N
      U S A U S A U S A
K E V L A R   A R C T U R U S
E L I S   A P L E Y   G A N T
B U R E N   U E Y   B E T T E
A D A   O E R   O S E   T R I
B E G S T H E Q U E S T I O N
  D O U B L E B O G F Y E D
    S P E E D S K A T E R
```

158

```
B A S   F L I P O N E S L I D
A C H   J U K E B O X H E R O
T R A   O R E G O N T R A I L
H O M B R E   W I E   I S N T
S P E E D   D O S   Y M H A
H O L E   P H O T O O P
E L E C   O L D S A W   H E R
B I S H O P     S L E A Z Y
A S S   D O G S I T   M I R A
      R E V O L T S   B R A N
  C B E R   K O S   T E M P O
P A R I   L A V   H E R E O N
O R A N G E P E K O E   T U E
S O V I E T U N I O N   A N A
T B O N E S T E A K S   L D L
```

159

```
A R M Y C A M P   U R G E S
R E A D A B O O K   T A U N T
P I N S T R I P E   T H E D A
E N E   A R S E N E   S L Y
L A D Y S   A T P A R   T E C
    O P A   H I P   F S S O
  L A K E P O E T   F A T S O
L O V E C O N Q U E R S A L L
I D O L S   P U P P E T R Y
L E I S   R A E   I T O
L S D   N U T S O   S N O U T
I T A   Y E R T L E   V S O
P O N T E   O I L T Y C O O N
U N C U T   L O I T E R I N G
T E E N S   N E A T I D E A
```

160

```
K A M A S U T R A   L O N G S
E G O M A N I A C   E N E R O
P E N N Y A N T E   L E G A L
T R O I S   T E R R A N O V A
    O A S   E N O T E S
S W M   H O U S E M D   I S T
T H I S   U S E R S   K A T Y
B A L L   P A X I L   O T O E
O L I O   N I E C E   P E N A
N E T   M A R S H E S   D E R
I B A N E Z     P O M
F O R E L I M B S   N A R C S
A N I L L   R A T I O N O U T
C E F L O   A L A N M O O R E
E S S E N   Z E N G A R D E N
```

161

```
T R A M P   C A B S   S P O T
R E B A R   Y O R E   P E N H
I N I G O   C L O G D A N C E
O E D I P A L   W E I R D E R
S E E   C L O D   R E S U M E
      J O L T E D     L O G
  C A M E R A O D S C U R A
  G O B I G O R G O H O M E
C R E S C E N T M O O N S
H E D   S H A K E S
R E D C A P   S T E M   M B A
I N O R D E R   I D A H O A N
S T R E A K E R S   K I O S K
T E M P   E D I T   E D S E L
O A S T   S O B S   R E E S E
```

162

```
A L C H E M I S T S   B A S E
P I R A T E S H I P   O M A H
S T A Y A T H O M E   S E M I
E R N S   H O W   D V O R A K
S E E T O   T D S   E M I R S
    A A A   O L A Y   C I A
B L A C K M A G I C   W A T T
R I S K S I T   M T S I N A I
O P T S   C O M E U N D O N E
A R R   J I M I   P E E
D E O R O   S N L   E R A S E
B A D E G G   I A N   I R A S
A D O S   A R C H A N G E L S
N E M O   W H A T A S H A M E
D R E W   D O M I N A T R I X
```

163

I	R	A	Q		C	A	V	E	R	S		O	D	S
R	A	C	E		A	D	I	D	A	S		J	O	T
I	D	I	D		L	I	V	I	N	G	W	A	G	E
S	I	N		A	L	E	R	T		T	H	Y	M	E
H	I	G	H	N	O	T	E	S		A	S	A	P	
		A	T	P				A	F	T				
T	R	A	D	I	T	I	O	N	A	L	I	R	A	S
M	A	L	A	R	I	A	P	A	R	A	S	I	T	E
E	M	O	T	I	O	N	A	L	O	U	T	L	E	T
N	A	T	I	O	N	A	L	A	N	T	H	E	M	S
	N	T	S		C	I	I							
A	B	B	E		T	E	X	A	S	S	I	Z	E	
T	O	R	A	H		O	V	E	R	T		V	I	A
S	T	O	R	E	F	R	O	N	T		W	A	L	T
I	O	N		R	O	C	K	I	E		O	N	C	E
X	X	X		R	E	H	E	A	R		K	A	H	N

164

L	A	B	A	M	B	A		A	T	A	V	I	S	T
I	P	A	D	A	I	R		S	I	S	E	N	O	R
R	E	T	W	E	E	T		K	T	H	X	B	Y	E
A	S	E	A		N	E	B	U	L	A				
		R	E	V		O	P	E	N	T	O	P		
S	U	P	E	R	E	G	O			T	A	B	L	E
N	N	E		S	N	A	K	E	B	I	T	T	E	N
A	C	R	E		U	N	C	L	E		S	A	D	D
G	O	O	G	L	E	G	L	A	S	S		I	T	O
S	I	N	G	E		U	N	T	I	L	N	O	W	
	L	I	O	N	C	U	B		D	R	E			
			S	E	N	S	O	R		F	O	W	L	
P	A	J	A	M	A	S		P	A	D	T	H	A	I
D	V	D	C	A	S	E		T	M	O	B	I	L	E
F	I	S	H	N	E	T		S	A	M	E	O	L	D

165

I	C	K	I	N	E	S	S		F	L	A	G	O	N
T	H	E	N	A	N	N	Y		T	A	T	A	M	I
C	I	T	A	T	I	O	N		C	I	T	R	I	C
H	A	T	S		S	W	E	E		D	E	A	T	H
			T	A	L	I		A	M	O	N	G	S	T
S	C	H	A	D	E	N	F	R	E	U	D	E		
E	R	A	T	O			R	E	N	T		D	E	A
M	A	Z	E		S	P	A	D	E		L	O	S	T
I	B	M		C	H	A	N		R	O	O	S	T	
	A	L	L	M	Y	C	H	I	L	D	R	E	N	
A	C	T	A	E	O	N		E	R	S	E			
R	A	S	T	A		E	C	T	O		S	E	A	S
B	R	U	I	N	S		R	E	B	O	T	T	L	E
O	V	I	N	E	S		A	R	O	M	A	T	I	C
R	E	T	O	R	T		N	O	T	G	R	E	A	T

166

J	A	I	L	B	R	E	A	K		M	E	C	C	A
A	P	O	L	L	O	X	I	I		S	T	O	L	I
C	A	N	D	Y	S	H	O	P		D	A	K	A	R
O	T	I	S		S	A	L		A	O	L	E	R	S
B	O	Z		B	I	L	I	O	U	S		Z	I	P
S	W	E	A	R		E	S	P	N		M	E	T	A
			T	I	C	S		S	T	E	A	R	I	C
M	O	J	I	T	O				I	N	T	O	N	E
O	P	U	L	E	N	T		B	E	E	T			
N	E	S	T		D	R	E	I		M	E	S	A	S
A	N	T		G	O	I	N	G	B	Y		E	R	E
R	A	D	N	E	R		C	H	A		L	A	I	T
C	R	O	O	N		G	O	O	G	L	E	B	O	T
H	E	I	S	T		A	R	A	G	O	N	E	S	E
Y	A	T	E	S		S	E	X	Y	S	A	D	I	E

167

G	O	T	A	B		S	O	B	S			C	P	R
S	A	H	I	B		E	N	E	M	Y		O	H	O
U	S	E	D	C	A	R	S	A	L	E	S	M	A	N
I	I	N		R	I	V	E	T		S	A	P	S	
T	S	O		A	M	I	C	I		E	L	L	I	E
		O	K	D		C	O	N	E	S		E	N	D
S	I	N	A	I		E	N	G	R		E	X	G	I
A	N	D	R	O	M	E	D	A	S	T	R	A	I	N
I	T	A	L		E	N	T	R		H	A	N	N	A
T	H	Y		L	A	T	H	E		E	T	A		
H	E	D	G	E		R	O	T	O	S		L	C	D
	W	E	R	E		A	U	R	A	L		Y	E	R
L	I	V	E	D	A	N	G	E	R	O	U	S	L	Y
A	L	I		S	A	C	H	A		T	R	I	L	L
M	D	L		S	E	T	T		S	I	S	S	Y	

168

H	O	L	M	E	S	I	A	N		T	B	A	R	S
A	T	A	G	L	A	N	C	E		A	R	P	E	L
K	I	S	S	Y	F	A	C	E		M	A	P	L	E
E	S	T		S	E	N	T		H	A	I	L	E	D
			T	I	L	E		H	O	R	N	E	T	S
S	U	B	W	A	Y		S	E	R	I	F	S		
A	L	A	I	N		H	U	M	A	N	R	A	C	E
C	E	N	T		W	A	R	P	S		E	U	R	O
S	E	A	T	M	A	T	E	S		P	E	C	A	N
		N	E	U	T	E	R		D	O	Z	E	N	S
S	M	A	R	T	E	D		A	A	R	E			
T	I	P	J	A	R		B	U	M	S		C	R	U
P	A	E	A	N		B	O	D	A	C	I	O	U	S
A	T	E	I	T		I	R	I	S	H	M	O	S	S
T	A	L	L	S		B	E	E	K	E	E	P	E	R

169

```
T O W E L S   B E S S E M E R
I N A P E T   E X I T L A N E
M E N A G E   T E X A S T E A
E S T   S N O W D E N   H R S
L I E V   O N E R S   L E G O
A D D I N   K E A   C A R Y N
G E I S O P E N   P U N
  D O I T B Y T H E B O O K
      T A J   W O R E T H I N
A S C O T   R O O   S T I N E
T B A R   G A F F S   E D D A
T A S   S I Z E U P   U L T
A R T M A J O R   M I N N I E
C R U M H O R N   A T O N E S
H O P E L E S S   C A V O R T
```

170

```
F L E W B Y   G E S T A T E S
R E D H O T   A L I E H A N I
I N W A R D   Z I P D R I V E
E N O L A   T E X A S   L I T
Z O O E X H I B I T   T O S S
E N D S   O D O R   M A R I O
      P R E S   S E X T O N
H E R A L D S   L E G I O N S
O P A Q U E   L E E S
M I N U S   T E A M   S A S S
E S A I   G R A P E J E L L Y
P O L   G R I F T   U P P E D
O D O N N E L L   O M A H A N
R E N T A B L E   A B L A Z E
T I G H T E S T   F O S S E Y
```

171

```
C A B B I E S   B U M M E R S
O R L A N D O S E N T I N E L
S O U R C E S O F I N C O M E
A W E D   N O M O   S E T U P
    C O D S   A R A   E S T
M E H T A   K L E B A N
A L I   M M I I   B L I M E Y
C A P T A I N P H I L L I P S
E N S I G N   I R E S   S E E
    M E S S R S   E T H E R
S A G   K E A   A T R A
C L E A T   E T A S   I N G E
A L E X A N D E R C A L D E R
L O S E O N E S M A R B L E S
P R E S S E D   S P R Y E S T
```

172

```
C O R N C O B P I P E   T A M
O N A C A R O U S E L   A L E
R A N A N E R R A N D   K T S
G I G A   D R O N E B E E S
I R E   A W E   A R E A R
    S T A R D O M   T I N S
S P H I N X L I K E   A M A H
Y O U D O   I C E   O R A I E
N O D E   I N T E G R A T E D
E L S A   T E A C O Z Y
  T O R T E   H B O   S U B
S A N M A R I N O   C A S E
E B B   D A N U B E R I V E R
A L A   A N C I E N T R O M E
U E Y   S T A T E S E C R E T
```

173

```
S A T E L L I T E S T A T E S
A D E L A I D E S L A M E N T
M A R I N E I N S U R A N C E
S I N G I N G T O G E T H E R
  R E I   S I E   I D I O
  S B A   T R O T   S U M O
    L I S   R O Z   R A H
S N E E R A T   G U E S S S O
H E X   E M I   T A C
A Z O V   M A P A   L A S
  R I M Y   A R M   R T S
S A C R I F I C I A L L A M B
A M I G L A D T O S E E Y O U
G A S O L I N E S T A T I O N
A N T S I N O N E S P A N T S
```

174

```
W H O A   P R I M A L U R G E
H A R M   L E G A L I Z E I T
A B A B   I D O B E L I E V E
T A L E S E   T E X T   F E R
I N E R T   A Y L A   R E I N
S E X S Y M B O L   L O R N E
I R A   L U L U   C U T
T O M K I T E   D U C H A M P
  I S T   P O R K   N A E
D E A T H   P A T T Y C A K E
O N E S   K E N S   M O T E L
O R R   T H E O   K E N O B I
F I O N A A P P L E   E L A N
U C B E R K E L E Y   Y I N G
S H E S A I D Y E S   S A K S
```

175

```
M O V E B A C K . B B K I N G
I R E A L I Z E . L I E S O N
D E L T A R A Y . U G A N D A
. V A D E R . P E G . T E T
S P E W E D . R A J A H .
I O T A S . F A C E M A S K S
G O R Y . K A F K A E S Q U E
H B O . K I T T E N S . U R L
T A P D A N C E R S . N A T E
S H E D T E A R S . D O R I C
. T E S T S . D I V E S T
A N N . M C S . C U R E D
T O O T O O . P O P E L E O X
T H E A S P . I D E C L A R E
N O L O S E . T E D T A L K S
```

176

```
C O L B E R T B U M P . C H E
E V E R S O S O R R Y . O A R
L E G I S L A T U R E . N I N
T R O T . A R S . O D I S T S
. I N S . M A O S U I T
A S G A R D . V I R G I L
H E E L S . D A R K S T A R S
A L O E . H A S T E . A T O I
B A C K B E N C H . F R E O N
. A S I A G O . S E T S T O
D O C E N T S . B A Y
O N H I G H . O A F . A W E S
L I I . H E A T S E N S O R S
C O N . A R C T I C O C E A N
E N G . M Y C O L O G I S T S
```

177

```
F O S H I Z Z L E . C A N S T
A T H E N A E U M . E P O C H
S T A N D I N G O . L I T H E
T O R . O R I G . G L A M O R
O M I T . E T A L I I . U L E
N A N A S . H G T V . S C A T
E N G I N E . E Y E . T H R O
. I N L A W . R U N A T
M A S T . T A B . P A Y O L A
A R C S . S N U B . P A L I N
N E A . P A S C A L . T O O T
M A R M O T . O M A R . O N O
A R I A L . A L A N A R K I N
D U N N O . L I K E C R A Z Y
E G G O S . E C O S Y S T E M
```

178

```
L E S S C O M P L I C A T E D
O N E A F T E R A N O T H E R
T H E G O B L E T O F F I R E
H A T E S . D W A R F . E I S
A N O S . D I R K . E L V E S
I C I . K E N A I . R E E S E
R E T . E G G P A N . E S T D
. I G A . U A R .
S N C C . S O M B E R . I C E
C O L O R . S I E V E . N A Y
A T O N E . M A J A . H A M E
C A S . S P O S E . B A S E L
C L E A N A S A W H I S T L E
H O S T I L E R E A C T I O N
I T T A K E S A L L S O R T S
```

179

```
C H I L L A X . G A G A R I N
H A V E A G O . A D R I A N A
U V I N D E X . T E R R I F Y
M R E D . S O P H S . E S O S
P E D A L . X K E . I D E M
. H O L O G R A M . H A D
D E J A V U . S E X S C E N E
E X E N E M Y . R I T A L I N
B A L D S P O T . O U T L A Y
S M L . E S U R A N C E
. P O E T . L I D . K R A U T
F A S T . G L O A T . W N B A
I P H O N E S . P A R A D O X
L E O N I N E . T R O U B L E
A R T S A L E . S T Y L E T S
```

180

```
C A M P . H O W D A R E Y O U
E V E R . I N A U G U R A L S
D I D O . M E L O N B A L L S
A L I T O . A T S E A . E A R
R A C E C A R D . W T S
. S U M M I T . O K B U T
E A S T L A . S E W . Y O K E
C A L V I N A N D H O B B E S
O R E O . A C E . A T O A S T
N E W T O . H Y D R O X
. E R N . W I F E S W A P
A R T . L I M O S . S E E M E
R E T R O V I R U S . A W A R
A N Y O N E E L S E . T O T O
B E L T S A N D E R . S N I T
```